A FORAY INTO THE WORLDS OF ANIMALS AND HUMANS

CARY WOLFE, SERIES EDITOR

Jakob von Uexküll

A FORAY INTO THE WORLDS

OF ANIMALS AND HUMANS

WITH *A THEORY OF MEANING*

Translated by Joseph D. O'Neil

Introduction by Dorion Sagan

Afterword by Geoffrey Winthrop-Young

posthumanities 12

University of Minnesota Press
Minneapolis · London

The University of Minnesota Press gratefully acknowledges
the generous assistance provided for the publication of this book
by the Margaret W. Harmon Fund.

Originally published as *Streifzüge durch die Umwelten von Tieren
und Menschen*, copyright 1934 Verlag von Julius Springer;
and as *Bedeutungslehre*, copyright 1940 Verlag von J. A. Barth.

English translation, Introduction, Translator's Introduction, and
Afterword copyright 2010 by the Regents of the University of Minnesota

Published by the University of Minnesota Press
111 Third Avenue South, Suite 290
Minneapolis, MN 55401-2520
http://www.upress.umn.edu

Library of Congress Cataloging-in-Publication Data

Uexküll, Jakob von, 1864–1944.
[Streifzüge durch die Umwelten von Tieren und Menschen. English]
A foray into the worlds of animals and humans ; with, A theory of
    meaning / Jakob von Uexküll; translated by Joseph D. O'Neil ;
    introduction by Dorion Sagan; afterword by Geoffrey Winthrop-
    Young.—1st University of Minnesota Press ed.
  p. cm.—(Posthumanities series ; v. 12)
Includes bibliographical references and index.
ISBN 978-0-8166-5899-2 (hc : alk. paper)
ISBN 978-0-8166-5900-5 (pb : alk. paper)
1. Animal behavior. 2. Psychology, Comparative. 3. Perception. I. Uexküll,
    Jakob von, 1864–1944. Theory of meaning. II. Title.
QL751.U413 2010
590.1—dc22   2010026059

Printed in the United States of America on acid-free paper

The University of Minnesota is an
equal-opportunity educator and employer.

31 30 29 28 27 26 25 24   10 9 8 7

CONTENTS

A THEORY OF MEANING

Dorion Sagan

ALTHOUGH LIFE BOTH TRANSFORMS MATTER and processes information, the two are not proportional: the touch of a button may ignite a hydrogen bomb, while the combined military efforts of Orwellian nations will fail to make a little girl smile. Thus life is not just about matter and how it immediately interacts with itself but also how that matter interacts in interconnected systems that include organisms in their separately perceiving worlds—worlds that are necessarily incomplete, even for scientists and philosophers who, like their objects of study, form only a tiny part of the giant, perhaps infinite universe they observe. Nonetheless, information and matter-energy are definitely connected: for example, as I was jogging just now, hearing my own breathing, I was reminded to share the crucial fact that the major metabolism that sustains us perceiving animals is the redox gradient,[1] which powers the flow of electrons between the hydrogen-rich carbon compounds of our food and the oxygen we take in from the atmosphere, a chemical difference which itself reminded me, in one of life's circumlocutionary moments, of its own existence.

Once upon a time, says Nietzsche, in a cosmos glittering forth innumerable solar systems, there was a star "on which clever animals invented knowledge [however] . . . After nature had drawn a few breaths the star grew cold, and the clever animals had to die." Their knowledge did not preserve their lifeform or lead to its longevity but only gave its "owner and producer . . . [a feeling of great] importance, as if the world pivoted around it. But if we could communicate with the mosquito [some translations give 'gnat'], then we would learn that it floats through the air with the same self-importance, feeling within itself the flying center of the world. There is nothing in nature so despicable or insignificant that it cannot immediately be blown up like a bag by a slight breath of this power of knowledge; and just as every porter wants an admirer, the proudest human being, the philosopher, thinks that he sees the eyes of the universe telescopically focused from all sides on his actions and thoughts."[2] How strange that our cleverness (which might be described as the linguistic, thought-based power to find—and forge—connections), which after all we possess only as a crutch to make up for our physical weakness, for we would have died without it, should lead us to consider ourselves masters of the universe. "[L]anguage is a thing:" writes Blanchot, "it is a written thing, a bit of bark, a sliver of rock, a fragment of clay in which the reality of the earth continues to exist."[3] But language is a thing with peculiar properties. Within a given animal's perceptual life-world, which the Estonian-born biologist Jakob von Uexküll (1864–1944) referred to as its *Umwelt*, signifying things trigger chains of events, sometimes spelling the difference between life and death. Consider the signifying honeybee. When bee scouts come back to a hive, before they do their famous figure-eight waggle dance, which tells their hivemates of the distance and location of resources needed by the group, they spit the water, pollen, or nectar they've collected into the faces of the other bees waiting at the entrance of the hive. What they spit to their fellows is essentially a sign of itself, but their dance says where and how far. Moreover, if the message is of something the hive needs, the bee will be the center of attention. In a hive starved for pollen, a scout bee may be welcomed enthusiastically by its fellows, and may do the famous waggle dance up to 257 times, for as long as half an hour.[4] But if it is later in the day, and the hive is cool, water is not needed and the ignored bearer of the information of the water source will tend to crawl about languidly. Even at the insect level such resource-related signifying—bringing good news or relaying useless messages—may coincide with feelings of depression or elation. Indeed the bee returning with pollen and the message of its whereabouts may even enjoy the sort of intersubjective bliss reserved in human beings primarily for matinee idols and rock stars.

The notion of a distinct perceptual universe for honeybees and other animals is Uexküllian. Uexküll sees organisms' perceptions, communications, and purposeful behaviors as part of the purpose and sensations of a nature that is not limited to human beings. Uexküll's conviction that nonhuman perceptions must be accounted for in any biology worthy of the name, combined with his specific speculations about the actual nature of the inner worlds of such nonhuman beings, is a welcome tonic against the view that nonhumans are machine-like and senseless. Uexküll also insists that natural selection is inadequate to explain the orientation of present features and behaviors toward future ends—purposefulness. Uexküll may be right. Natural selection is an editor, not a creator. The whittling away of relatively nonfunctional forms by their perishing and leaving no offspring (that is, by natural selection) would seem to provide an incomplete explanation. Uexküll's postulation of a human-like consciousness orchestrating natural purposes from a vantage point outside of time and space will seem bizarrely Kantian or too creationistic for most modern readers. Worse still, Uexküll's talk of a "master plan" may sound outright Nazi—although this may be partly the result of translation.[5] If the real world of human toes, parasitic wasps, and penguin wings suggests more a cosmic hack than an all-powerful creator, the history of Faustian eugenics at the time Uexküll was writing renews the question of where Uexküll, in his view of life as a unified entity, thought purposeful life was going. And yet Uexküll's exposition of purpose and perception, of cycles and signaling, of the relationship of part to whole attends to precisely those subjects that have been neglected in the development of biology after Darwin. Perception and functionality pervade living things, and ignoring them, while convenient, is not scientific. Thus Uexküll's careful inventory of such phenomena is to our lasting benefit. Uexküll's examples remain fresh and interesting to modern theorists coming back to construct a broader, more evidence-based biology—a biology that embraces the reality of purpose and perception without jumping to creationist conclusions.

Uexküll is among the first cybernetic biologists, ethologists, and theoretical biologists, as well as being a forerunner to biosemiotics, and a neo-Kantian philosopher.[6] The scientist most cited by Heidegger, Uexküll and his Institute studied the differences of human and other animals' perceptual worlds. The nature of the alleged gulf between humans and (other) animals of course has ethical implications, because it helps determine how we treat them, and was a problem that absorbed Derrida during his dying days. Uexküll's analyses are important to Deleuze and Guattari, among other philosophers. In literature he influences Rainer Maria Rilke and Thomas Mann, in ecology Arne Næss, and in systems theory Ludwig von Bertalanffy.[7] Uexküll's example-rich discourse of life perceived by various species is relevant to epistemology; it expands phenomenology; and it integrates the primary data of perceptual experience into behavioral psychology. Uexküll's notion of the Umwelt and his work in general was popularized and developed by Thomas Sebeok, who spoke of a "semiotic web"—our understanding of our world being not just instinctive, or made up, but an intriguing mix, a spiderlike web partially of our own social and personal construction, whose strands, like those of a spider, while they may be invisible, can have real-world effects. Sebeok calls Uexküll a "cryptosemiotician," semiotics—the study of signs—being, according to John Deely, "perhaps the most international and important intellectual movement since the taking root of science in the modern sense in the seventeenth century."[8]

Scientific innovator though he be, Uexküll, while not explicitly anti-evolutionist, disparages Darwinism. He dismisses the notion that natural selection can account for the character of life he considers most important: the interlinked purposeful harmonies of perceiving organisms. The existence of rudimentary organs is "wishful thinking."[9] Uexküll compares functional features to a handle on a cup of coffee, which is clearly made for holding. He calls our attention to angler fish with lures built into their heads that attract smaller fish which, approaching, are literally sucked in by a whirlpool when the angler suddenly opens its mouth. He points out butterflies whose wing-placed eyespots startle sparrows because to them the spots look like a "cat's eyes." He makes much of beetle larvae that dig escape tunnels in hardening, maturing pea plants, so that when they metamorphose their future forms, about which they know nothing, can eat their way out of the rigidified vegetable matter, which would otherwise become their green coffins.[10]

Organisms in their life-worlds recognize not only sensory inputs, but also functional tones, the use they need to make of certain stimuli if they are to do what they need to survive. The hermit crab has developed a long tail to grab snail shells to use as a temporary home. "This fitting-in cannot be interpreted as a gradual adapt[at]ion through any modifications of anatomy. However, as soon as one gives up such fruitless endeavors and merely ascertains that the hermit crab has developed a tail as a prehensile organ to grasp snail shells, not as a swimming organ, as other long-tailed crabs have, the hermit crab's tail is no more enigmatic than is the rudder-tail of the crayfish."[11]

But of course evolution implies evolution of function, with new purposes coming into being. Consider the surprising result that the life spans of animals such as rats increase not only, as is well known, if they eat less, but can also increase if they don't *smell* food. Houseflies exposed to the odor of yeast paste are deprived of longevity at approximately 40 percent the rate of their calorically restricted brethren. The smell of food, although vanishingly tiny compared to what it signifies, functions as a molecular sign. An evolutionary explanation is that the smell of food is an indicator of dense populations. Foregoing feeding and dying sooner under such circumstances would tend to preserve resources and allow rodent populations to be refreshed with stronger, more youthful members. The fitting in, the matching of food giving away its presence by an "olfactory sign" (the food in effect being a sign of itself[12]) to increased rodent senescence, is beyond individual rat consciousness but selected for by the superior robustness of populations whose members interpreted excess food as a biosign. Such meaning-making, or semiosis, evolves between organisms and their environments, among organisms of the same species and across species, and within individual organisms such as humans attempting to understand the symptoms of their bodies. Signs are read in a language older than words. An embarrassed person's face flushes, showing something about his relationship to the group. That men produce more sperm if they believe their spouses are cheating reflects not a conscious but an unconscious semiosis, at the level of the body. An itch signifies the possible presence of an insect, which evolutionarily was often enough fatal due to adventitious inoculations of pathogens during the blood sucking of insects. Emotions and feelings carry meaning at a prelinguistic or preverbal level in ways illuminated by a consideration of evolutionary history.

While all organisms may have minor goals, such preparations for the future as that of a beetle larva, along with "our personal Umwelts, are part of an all-embracing master plan."[13] Yet one need not adhere to the idea of a master plan—so consonant with German philosophy (e.g., G. W. F. Hegel's writings), Nazi ideology, and monotheism—to recognize the pervasiveness of purposeful activity in biology. More than once in his corpus Uexküll mentions Noah's Ark (e.g., "we have seen them leave the ark of Noah in pairs").[14] Invoking "transensual, timeless" knowledge that allows organisms without human foresight to act in ways that match present action to future needs, he genu-flects to a musician-like "composer" of awareness who is "aware" and can "shape future life-requirements," with a "master's hand":[15] it is clear that he has not completely abandoned tradi-tional monotheistic ideas of design, although this may be more a reaction to the perceived inadequacy of Darwinism to explain function than an unqualified embrace of creationism. Uexküll wheels out musical metaphors. Organisms are instruments in a sort of celestial music show of which we hear only strains.

Thus, Uexküll is divided: on the one hand he reserves in his neo-Kantianism a transcendental dimension beyond space and time that seems quite anachronistic in terms of modern science, and yet on the other he catalogs details of animal be-havior deducing the reality of their perceptual life-worlds in a manner more naturalistic than that of behaviorists, mecha-nists, and materialists who treat the inner worlds of animals (for *functional* reasons of scientific investigation!) as if they don't exist. A systemic view, which gives some causal agency to the whole over the parts, is not only consonant with modern thoughts of emergence, systems biology, and thermodynamics, but vindicates Uexküll's dogged persistence against natural se-lection as a sufficient explanation for the extremely nuanced, functionally oriented life-forms covering our planet. One need not embrace a transcendental master plan or nature moving toward a unified single goal (e.g., God, or the end of history) to see purposeful activity deeply embedded in living things, and emerging often in diverse, unpredictable ways.

Pre-Uexküllian ignorance of animal Umwelten should be seen in terms of the history and methodology of science: focus-ing on one aspect of the environment, as science does to isolate objects for study, presents an abstracted, truncated version of the elements under study that eventually comes back to haunt those who overgeneralized on the basis of an incomplete sam-ple. For example, Max Delbrück's decision to investigate life's molecular mechanism by studying bacteriophages (bacterial viruses that do not have their own metabolism, making them easier to study) helped lead to an overemphasis on genes as the all-explanatory secret of life.[16] So, too, particle physics discovered the necessity of including the observer, her apparatus, and measurements to fully account for observed behavior. And in thermodynamics, the initial simplified studies of matter and energy in thermally scaled systems were prematurely extrapolated to suggest that all natural systems inevitably become more disordered, even though most systems in the universe, including those of life, are not isolated in experimental boxes but open to material and energy transfer.

The phenomenon might be described as the return of the scientifically repressed: what is excluded for the sake of experimental simplicity eventually shows itself to be relevant after all. Behaviorism, explaining animals in terms only of their external behavior, is a logical development of the expeditious exclusion of the dimension of living perception, methodologically bracketed by a church-savvy Descartes, and swept under the rug by a Faustian science drunk on the dream of an all-encompassing materialistic monism.[17] With Uexküll the inner real comes back in the realization that not only do we sense and feel, but so do other sentient organisms; and that our interactions and signaling perceptions have consequences beyond the deterministic oversimplifications of a modern science that has bracketed all causes that are not immediate and mechanical.

"The process by which the subject is progressively differentiated from cell-quality, through the melody of an organ to the symphony of organism, stands in direct contrast to all mechanical processes, which consist of the action of one object upon another."[18] Here Uexküll remarks the ineffectiveness of immediate cause and effect to explain the long-range development of organisms. Uexküll doesn't see, for example, how natural selection can explain the growth of an acorn into an oak, or an egg into a hen, because, "Only when cause and effect coincide in time and place can one speak of a causal connection."

Despite his musico-creationistic vocabulary, his seeming lack of understanding of how natural selection can radically alter function and eliminate the nonfunctional, as well as his death (1944) prior to the massive advances in chemical understanding of effective causation at the level of replicating genes in the 1950s, Uexküll's emphasis on the need to better integrate functionality into biology is, I believe, correct.

Although functionality can certainly change (think, for example, of using car ashtrays to store change), the functional characteristics of organisms have been illuminated in recent years by nonequilibrium thermodynamics. This science provides the backdrop for life's origin and evolution, and for its overall character of being highly functional and goal-oriented. Perhaps it is best to give at the outset what I consider to be one of the best examples of the misreading of teleology—purpose—in biology, which I hereby christen "Turing Gaia." First it is crucial to realize that there is a huge taboo against a teleological understanding of organisms and/or their organs being genuinely "for" something—except, of course, for surviving, which is not an explanation in terms of immediate cause and effect, but is allowable because natural selection in the past gives the impression of present, to use an Uexküll term, harmony. The reason for the antiteleological bias is obvious enough: purpose smacks of God's plan, religion, and design, anathema to scientists. But "Turing Gaia" shows that what looks like purpose and in fact may be purposeful need not have *either* a creationist *or* a Darwinian explanation. Gaia is shorthand for the realization that in the biosphere major environmental variables such as global mean temperature, reactive atmospheric gas composition, and ocean salinity are regulated over multimillion-year time spans. Indeed, Earth's surface resembles a giant organism, whose surface regularities and complex biochemistry look engineered, behave purposefully, and would never be predicted on the basis of chance alone.

But the environmental regulation has a natural thermodynamic explanation. When sensing organisms react by growing or not growing within certain ranges, for example of temperature, this will lead to global environment regulation. The simplest computer model to show how this works is the Daisyworld model.[19] Growing and absorbing heat when conditions are cool (but not too cool) patches of black daisies (say) heat things up. Then, when they get too hot, they stop growing, leading to planetary thermoregulation. White daisies do the same, working in reverse. The real Earth multiplies uncounted variations on this theme of open systems growing and not growing within constraints in such a way that regulation and intelligent-seeming behaviors occur. There is no mysticism, just the growth of organisms within a certain temperature range or other conditions.

Nonetheless, such planetary regulatory behavior could not be understood by hard-core Darwinians because they could not see how organisms could arrive at a "secret consensus" (Ford Doolittle), or regulate as a single being without natural selection having acted at a planetary level, implying an astronomical environment littered with dead or less functional planetary individuals (Richard Dawkins). In short, fear of teleology as nonscientific leads scientists to accept true purpose only at the level of evolved structures or human consciousness. But growing at such and such a temperature, and not at another, leads directly to planetary regulatory behavior that looks so purposeful it was dismissed as impossible evidence of consciousness, teleology, and intent. The behavior is also implicitly semiotic, as temperatures are interpreted as signs. The reason I call this example Turing Gaia is that Alan Turing defined a conscious computer as one that would be able to consistently persuade humans that it had a genuine inner self, a cyber-Umwelt. As hard-core Darwinians mistook for conscious foresight simple thermodynamic behavior modeled on a computer, growth within constraints has in effect passed the Turing Test. Simple behaviors can easily appear purposeful and conscious.

There is indeed a functional tone to the whole of life. But

it probably owes far less to Uexküll's transcendental celestial counterpoint than it does to the vicissitudes of energy flow in complex systems. Uexküll's focus on perceptions that lead to actions has a thermodynamic context because complex systems (such as daisies) appear only under certain conditions, which they implicitly recognize as signs. They do not appear when those physical conditions, which again act as signs, are not present.

Uexküll may not have liked Darwinism's Englishness, its truncation to a bare-bones mechanical view of a broader German *Naturphilosophie*. Uexküll argues the British popularizer of Darwinism Herbert Spencer "made a basic error" when he put forth "'survival of the fittest'" rather than "survival of the normal" to "support the theory of progress in the evolution of living beings."[20] As for many German scientists, Uexküll's thought grew out of Kant, who argued there was no direct apprehension of things in themselves. We bring our own categories—for Kant, time, space, and causality—to the world we appear to observe directly. Ironically, this emphasis on mental construction and the impossibility of a true objectivity may have helped make Uexküll be more objective, thinking about the categories under which other animals perceived the world.

Defying the rise of biological reductionism epitomized by natural selection as an explanatory principle, Uexküll emphasized the influence of the whole: whereas, he says, "When a dog runs, the animal moves its feet, i.e., the harmony of the footsteps is centrally controlled. But in the case of a starfish we say: 'When a starfish moves, the legs move the animal.' That is, the harmony of the movement is in the legs themselves. It is like an orchestra that can play without a conductor."[21] The starfish's legs take the starfish along, whereas you decide where you want your feet to go.

Uexküll's view here is holistic, anticipating systems biology and cybernetics. Ironically, considering the ascendance of

Gaia science (or "Earth systems science" as it has been appropriated in geology departments) as "geophysiology," Uexküll identified physiology as the life science challenged by its focus only on parts, whereas biology proper was for him the life science of the whole. (However, Uexküll tended to focus more on individuals than ecosystems.) The scientific trend against which Uexküll was reacting, of explaining everything in terms of local cause and effect, stimulus and response, the material interaction of connected parts, he identified with physiology: "In the introduction to his first book about the experimental biology of water animals, Uexküll distinguished between physiology, which organizes the knowledge about organic systems on the basis of causality, and biology, which does it on the basis of purposefulness (*Zweckmessigkeit*)."[22]

Uexküll pushed for a biology that would systematically account for the perceiving beings that had been left out in the rush to explain living "things" (as we sometimes say) as effectively and scientifically as Newton had explained celestial motions by mechanics. The law of natural selection does not explain the inner world of animals—our original and enduring encounter with reality—with anything like the accuracy that the laws of motion explain the external behaviors of plants. Cartesian philosophy dismissed the inner world of animals (let alone plants and microbes[23]), treating them, conveniently enough, as soulless, unfeeling machines. Behaviorism in psychology, such as Pavlov's experiments on dogs, investigated animals as mechanisms without attending to their inner processes. Uexküll's work, however, integrated inner experience. Take the Umwelt of "man's best friend," the dog. How do dogs perceive? Uexküll shows us the difference in the Umwelten of the shy dog and the "spirited" dog, urinating away, marking his territory. Whereas Chekhov writes of a dog sniffing all the corners of a room and, from the dog's viewpoint, of the unquestioned superiority of human beings, and Nietzsche talks about a dog coming up to the philosopher as if to ask a question, but then forgetting the question, Uexküll more closely enters the question of what it is like to be a dog.

Pavlov's experiments showed dogs could be made to salivate in expectation of food at the ding of a bell, and by extension at a spoken word such as "food"—but that doesn't mean they understand the meaning of the word. Contrariwise, as Uexküll points out, referencing the work of a colleague, that dogs trained to sit on a special chair at the command "Chair!" will look for something else to sit on if the call is repeated but the chair removed. This suggests that dogs use signs, which can be used to convey a notion of a "sitting-quality," and Uexküll adds that, while linguistics is beyond him, making a "biological science" of it is the "right path"—although it may be that "true" (human-style) language, which includes a childhood ability to learn grammar, and a cultural ability to play in a semiotic space that can virally spread new and discard old words as well as other abstract signs, depends on the ability to realign neuronal models with external models, and thus that it starts with brains and not, as Uexküll's son Thure von Uexküll suggests, with the "living cell" as the "'semiotic atom.'"[24] The superiority of certain modeling tasks human beings have thanks to our neuron-packed cerebral cortices should not be confused with either a complete perspective or a lack of complex sensory processing in nonhuman beings. Novelist, painter, and biological theorist Samuel Butler, in his *Note-Books* (derived from his habit of carrying one with him and making notes whenever an idea struck him), points out the anthropocentrism of the very notion of language. Doing the etymological analysis, he shows that language, the word, comes from the French *langue*, meaning "tongue." But, Butler points out, when a dog looks at you, then looks at a door, then looks at you in anticipation, he is also talking, not with his tongue but with his eyes—and this Butler, a clever wordsmith, deigns to call "eyeage."

Compared to that of dogs, the human Umwelt is superabundant in signs but poor in smells, the genes for which, indeed, have been disappearing in our lineage. A dog is hungry, he eats, he is no longer hungry. The desire to replenish, to do something to continue or fortify the systems we call living, is linked to their circular state, the cycle linking perception to action that Uexküll calls *Funktionskreis* ("functional circle").[25] Because the living being is not a finished state but a continuous process that must replenish and keep integrated its parts, and ultimately reproduce before they fall into disrepair, succumbing to the wear and tear formalized in the second law of thermodynamics, there is, given awareness, a continuous sense of anticipation of one thing leading to the next, as well as surprise, disappointment, fear, and so on when they don't. Julius Fraser, who has made a professional study of time, takes a cue from Uexküll to argue that time neither flows nor should be understood in terms of eternity but rather reflects certain basic, sometimes animal-less, Umwelten.[26] The experience of time, space, and language probably differs from species to species. Wittgenstein rhetorically asks why we would say a dog is afraid his master will beat him but not that a dog is afraid his master will beat him tomorrow? Wittgenstein also says that if a lion could speak we would not understand him—a comment that no doubt cannot be not (mis)understood.

Semiosis, meaning-making, comes from the Greek word *semeion*, as does the word "sign"—"something that suggests the presence or existence of some other fact, condition, or quality," as defined by the 2006 edition of the *American Heritage Dictionary*.[27] For Derrida, writing is "general"; "Il n'y a pas de hors-texte": there is no outside of the text.[28] For Heidegger "man is not only a living creature who possesses language along with other capacities. Rather, language is the house of Being in which man ek-sists by dwelling, in that he belongs to the truth of Being, guarding it."[29] From this pan-linguistic, post-structuralist standpoint, everything would seem to have a semiotic component. Even the orthodox thought that there is a realm to which language does not extend is necessarily expressed in language.

When Derrida died, he had already been selected by Blanchot to read the latter's eulogy, as Blanchot trusted no one else to do it right. But apparently the eulogy, delivered among the family, came across as awkward and boring, and thus Derrida made sure to write his own eulogy, which his son delivered graveside. The key passage, as related by Avital Ronell in Manhattan shortly after the philosopher's death, reads: "Know that, wherever I am now, I am smiling."[30] Which "undecidably" (to use a Derridean adverb) signifies both a spiritual passage into the (fictional) afterlife and a presentiment of the scene in which the departed eulogy writer smilingly composed his doubly meaningful lines. Relatedly, I had earlier heard from a professor at De Paul University in Chicago that Derrida was accused in Kansas of practicing willful obscurantism by a pointing fellow, who said words to the effect, "We know what you're up to—you're like the one in the movie, *The Wizard of Oz*!"

"*Ou?*" replied Derrida in his French accent, "zhe dawg?"

Some would argue that dogs don't have language because, while they use signs, they don't know they're using them—they have no relationship to the symbolic realm as such, let alone living, as we do, in language. In discussing the Umwelt of *Canis familiaris*—the "dawg"—Uexküll contrasts the relative barrenness of a room, whose chairs to sit on and plates indicating potential food are meaningful in the canine world, but whose scholarly books and writing desks are all but irrelevant. (Of course for puppies and teething toddlers, almost anything can be endowed with a lovely "chewing tone.") Yet the dog is not stupid. It has in its mind an idea, a "search image" of the stick it is looking for before it finds it. (Even an earthworm has a search image, says Uexküll, and knows, by smell, which end of a leaf fragment to pull on to bring it to its burrow.[31]) And certain impediments for some humans, such as the curb of a sidewalk for a blind man, a dog navigates without a second thought. So, too, as dog whistles attest, the ears of a canine perk up at the sound of ultrasounds we miss. With regard to language, as Uexküll points out in a letter, some languages are innate, making it possible for pheasant chicks to be raised by turkey hens, whose warning cries they respond to, but not to ordinary hens, whose alarm call they don't understand.[32]

The capacity to learn new associations varies. Nonetheless, even if brains are necessary to process language proper, organisms in their bodies as well as their behavior show clear evidence of finely honed functionality. An air bladder used for stabilizing fish evolves into gills, with a function that comes to be even more crucial. Penguins cannot fly, but their fat wings help them steer on ice and swim in icy waters. The heart may have other functions, but one is clearly to circulate the blood. As Salthe and Fuhrman point out, the genitals and breasts have a function that rightly belongs not to the present but to the next generation, to keep going the basic functionality and form of a system whose parts, if they were not reproduced in new models, would perish of thermodynamic disrepair.[33] The whole organism, along with and as its integrated parts, functions to deplete energy gradients. Gleaning this functionality may have misled Uexküll to espouse his musical creationism. Less sophisticated creationists also use the neglect of the obvious evidence of purpose in anglo-American evolutionism to dismiss the entire evolutionary enterprise. Unfortunately, evolutionary biologists as authoritative and as ideologically opposed as Richard Dawkins and Stephen Jay Gould both portray a largely random biological world devoid of purpose, direction, or progress. However, these traits exist and are demonstrably thermodynamical adjuncts of the development of complex systems effectively and naturally depleting energy sources, rather than necessarily implying the awkward thesis of humanoid design. Not just the functionality of organs and behaviors that Uexküll catalogued (and are indeed partially the result of natural selection), but many clearly nonrandom trends mark the evolutionary process: increasing number of taxa, amount of energy use, energy storage, memory storage and access, area colonized, number of individuals, efficiency of energy use as indexed by respiration efficiency in representative samples of more recently evolved taxa as we move forward in time[34] and, despite clades that have experienced decreases in brain-to-body ratios, a secular increase (albeit with setbacks during mass extinctions) toward increasing intelligence, semiotic transfer and data processing capacities, ability to represent past and predict future states, number of chemical elements involved in biological processes, and maximum energy levels achieved are among the abilities life has progressively augmented. These progressive tendencies are of a piece with the purposeful behavior of even simple energy systems, which have as their natural end-state equilibrium, but which may undergo quite complex processes "to" move toward achieving that state. Even nonliving systems use up available energy, cycling matter and growing until their natural teleological task is finished.

Because of a new wave of mechanical understanding of living things based on molecular biology and replicating DNA and RNA, Uexküll's emphasis on the importance of integrating purpose, function, and nonrandom directionality is if anything more germane now than when first he enunciated it. Genetic determinism does not tell us how, if I tell you to close your eyes and think of a pink tree, you can do that, any more than it tells us how you can understand that you are alive in a world that exists. And yet Darwin was himself Uexküllian in the berth he gave to the inner worlds of animals.[35] Both Darwin's *The Expression of the Emotions in Man and Animals* and his *The Descent of Man and Selection in Relation to Sex* discussed the inner worlds of organisms, some, such as choices by females in selecting mates whose traits would thereby persist, affecting evolution. Should not Uexküll's insights, such as his emphasis that we perceive things like bells not only in terms of their colors and sounds but most importantly (ignoring such features) in terms of the more primordial question what they are for, be integrated into our evolutionary view?[36]

Although Uexküll seems to have retreated toward an outmoded idealism and creationism, in comparing the wholeness and functionality of organisms to the wholeness of instruments in an orchestra, he in a way leapfrogs to an older understanding of the word organism, *organon*, Greek for instrument. For Uexküll we organisms are not cosmically random. Uexküll's Umwelt music might strike the modern listener as quaint or romantic but it reminds us to see life in terms of wholeness, perception, and purpose. Far from being impeded by the development of complex systems, our activities along with those of other complex systems expand the natural end-directed processes of energy to be used up and spread implicit in the second law. Life has also hit upon many ways to moderate its use of available energy, which has allowed it to last far longer than nonliving complex systems that deplete energy.

Life on Earth has been transforming the energy of the sun for almost four billion years now. Complex systems, though they grow their own complexity, more effectively export heat to their surroundings. And this natural finalism or teleology coordinates with life's detection, sensation, and perceptual modeling abilities. It has a perceptual connection. By metabolizing and spreading organisms produce entropy, mostly as heat, keeping themselves relatively cool in the process. The biosphere in general, and complex ecosystems (such as rainforests) in particular, measurably reduce the energy gradient between the 5700 kelvin sun and 2.7 kelvin space.[37] (0 kelvin is absolute zero, the theoretical temperature of absolute atomic stillness.) Nonequilibrium thermodynamics thus deconstructs the line between life and nonlife, much as Darwinism deconstructs the barrier between humans and other organisms by showing our behavioral, morphological, and biochemical continuity to other organisms.

We can thus suggest life is a natural thermodynamic process with a natural "plan," the same coordinated tendency of matter to join and cycle to bring about equilibrium seen in nonliving complex systems. Complex systems showing harmony, wholeness, and a subservience of the parts to the whole, which have the natural function of producing molecular chaos (thermodynamic entropy) as they grow, are not confined to life. They include Belousov-Zhabotinsky reactions and other chemical clocks, manmade Taylor vortices that "remember" their past states, whirlpools such as hurricanes and typhoons that grow as they reduce air pressure gradients, and Bénard convection cells that actively reduce temperature gradients. These systems, like the daisies of Daisyworld, grow only under certain conditions, making them effectively semiotic.[38] Living beings enhance this thermodynamic process by reproducing. They "relight the candle"—life as life persists as a thermodynamically favored, implicitly teleological process that uses genetic replication. As stable vehicles of degradation, our kind sustains and expands natural processes of entropy production and gradient destruction.[39]

From a nonequilibrium thermodynamic our ceaseless striving has no metaphysical significance in terms of good and evil or ultimate meaning, but just reflects our being caught up in a more efficacious, but constantly threatened, process of gradient reduction by complex systems. Although we may semiotically separate ourselves from the process, whilst we live such striving is part of a function-oriented systemic process that occurs unconsciously and underconsciously, and includes learning, such that the directed goals toward which animals strive— say a baby squirrel trying to climb a cement wall to reach its mother, or a six-year-old trying to stay on a bike—can retreat from conscious effort to subliminal mastery. Some anciently evolved behaviors, such as breathing, occur automatically but remain open to conscious intervention. It is as if consciousness is a limited ability that takes hold uncertainly in uncertain situations.

Uexküll's humble ("This little monograph does not claim to point the way to a new science . . .") *Foray into the Worlds of Animals and Humans* is a bit of a conundrum. On the one hand, we have an intrepid philosophical act of observation, intuition, and deduction of the perceptual worlds of other species. Shamanically, he'll tell us what it's like to be a blind, deaf tick waiting in darkness for the all-important whiff of butyric acid, prior to a drop from the top of a blade of a grass, hopefully onto a warm, blood-filled animal. He tells us what it means to be a scallop, or what flowers look like to bees in a spring meadow. On the other hand, he is simply saying that other animals perceive, that they too have worlds, and trying to figure out what those worlds are like. Thus at one and the same time Uexküll is a kind of biologist-shaman attempting to cross the Rubicon to nonhuman minds, and a humble naturalist closely observing and recording his fellow living beings.

Not only for us but for every living being, the world may seem perplexing but also somehow complete. Uexküll's vision entails what I've called "Procrustean perception"—after the Greek robber who cut people's legs off to fit them in bed: so, too, evolutionary expediency forces us (unless we are mad or drugged) to conceive of this world as whole despite being formed from data fragments.[40] For example, you only have eyes in front of your head yet your conception of the space around you is not marked by a huge gap corresponding to the back of your head. Incomplete beings, we are "Procrustean" in that, although we take in only tiny parts of an immensity whose totality we cannot possibly perceive, we nevertheless cannot help but fill in the blanks, constructing a whole we then take to be real. This premature completeness allows organisms to be fooled by signs, the parts and sensations they take for wholes. Uexküll shows us the sea urchin extending its spines to the stimulus of passing ship and cloud, which the sea creature misinterprets as a potentially deadly predator fish. He intuits the plight of the fly, its vision unable to resolve the strangling strands of the spider's web, or the jackdaw fooled by a cat carrying a rag. Even the world of the blind, deaf tick, sensing mammals by the slight amount of butyric acid[41] their bodies give off, is uncovered by Uexküll's shamanic Umwelt vaulting.

Uexküll's vision reminds me of the Net of Indra in Indian Mahayana and Chinese Huayan Buddhism. Indra's net is an infinite web with a dewdrop-like eye glimmering in the middle of each compartment. Each jeweled eye contains all the others and their reflections. Similarly, each of us contains a view, albeit particularized, of the entire world. As Leibnizian monads, we do not have windows, direct access into the sensory flow of others, though there are examples in fiction, such as Mr. Spock's Vulcan "mind meld" in *Star Trek*. Fiction itself, creating characters with whom we can identify, creates at least the illusion of experiencing foreign sensoria. In Tibetan Buddhism, *lojong* is the art of putting yourself in another's shoes. Thus while assuming the sensorium of other organisms has long been claimed in shamanic circles, and has been explored in fiction, for example in Carlos Castaneda's Don Juan books, in John Varley's "Overdrawn at the Memory Bank," where the protagonist is "doppeled" into a wild baboon, Gregor Samsa the cockroach in Kafka's *The Metamorphosis*, and of a variety of animals inhabited by gods in Ovid's *Metamorphoses*, such explorations, such "embodiments" remain rare in the scientific literature. It is as if after Descartes, who famously compared the cries of animals to the squeaking of parts in an unfeeling machine, any imputation of complex awareness or humanlike consciousness in nonhuman entities might take away the license of researchers to tinker with suffering nonhuman bodies. In Disney cartoons animals must be clothed like humans and talk like humans before we accept them as sufficiently human to take them seriously—which even then we don't because they're only cartoons.

In addition to Uexküll's stick-searching dogs, hypothesis-generating scientists, and starfish-avoiding scallops, there are an estimated ten to thirty million extant species: water scorpions with built-in fathometers sensing hydrostatic pressure gradients, plants with gravity sensors, algae perceiving barium sulfate and calcium ions, fish that gauge the amplitude and frequency of turbulent waters with dipole electrostatic field generator-and-sensors, magnetosensitive bacteria, homing pigeons and polarized light-detecting bees whose peregrinations are not impeded by clouds, male silkworm moths sensing sexually mature females miles away, and deep-sea fish with luminous lures attached to their heads that attract each other as well as provide bait to dupe their prey into an ugly mouth. Luminous algae in the waves and moss in the woods have inspired poets and the tellers of ghost stories. Fireflies recognize each other's flashes, and some species use specific mating patterns for one species to lure males of another. Once, in the woods, a firefly appeared to mistake the tip of my cigarette for an attractive conspecific.

Procrustean perception assures mistakes on the basis of preconceptions and signs. In Poe's story "The Sphinx," a frighteningly bizarre hairy giant animal with tusks and a skull marking on its great back is confirmed seen, the second time prowling the woods beyond a scholar's window as the perceiver risks revealing the possible hallucination of a private Umwelt. The scholar, reading from a book, solves the mystery: the beast turns out to be nothing but a death's-head moth, *Acherontia atropos*, on the glass of the window but mistakenly thought to be farther away.

Although we have learned to augment our senses with technological instruments from infrared cameras to X-ray telescopes, the naked human eye sees only visible light, a relatively small region of the electromagnetic spectrum consisting of light waves from 400 to 700 nanometers. Photosynthetic bacteria and their descendants such as algae and plants, as well as most animals, also sense this same range of wavelengths, which comes to us as all the colors of the rainbow ranging from the shortest wavelengths, purple, to the longest, red. Many pollinating insects detect flowering plants through signs invisible to those who cannot see in the ultraviolet range below 400 nanometers in wavelength. At the other end of the spectrum, pit vipers such as rattlesnakes detect infrared radiation (heat) too subtle for us to notice. Bats determine the size, location, density, and movement of prey such as fruit flies 100 feet away in a pitch-black cave by use of sonar, emitting through their mouths and nostrils ultrasound vibrating at frequencies of some 100,000 cycles per second, about five times what we can hear. Dolphins echolocate in the water by making click sounds, and humpback whales sing to each other in songs that completely change over a five-year period, using some of the same rules human composers do. The metabolically advanced, quorum-sensing, gas-exchanging bacteria grow and trade genes globally, not unlike a more-than-human, genetic version of the information-expanding Internet.[42]

If we grant that language is a group-evolved phenomenon that records signs older than and more time-tested than any individual human, we must boggle at the bewildering possibilities of potential biocommunication systems of an estimated extant ten to thirty million species, trading signs with each other and across species boundaries. As Nietzsche intimates, it begins to look increasingly ridiculous for us to indulge our delusions of possessing a radical cleverness, some sort of ur-Umwelt that would separate us as if by an "abyss" (as Heidegger puts it) from other animals. How, for instance, do we stack up against blue whales, whose brains are far bigger than ours, and who (at least until recently, with the constant roar of ship engines) communicate with each other across the oceans over thousands of miles? For any punk rock or heavy metal fans out there, consider this. The threshold of pain to the human ear is 120 to 130 decibels. A jet engine is about 140 decibels. Concert music, at its loudest, is 150 decibels. Blue whales, comparatively, belt out their vocals at 188 decibels. Their communications are time-delayed because of water. They may, in their giant Umwelten, have fabulous multisensory pictures of major portions of the ocean, images that, even if we had direct access to them, we couldn't process, because our brains are too small. They may experience time in an extended way compared to our sense of time, even as their native ocean-imaging abilities likely far surpass our own.

Together the biospheric network of interacting, sensing, proto- or fully semiotic organisms, many if not all of which have their own Umwelten, maintain the complexity and regulate the environmental conditions of Earth's biosphere away from chemical and thermodynamic equilibrium. Contrary to creationist beliefs and neovitalist "negentropic" scientific models, organisms are perfectly natural within the energetic context of producing entropy in accord with thermodynamics' inviolate second law, which says that energy will move from a concentrated to a spread-out state, becoming unavailable for work over time. Semiosis, insofar as it recognizes regions of energy flow and material substrates to go, is integral to life's process. As James Clerk Maxwell (in the *Encyclopaedia Britannica*, 1878) pointed out, the potential energy of reactive particles in a mixture depends on intelligence to be tapped: "Dissipated energy is energy which we cannot lay hold of and direct at pleasure, such as the energy of the confused agitation of molecules which we call heat. Now, confusion, like the correlative term order, is not a property of material things in themselves, but only in relation to the mind which perceives them. . . . It is only to a being in the intermediate stage, who can lay hold of some forms of energy while others elude his grasp, that energy appears to be passing inevitably from the available to the dissipated state."[43]

Maxwell's Demon was an attempt to get rid of the third interpretive third party, by replacing it with a physical differentiator that could create gradients and therefore, through the operation of a pure intelligence-sensation, reverse the dissipation of energy. This would, however, effectively be the production of a perpetual motion machine, and has been deemed impossible, not just theoretically but practically, in the U.S. Patent Office's refusal to accept applications for them. However, the thought experiment was quite instructive, helping lead to the recognition that a differentiating machine can process information. No machine or organism, however, can restore gradients from scratch; all require external inputs of high-quality energy. In retrospect, we can recognize life as a sort of reverse perpetual motion machine, a Maxwellian Angel that uses information to build itself up as it dissipates gradients—until it runs out of resources. Humanity is a most impressive but necessarily stable example of this natural semiosis. Maxwell, who linked electricity and magnetism, shows here a link between matter and mind.

Animals who identify the particularly colored, scented flowers, fruit, or fungi upon which they need to feed breed and succeed relative to those who make mistakes in identifying food sources. The ability to detect concealment and camouflage, as well as to sense fine differences in colors, such as the color orange associated with vitamin A, brought about a natural increase in sensibilities, a fine-tuning of Umwelten within the thermo-evolutionary space. This space provides the backdrop for the beloved Byzantine textual practices of literary critics, hermeneuticists, and scholastic intelligences. The keen-eyed wolf, the bacteria swimming toward sweetness and light (in order to degrade sugars and make energetic use of high-quality electromagnetic energy), the hard teeth of the australopithecine ancestor used for grinding and crunching, crushing and slicing vegetable tissue in mastication prior to digestion—these and other obviously semiotic, purposeful activities must be seen in their thermodynamic context.

Uexküll's scientific formulation of the Umwelt can and should be developed within an evolutionary-semiotic context. As Uexküll suggests in the final section of his essay, where he discusses the worldviews of the astronomer, the chemist, and the physicist, science also has its Umwelten. Forming scientific pictures of the universe with the aid of instruments and the cross-checking and peer reviews of scientists, despite political and corporate corruption of scientists, can be seen as the development of a metahuman neural network adding another powerful eye to the evolving Net of Indra. Uexküll's pioneering investigations focus our attention on the perceptions of nonhuman others, some of whose perspectives, as profound as they are alien, we will probably never understand, nor get the chance to, given the present epoch of human-generated mass extinction.

In the opinion of Deely, Uexküll's work, while not fully developed, provides an opening onto the most important revolution in intellectual history since the origin of science.[44] Uexküll gives the lie to the idea of scientific objectivity divorced from the perspectival, perceptual subjectivity of the observers themselves and the signs they use. The idea of an independently existing external reality divorced from minds occurs only within minds.[45] Following an illustrious intellectual history that does not shirk medieval jaunts through scholastic ontology or religious philosophy, Deely argues the world is intelligible. We have, you might say, a sense of being: just as the primary datum of the sense of vision is light, and hearing sound, so the human instrument receives, via the intellect, the basic knowledge that the universe exists. We are alive and know we are alive, whatever that may mean. Following Heidegger (who calls animals "benumbed"[46]) to a certain extent, Deely however doubts that this knowledge of the world as world exists for animals, who are semiotically underdeveloped compared to us. According to Deely, while animals may and do communicate, they do not have language as such, which he defines not just as the ability to use signs (like Butler's dog, signaling with his eyes), but understanding of those real, but nonetheless invisible, linguistically constructed relations among signified things.

For Charles Sanders Peirce, whom Deely recognizes as the founder of semiotics, "firstness" refers to existence, "secondness" to contiguity of relations therein, with "thirdness" and the possibility of semiosis occurring only with an interpretant reacting to the sign. A third "party" in other words is necessary to make sense and recognize the relations of one thing to another. The mute interaction of one thing with another opens the possibility of signification, especially in the living, where material complexity and thermodynamic lag ensures that the appearance of one substance will follow another. The simplest and best example of this is food, as it "represents" the attended-to substrate on which an organism's continued livelihood depends. Its "meaning" is simple enough—continued survival itself, along with the continued ability to recognize that upon which the organism, originally or originarily a bacterium, depends. The example of such a bacterium swimming up a sugar gradient shows the basic semiotic operation, which is also a purposive and cybernetic act, and how it differs in living things. As the bacterium swims toward its source of increasing nutriment, it recognizes, implicitly or with the tiny awareness and limited purposefulness that Samuel Butler imputed to even the smallest beings, the signs that it must follow to ensure its survival. If it fails to be aware of the chemical and energetic concentrations upon which it depends, it may perish. If it successfully "hermeneuticizes," following the tracks of the material signs upon which its continuous thermodynamic degradation depends, it will tend to leave more semiotically adept ancestors than its less sensitive, less aware (or aware-acting) brethren. The living being is thus aware of the signs of its own continued being and thus contrarily its own potential demise. Here we may locate a segue between signification and primitive sensations, such as hunger and thirst, as well as proto-emotions such as depressed activity due to lack of stored energy, and fear of death, which may exist in Umwelten in some manner nearly from the beginning.[47]

Perhaps the most influential philosopher of the twentieth century, Martin Heidegger, speaks of being-toward-death as proper to *Dasein* (literally "being there"), his version of the human perceptual world, our Umwelt that we tend to raise up over those of other species, just as we tend to put our own concerns, and those of our loved ones, and our nation, over those of other people, races, and countries. Philosophers vary in the extent to which they would separate the Umwelt Heidegger calls Dasein from those of other animals. In Deely's terms we engage in anthroposemiosis, which is distinct from zoosemiosis although it is a part thereof. An internet interlocutor, responding on a blog hosted by the novelist-philosopher "Kvond," defends this long-standing philosophical tradition that erects a special place for our species, against the blog's host, who begs to differ, quoting Spinoza to the effect that humanity is not so separate but rather constitutes a "kingdom within a kingdom":

> It seems to me that for both Bains and Deely, and the authors on whom Deely relies (notably Aquinas, Scotus, Poinsot and Peirce), all mental action is, as you say, transspecific (though not panpsychic). All beings capable of even the lowest level of sensation are characterizable as cognitive, noetic, mental, or what have you. Rational, intellectual, semiotic mentality is a special kind of mentality, but it is not a division autonomous from the sphere of the mental generally. Rather, it is a division that occurs within the mental sphere. Why is this division crucial? Because it explains what is most distinctive of human beings. All animals employ signs, but only humans are aware of the nature of signs as triadic relations (cf. Poinsot, Maritain and Peirce). All animals are semiosic, but only human animals are semiotic. Semioticity is a property that one either has or does not have, much like being pregnant. Does this privilege human beings? Yes and no. If you consider the world of culture, art, the sciences, etc. to be privileges, then we are privileged through our semiotic capacities to be able to participate and enjoy in these aspects of "world" that these capacities have enabled. However, this is not to say that animals are not privileged in other ways. As even Heidegger is willing to say, "this does not mean that [nonhuman] life represents

something inferior or some kind of lower level in comparison with human Dasein. On the contrary, life is a domain which possesses a wealth of openness with which the human world may have nothing to compare.[48]

Uexküll himself writes that the first principle of Umwelt theory is that "all animal subjects, from the simplest to the most complex, are inserted into their environments to the same degree of perfection. The simple animal has a simple environment; the multiform animal has an environment just as richly articulated as it is."[49] Heidegger's notion, that "*the* [*sic*—italics added] animal" (again: we are animals) is "poor in world"—while also maintaining that other species are not on "some kind of lower level"—seems an example of what Theodor Adorno calls Heidegger's "peasant cunning."[50] Derrida, the closest and most respectful reader of Heidegger, nonetheless reviles his claim of an "abyss" between the human and the animal, calling it "violent and awkward."[51]

Academic hairsplitting is a common enough phenomenon to merit the derogatory idiom, but is also simultaneously indicative of humanity's semiotic strength. The categories into which we divide things, based on the relations Deely would credit us with realizing exist in contradistinction to the benighted animal world, do not always work in our favor. Earth seen from space sports none of the color-coded boundaries among nations we see on the typical map of the world. Nature does not weep over academia's fractious territorialisms, nor take pleasure in the university's attempts at interdisciplinary cross-fertilizations. Our strength at connecting one thing to another, arbitrarily, by inventing signs, such as the color schemes displayed by countries on their flags, may well be our special strength, our Nietzschean cleverness, the key of thought which opens our Umwelt. But it is a strength based on a kind of lie, the power of invention that we then take to be real, forgetting the history of our associations, the connections forged by thought. Chemistry and physics and biology, the human and social and sciences proper, are all already always abstracted from nature's wholeness, which haunts typological thought like the plump belly of the Buddha sitting serenely in silent meditation. We have ignored the viewpoints of other beings, which like our own reflect the whole, for the sake of our simplified, goal-directed analyses. Our metastasizing terminologies may or may not have real-world effects. Our gift of making signs and sense, and partial and postmodern forms of (non)sense is, as Nietzsche reminds us, not an unqualified encomium, but the only way we've found to spread, as a relative weakling primate, across all the continents and seven seas. Although it has inspired amazing things, it has also wreaked major havoc, both to our own species, to other beautiful animals and arguably to the global biosystem, whose present stage of development was required for human evolution but may, because of human activities, be coming to an end.[52]

Humanity's technical intelligent civilization is extremely adept at energy extraction, but that does not mean it has staying power. The most confounding quality of our "intelligence" is its lack of wisdom: we use our know-how to plunder as quickly and greedily as possible, cheating each other, hoarding luxuries, organizing corporations on the basis of quarterly reports, and in general acting like Jonathan Swift's Yahoos, whose most memorable trait was to defecate impressively from treetops. Life as an Umwelt-studded system is some 3.5 billion years old. Whether we can survive within it, let alone at our current and growing levels of energy depletion, is another story. The two primary activities in which living beings are involved are gradient reduction and survival. Semiotic cleverness may be exceedingly good at the first task but ultimately fail at the second.

The opposite of Heidegger's abyss is Alan Watts's claim that all organisms think they're human. To deconstruct the would-be yawning gulf between the human and the nonhuman requires sensitizing ourselves not only to the evolutionary continuity between humans and other organisms, not only appreciating the ecological contiguity of life forms on a connected biosphere, but also remarking the mind-like processes observable in far-from-human systems, including nonliving systems, to which we have (as indeed we have toward each other) no direct phenomenological access. In Alan Turing's test of computer consciousness, a program that persuades us by its behavior that it is self-aware must be considered aware. I thus believe your foreign Umwelt is real because you persuade me as such. The alternative is solipsism. I can imagine, but not directly know, what it's like to be you.

In *Do Androids Dream of Electric Sheep?*, Philip K. Dick plays in multiple ways with this quixotic notion of the imputed Umwelt. Rachael Rosen, his (character's) beautiful single-malt–drinking love interest, is an android whose fabricators at the Rosen Association have implanted artificial memories in her that make her initially think she's human. Real animals are a symbol of status, ecologically rare, and replaced by very lifelike flesh-and-blood replicas. Rick Deckard (a partial homonymic anagram of the author's name, Dick) is a bounty hunter with an electric sheep and a depressed wife. He is charged with hunting down escaped Nexus-6 robots. Deckard is told by the self-serving Rosen Association that Rachael is actually a real human but schizoid, meaning that his initial test of her status calls into question the testing protocol to distinguish androids from humans. The Voight-Kampff tests differentiating between real humans and the ersatz fugitives (their escape implying free will) Deckard must "retire" paradoxically measure not only involuntary eye movement and blushing, but the level of emotions in responses to questions about harming animals. Thus Rachael Rosen, an android who believes otherwise, has a real Umwelt in which she comes to realize she is not authentic, whereas her heartless corporate keepers, lying and conniving, scheme to elude the empathy testing protocol that would identify bona fide beings with the right to exist. Rachael confesses she feels empathy for a fellow android of her make, and that she loves Deckard. Later she kills the real goat he had purchased while he, in the radioactive Oregon desert, finds a toad thought to be extinct. Exhausted, he brings the toad home to his wife, who finds it is also electronic–thus defying French biologist Jean Rostand's couplet: "Theories pass. The Frog remains."[53]

While Heidegger points to the abyss between human and animal Umwelten, and Deely separates physiosemiosis from zoosemiosis from anthroposemiosis, Derrida is busy deconstructing the figures of speech that allow us to show how one thing differs from another.[54] In "The Flowers of Rhetoric" section of the piece "White Mythology" in *Margins of Philosophy*, he does this in part by introducing the word "heliotrope." A trope is a figure of speech, etymologically deriving from the Greek tropos, "to turn." The heliotrope has three main meanings, first, of a type of flower, second, of a stone (bloodstone), and third a color, ranging from pale violet to a deeper reddish-purple color. Beyond specific flower, rock, and color, however, the word means any plant that turns toward the sun. Etymologically and literally, if not by extension, a heliotrope is that which turns sunward. It thus becomes a kind of metatrope for polysemy in general and also for a semiosis or metasemiosis beyond discrete meaning that refers to a physical process involving the sun. Here one can probably detect, although Derrida eschews talk of "influence" (perhaps it is his desert cunning), the influence of that great theorizer of a solar influence behind, beyond, and creating the condition of meaning, Georges Bataille. In 1929 Bataille read Soviet geochemist Vladimir Vernadsky's *La Biosphère*, a book in which the activity of life on Earth is discussed as a unified transformation of solar energies, manifesting, for example, in the power of living beings, as birds and human munitions, to defy the determinism of gravity by taking to the skies. Indeed, while Vernadsky described living matter (he avoided the term "life") as a kind of moving mineral, and Lovelock described Earth's surface as a planet-sized organism, both break down, as does Derrida from a completely different direction, the would-be ironclad (heliotrope-colored) distinction between life and nonlife.

Such deconstructions no doubt reflect a moment in the evolutionary trajectory of which we are a part. As we grow, and our knowledge increases, and life begins to impinge upon the cosmic environment from which it derives and to which it has always necessarily been connected, our understanding of ourselves not as divine isolates, but part of an interconnected natural thermodynamic system, increases. We may as well speak of technosemiosis or paranthroposemiosis when speaking of humanity in its technological phase as a growing telecommunicating mass whose Umwelt connects us at the speed of light to once-remote regions of the world, and through satellite telemetry and the Hubble Telescope to a Gaian and astronomic Umwelt whose bubble, to use Uexküll's term, extends beyond this sphere 27,000 miles in circumference billions of years backwards in time to the microwave radiation left over from the Big Bang, and forwards to speculative physicists' visions of coopting the energy of galaxies for the purposes of life.

In the meantime, less grandiosely, it is worth pointing out that there is something almost spookily semiotic about nonliving complex thermodynamically driven processes. They need not even be complex. Close to equilibrium situations, such as hot air in an imperfectly sealed container, will appear to "figure out" how best to equilibrate[55]—reduce the gradient, spread the energy—"in order to" (preanimate teleology) achieve the temporary end state of gradient reduction implicit in extended versions of the second law. As Fraser says, "the poltergeists of yesterday are the creaking steps of today."[56] The creaky stairs, no less than directed gusts of wind (perhaps appearing with ghostly miens due to a light tracking of dust) in Victorian houses, especially poorly insulated ones equilibrating as the sun goes down at night, may well—especially in conjunction with human tendencies to personify—be a large part of the physical explanation behind historical reports of ghosts. As Uexküll presciently stressed, biology must take full account of the real processes of purposiveness observant biologists have catalogued in the growth and behavior of living forms. Ironically, however, identification of mind-like processes indicative in us and Rachael Rosen and others of genuine semiosis seems also to exist in the natural teleology of thermodynamic processes to which few would be willing to grant an Umwelt. If it is too late to say with Plato that the celestial spheres move in perfectly circular orbits of their own volition, it is too early to say definitively who, or what, does and does not have an Umwelt.

THE COMPLICATIONS OF TRANSLATING Jakob von Uexküll's text begin with its title. The text describes itself as a series of *Streifzüge*, of forays, of rambles, a walk-through. An earlier translation by Claire Schiller gave an English title as "Strolls through the worlds of animals and men."[1] While my translation as "foray" may seem curious, "stroll" is too casual for both the scientific curiosity and the rigor with which Uexküll elaborates what is nonetheless a popularization of his theory of animal cognition. While Schiller's translation of *Menschen* as "men" reflects a bygone use of language, the real issue arises with the word *Umwelten*. While the choice of "worlds" in the title will hopefully make the work more appealing, I have chosen to translate this in the body of the text as "environments," first because this is the literal translation of *Umwelt*, and second because this echoes the language of the system/environment distinction in systems theory, of which Uexküll's theory is a forerunner and of which Niklas Luhmann's social systems theory is the culmination.

For all that, the title of this volume accurately reflects a key aspect of the term *Umwelt*, if one assumes that "world" is always the world of or for some subject. As Goethe's Faust exclaims as he looks around his cluttered study, "Das ist deine Welt! Das heißt, eine Welt!" "That is your world, that is, one world."[2] For Uexküll as in *Faust*, this means one, closed world, among many others which Faust fails to grasp. In Uexküll's language, *Umwelt* does not quite map semantically onto the system/environment distinction in systems theory because it seems to define what the latter will call "system": the world as constructed by the subject. In other words, Uexküll does not invite us to travel through the environment except insofar as it is the environment of some species, i.e., the system of distinctions by which that species orients itself functionally in *its* world. Uexküll distinguishes in this sense between "environment" (i.e., an order created by the subject's specific disposition and activity) and "surroundings" (*Umgebung*). This is why he stresses that his work is in the Kantian epistemological tradition, in which knowledge is always conditioned by a priori synthetic judgments which refer back to the subject's own capacities and dispositions.

The functional cycle of the animal presents further complications for a translation that is both accurate and respects colloquial usage in each language. The terms of this cycle are differentiated by their prefix, *Merk-* or *Wirk-*, and connected by their stem: *Mal* or *Zeichen*. These prefixes denote passive and active features, respectively, as in Schiller's translation in terms of "effectors" and "receptors," but the stems indicate nuances of the distinction between a mark (*Mal*) and a sign (*Zeichen*). Moreover, Uexküll also uses the terms *Rezeptor* and *Effektor*, which have a different location in his functional topology and which I translate as "receptor" and "effector." For the sake of consistency and for want of the compounding options available in German, I concatenate nouns ("perception mark," "effect sign") rather than attempt to render these terms with adjectives.

Mal can be any mark, not necessarily a sign of something, while *Zeichen* has a referent; it belongs clearly to the province of semiotics as a sign of something. While, in common usage, *Merkmal* is almost universally translated as "feature," I translate *Merkmal* consistently as "perception mark" and *Merkzeichen* as "perception sign" because it clearly denotes not primarily something about the object, its features, but something about the way in which the subject organizes its Umwelt through selective perception of those features, which are only relevant insofar as they are relevant for the subject (or the subject's species). In the Introduction, *merken* clearly refers to the perceptive activity of the subject, as the *Merkzeichen* is produced by the sensory organs of the subject. Torsten Rüting's suggested translation as "feature sign" echoes *Merkmal* but is pleonastic, introduces "sign" where the common and specifically semiotic term *Zeichen* is not present in the text, and does not refer to the subject's activity of perception as contrasted with that of producing effects, *wirken*.[3]

Mal is generally only significant in the manner of a sign when specified by a prefix (*Merkmal*, *Denkmal*, *Wundmal*, *Mahnmal*, *Kainsmal*, *Muttermal*, etc.). *Merkmal* therefore specifies that this is a mark of which one takes notice, just as *Merkzeichen* specifies perception as active noticing (*Merken*), which is only passive relative to its counterpart, the active production of effects (*Wirken*) and is not simply perception as cognition (*Wahrnehmung*). In the diagram of the functional cycle, Urmas Sutrop translates "Merk-" as "sense": "sense feature," and so on.[4] The German for "sensory organ" would be *Sinnesorgan* and has to do more with gross anatomy than with the sort of phenomenology of system/environment relations described by Uexküll. Uexküll also distinguishes between the *Sinnesorgan* and the functions of *Merken* and *Wirken*; the sensory organ receives stimuli, but it does not yet organize the environment. I therefore stick with the terms "perceptive" and "perception," especially since *Merken*, while passive in comparison to *Wirken*, is still an act of attention to something, in this case something that constitutes the specific, closed world, in Uexküll's language, the environment of the animal as subject.

The most interesting set of problems, and perhaps the most vexing for my desire to furnish a readable English translation, concerns Uexküll's use of terminology in *The Theory of Meaning*, the second of the two texts in this volume. In the later work, in apparent contrast to the Kantian synthesis of animal subjectivity, Uexküll claims that there is an overarching and (for the scientist) perceptible unity in Nature, which is a sort of mega-subject integrating all other subjects. Uexküll's running critique of Darwinian biology, already evident in *Foray*, rests on this sort of argument from design, which enlarges the scope of subjectivity well beyond that of the philosophical "I." For this reason, and in both works, I always capitalize Nature when it could possibly refer to this entity, as opposed to the particular nature of a thing. I translate the prefix *Natur-* as "natural" when it seems to be a matter of the latter, less emphatic use, and as "of Nature" when it seems to refer to the collective subject in the former, more emphatic sense.

Uexküll underscores this turn in *The Theory of Meaning* to the mega-subject Nature through extended metaphors and conceits which amount to an allegory of the natural world in terms of music, but also in a reiteration of terms which are very close in meaning: *Bildung* and *Gestaltung*, which both have to do with development and formation and are as close as their stems *Bild* and *Gestalt*, "image" and "figure or form," respectively. While it has a certain rhapsodic beauty, his musical allegory is not very elegant. Uexküll refers to "*die Klaviatur des Lebens*," "the clavier of life," on which symphonies and great polyphonic works, i.e., the environments of animals and their interrelations, are composed. He also describes natural processes repeatedly in terms of a melody, by which he means the structure of an animal's relation to its environment. For instance, he speaks of a "bumblebee melody" and a "snapdragon melody," and *Zellglocken*, "cellular bells," contribute to these as they are played on a *Glockenspiel*, "carillon," or the *Klaviatur*, "clavier" of Nature. All of this is combined with visual perception of environments from different perspectives in a synthesis not just of ideas but of the senses. In these cases, as in the perhaps awkward renderings of his more technical terminology, I have chosen to provide a version which does not smooth over Uexküll's insistence on these particular terms and their consistent development as a system. To do otherwise would have been to assimilate his thought in both its precision and its excess to another system or, in other words, to read his discourse as if it were coming from some environment other than that of Jakob von Uexküll.

A FORAY INTO THE WORLDS

OF ANIMALS AND HUMANS

FOREWORD

THE PRESENT BOOKLET does not claim to serve as the introduction to a new science. Rather, it only contains what one might call the description of a walk into unknown worlds. These worlds are not only unknown; they are also invisible. Furthermore, the justification for their existence is denied by many zoologists and physiologists.

While this assertion will sound odd to anyone familiar with those worlds, it can be explained by the fact that not everyone has access to those worlds. Certain convictions are able to bar the entrance to those worlds so securely that not even one ray of all the splendor that spreads over them can penetrate it.

Whoever wants to hold on to the conviction that all living things are only machines should abandon all hope of glimpsing their environments.

Whoever is not yet an adherent of the machine theory of living beings might, however, consider the following. All our utensils and machines are no more than aids for human beings. Of course there are aids to producing effects [*Wirken*], which one calls tools [*Werkzeuge*], a class to which all large machines belong, such as those in our factories that process natural products and furthermore all trains, automobiles, and aircraft. But there are also aids to perception [*Merken*], which one might call perception tools [*Merkzeuge*]: telescopes, eyeglasses, microphones, radio devices, and so on.

From this one can readily assume that an animal is nothing more than a selection of suitable effect-tools and perception-tools, which are bound up into a whole by a control device which, though it remains a machine, is nonetheless suitable for exercising the vital functions of an animal. This is in fact the view of all machine theorists, whether they are thinking of rigid mechanics or flexible dynamics. Animals are made thereby into pure objects. In so doing, one forgets that one has from the outset suppressed the principal factor, namely the *subject* who uses these aids, who affects and perceives with them.

By means of the impossible construction of a combined effect-perception tool, it is not only in the case of animals that one has stitched together the sensory and motor organs like machine parts (without taking into account their perceptive and effective functions). One has also gone so far as to mechanize human beings. According to the behaviorists, our sensibility and our will are mere appearance. In the best case, they are to be valued only as background noise.

Whoever still holds the view that our sensory organs serve perception and our motor organs serve the production of effects will also not see in animals simply a mechanical assemblage; they will also discover the *machine operator* who is built into the organs just as we are into our body. But then he will address himself to animals not merely as objects but also as subjects, whose essential activities consist in perception and production of effects.

But then, one has discovered the gateway to the environments, for everything a subject perceives belongs to its *perception world* [*Merkwelt*], and everything it produces, to its *effect world* [*Wirkwelt*]. These two worlds, of perception and production of effects, form one closed unit, the *environment*.

The environments, which are as diverse as the animals themselves, offer every nature lover new lands of such richness and beauty that a stroll through them will surely be rewarding, even though they are revealed only to our mind's eye and not to our body's.

We begin such a stroll on a sunny day before a flowering meadow in which insects buzz and butterflies flutter, and we make a bubble around each of the animals living in the meadow. The bubble represents each animal's environment and contains all the features accessible to the subject. As soon as we enter into one such bubble, the previous surroundings of the subject are completely reconfigured. Many qualities of the colorful meadow vanish completely, others lose their coherence with one another, and new connections are created. A new world arises in each bubble.

The reader of this travelogue is called upon to come along as we wander through these worlds. The authors have split up their tasks in such a way that one (Uexküll) wrote the text and the other (Kriszat) was responsible for illustrations.

We hope that, with this travelogue, we will take a decisive step forwards and convince many readers that such environments exist and that a new, infinitely rich field of research is opening up. At the same time, this book should attest to the spirit of research shared by the colleagues at the Institute for Environmental Research in Hamburg.[1]

We owe a special debt of gratitude to Dr. K. Lorenz, who greatly advanced our work by providing the images that document his rich experience with jackdaws and starlings. Professor Eggers kindly sent us a thorough report on his experiments with nocturnal butterflies. The well-known watercolorist Franz Huth created the images of the room and the oak. Figures 42 and 55 were created by Th. von Uexküll. We would like to express our heartfelt gratitude to all of them.

JAKOB VON UEXKÜLL
Hamburg, December 1933

INTRODUCTION

ANY COUNTRY DWELLER who traverses woods and bush with his dog has certainly become acquainted with a little animal who lies in wait on the branches of the bushes for his prey, be it human or animal, in order to dive onto his victim and suck himself full of its blood. In so doing, the one- to two-millimeter-large animal swells to the size of a pea (Figure 1).

Although not dangerous, the tick is certainly an unwelcome guest to humans and other mammals. Its life cycle has been studied in such detail in recent work that we can create a virtually complete picture of it.

Out of the egg crawls a not yet fully developed little animal, still missing one pair of legs as well as genital organs. Even in this state, it can already ambush cold-blooded animals such as lizards, for which it lies in wait on the tip of a blade of grass. After many moltings, it

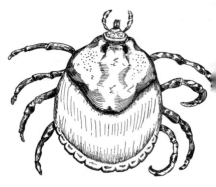

FIGURE 1. Tick

has acquired the organs it lacked and can now go on its quest for warm-blooded creatures. Once the female has copulated, she climbs with her full count of eight legs to the tip of a protruding branch of any shrub in order either to fall onto small mammals who run by underneath or to let herself be brushed off the branch by large ones. The eyeless creature finds the way to its lookout with the help of a general sensitivity to light in the skin. The blind and deaf bandit becomes aware of the approach of its prey through the sense of smell. The odor of butyric acid, which is given off by the skin glands of all mammals, gives the tick the signal to leave its watch post and leap off. If it then falls onto something warm—which its fine sense of temperature will tell it—then it has reached its prey, the warm-blooded animal, and needs only use its sense of touch to find a spot as free of hair as possible in order to bore past its own head into the skin tissue of the prey. Now, the tick pumps a stream of warm blood slowly into itself.

Experiments with artificial membranes and liquids other than blood have demonstrated that the tick has no sense of taste, for, after boring through the membrane, it takes in any liquid, so long as it has the right temperature.

If, after sensing the butyric acid smell, the tick falls onto something cold, then it has missed its prey and must climb back up to its lookout post.

The tick's hearty blood meal is also its last meal, for it now has nothing more to do than fall to the ground, lay its eggs, and die.

The clearly known life processes of the tick afford us a suitable criterion in order to demonstrate the soundness of the biological point of view as opposed to the previously common physiological treatment of the subject. For the physiologist, every living thing is an object that is located in his human world. He investigates the organs of living things and the way they work together just as a technician would examine an unfamiliar machine. The biologist, on the other hand, takes into account that each and every living thing is a subject that lives in its own world, of which it is the center. It cannot, therefore, be compared to a machine, only to the machine operator who guides the machine.

We ask a simple question: Is the tick a machine or a machine operator? Is it a mere object or a subject?

Physiology declares the tick to be a machine and says

that one can differentiate receptors, i.e., sensory organs, and effectors, i.e., activity organs, in the tick. These are connected with one another through a control apparatus in the central nervous system. The whole thing is a machine, with no trace of a machine operator.

"Exactly therein lies the mistake," says the biologist. "Not one part of the tick's body has the character of a machine. There are machine operators at work all over the place."

The physiologist will continue unperturbed: "Precisely in the tick, it can be shown that all actions depend solely on reflexes,[2] and the reflex arc forms the foundation of every animal machine (Figure 2). It begins with a receptor, i.e., with an apparatus that admits only certain external influences, such as butyric acid and heat, and disregards all others.

"The arc ends with a muscle which sets an effector into motion, whether this is the apparatus for locomotion or for boring.

"The sensory cells, which activate sensory stimulation, and the motor cells, which activate the movement impulse, are only connectors which transmit the completely physical

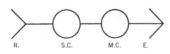

R.   S.C.   M.C.   E.

FIGURE 2. Reflex arc: receptor, sensory cell, motor cell, effector

waves of excitation, produced by the receptor in the nerves in response to an external impulse, to the muscles of the effector. The whole reflex arc works with the transfer of motion, just like any machine. No subjective factor, as one or more machine operators would be, is apparent anywhere."

"Exactly the opposite is the case," the biologist will reply. "Everywhere, it is a case of machine operators and not of machine parts, for all the individual cells of the reflex arc act by transfer of stimuli, not by transfer of movement. But a stimulus has to be *noticed* [*gemerkt*] by the subject and does not appear at all in objects."

Any machine part, for example the clapper of a bell, only

operates in a machine-like manner if it is swung back and forth in a certain way. All other interventions, such as, for example, cold, heat, acids, alkalis, electrical currents, it responds to as any other piece of metal would. But we know since Johannes Müller,[3] however, that a muscle behaves in a completely different way. It responds to all external interventions in the same way: by contracting. Any external intervention is transformed by the muscle into the same stimulus and responded to with the same impulse, by which its body of cells is made to contract. Johannes Müller showed further that all external effects that hit our optic nerve, whether these are waves in the ether, pressure, or electric currents, cause the sensation of light, i.e., our sight-sense cells answer with the same "perception sign" ["*Merkzeichen*"].[4]

From this, we can conclude that every living cell is a machine operator that perceives and produces and therefore possesses its own particular (specific) perceptive signs and impulses or "effect signs" ["*Wirkzeichen*"]. The complex perception and production of effects in every animal subject can thereby be attributed to the cooperation of small cellular-machine operators, each one possessing only one perceptive and one effective sign.

In order to make an orderly cooperation possible, the organism uses brain cells (which are also elementary machine operators), grouping half of them in differently-sized groups of "perception cells" in the part of the brain that is affected by stimuli, the "perception organ." These groups correspond to external groups of stimuli, which present themselves to the animal subject in the form of questions. The organism uses the other half of the brain cells as "effect cells" or impulse cells and arranges them in groups by means of which it controls the movements of the effectors, which impart the animal subject's answers to the outside world. The groups of perception cells fill up the "perception organs" of the brain, and the groups of effect cells form the "effect organs" of the brain.

If we may, on this account, imagine a perception organ as the site of changing groups of these cell-machine operators, which are the carriers of different perceptive signs, they are still spatially separated individuals. Their perceptive signs would remain isolated if it were not possible for them to coalesce into new units outside the spatially fixed perception organ. This possibility is in fact present. The perceptive signs of a group of perception cells come together outside the perception organ, indeed outside the animal's body, in units that become qualities of the object that lie outside the animal subject. We are all quite familiar with this fact. All our human sensations, which represent our specific perception signs, join together to form the qualities of the external things which serve us as perception marks for our actions. The sensation "blue" becomes the "blueness" of the sky, the sensation "green" becomes the "greenness" of the lawn, and so forth. We recognize the sky by the feature "blue" and the lawn by the feature "green."

Exactly the same thing takes place in the effect organ. Here, the effect cells play the role of the elementary machine operators, which in this case are arranged into well-articulated groups according to their impulse or productive sign. Here, too, it is possible to group the isolated effect signs into units that, in the form of self-contained motor impulses or rhythmically arranged melodies of impulses, produce effects in the muscles subject to them. At this, the effectors activated by the muscles impress their "effect mark" ["*Wirkmal*"] on the objects that lie outside the subject.

The effect mark that the effectors of the subject impart to the object is immediately recognizable, just like the wound which the tick's mouthparts inflict upon the skin of the mammal on which it has landed. But only the laborious search for the features of butyric acid and warmth completes the picture of the tick as active in its environment.

Figuratively speaking, every animal subject attacks its objects in a pincer movement—with one perceptive and one effective arm. With the first, it imparts each object a perception mark [*Merkmal*] and with the second an effect mark. Certain qualities of the object become thereby carriers of perception marks and others carriers of effect marks. Since all qualities of an object are connected with each other through the structure of the object, the qualities affected by the effect mark must exert their influence through the object upon the qualities that are carriers of the perception mark and have a transformative effect on the perception mark itself. One can best sum this up this way: The effect mark extinguishes the perception mark.

In addition to the selection of stimuli that the receptors allow to pass and the order of muscles which give the effectors certain potentials for activity, the decisive factors for any action by every animal subject are above all the number and order of perception cells that distinguish the objects of the environment by assigning them features with the help of their perception signs, and the number and order of the effect cells that furnish the same objects with effect marks.

The object only takes part in this action to the extent that it must possess the necessary properties, which can serve on the one hand as feature carriers and, on the other, as effect sign carriers, and which must be in contact with each other through a reciprocal structure.

The connection of subject to object can be most clearly explained by the schema of the functional cycle (Figure 3). The schema shows how subject and object are interconnected with each

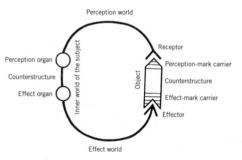

FIGURE 3. Functional cycle

other and form an orderly whole. If one further imagines that subjects are linked to the same object or different ones by multiple functional cycles, one can thereby gain insight into the fundamental principle of the science of the environment: All animal subjects, from the simplest to the most complex, are inserted into their environments to the same degree of perfection. The simple animal has a simple environment; the multiform animal has an environment just as richly articulated as it is.

Now, let us place the tick into the functional cycle as a subject and the mammal as its object. It is seen that three functional cycles take place, according to plan, one after the other. The mammal's skin glands comprise the feature carriers of the first cycle, since the stimulus of the butyric acid sets off certain perception signs in the [tick's] perception organ, and these signs are transposed outward as olfactory features. The processes in the perception organ bring about corresponding impulses by induction (we do not know what that is) in the [tick's] effect organ which then bring about the releasing of the legs and falling. The falling tick imparts to the mammal's hairs, on which it lands, the effect mark "collision," which then activates a tactile feature which, in its turn, extinguishes the olfactory feature "butyric acid." The new feature activates the tick's running about, until this feature is in turn extinguished at the first bare patch of skin by the feature "warmth," and the drilling can begin.

This is no doubt a case of three reflexes, each of which is replaced by the next and which are activated by objectively identifiable physical or chemical effects. But whoever is satisfied with that observation, and assumes he has therefore solved the problem, only proves that he has not seen the real problem at all. It is not a question of the chemical stimulus of the butyric acid any more than it is of the mechanical stimulus (activated by the hair) or of the thermal stimulus of the skin. It is only a question of the fact that, among the hundreds of effects that emanate from the mammal's body, only three become feature carriers for the tick. Why these three and no others?

It is not a question of a contest of strength between two

objects but, rather, of the connection between a living subject and its object. These take place at an entirely different level: between the subject's perception signs and the object's stimulus.

The tick hangs inert on the tip of a branch in a forest clearing. Its position allows it to fall onto a mammal running past. From its entire environment, no stimulus penetrates the tick. But here comes a mammal, which the tick needs for the production of offspring.

And now something miraculous happens. Of all the effects emanating from the mammal's body, only three become stimuli, and then only in a certain sequence. From the enormous world surrounding the tick, three stimuli glow like signal lights in the darkness and serve as directional signs that lead the tick surely to its target. In order to make this possible, the tick has been given, beyond its body's receptors and effectors, three perception signs, which it can use as features. Through these features, the progression of the tick's actions is so strictly prescribed that the tick can only produce very determinate effect marks.

The whole rich world surrounding the tick is constricted and transformed into an impoverished structure that, most importantly of all, consists only of three features and three effect marks—the tick's environment. However, the poverty of this environment is needful for the certainty of action, and certainty is more important than riches.

As one can see, the fundamental aspects of the structure of the environments that are valid for all animals can be derived from the example of the tick. But the tick has one more remarkable capability that allows us a greater insight into environments.

It is immediately evident that the happy occasion that brings a mammal to pass beneath the branch on which the tick sits occurs most seldom. Even the great number of ticks lying in wait in the bush does not compensate for this disadvantage in such a way as to secure the reproduction of the species. In order to increase the probability that its prey will pass by, the tick must be capable of living a long time without nourishment. And the tick is capable of this to an unusual degree. At the Zoological Institute in Rostock, they kept ticks alive that had gone hungry for eighteen years.[5] The tick can wait eighteen years; we humans cannot. Our human time consists of a series of moments, i.e., the shortest segments of time in which the world exhibits no changes. For a moment's duration, the world stands still. A human moment lasts one-eighteenth of a second.[6] We shall see later that the duration of a moment is different in different animals, but, no matter what number we assign to the tick, it is simply impossible for an animal to endure an unchanging environment for eighteen years. We shall therefore assume that the tick is, during its waiting period, in a state similar to sleep, which also interrupts our human time for hours. But time stands still in the tick's waiting period not just for hours but for years, and it starts again only when the signal "butyric acid" awakens the tick to renewed activity.

What have we gained by this knowledge? Something very significant. Time, which frames all events, seemed to us to be the only objectively consistent factor, compared to the variegated changes of its contents, but now we see that the subject controls the time of its environment. While we said before, "There can be no living subject without time," now we shall have to say, "Without a living subject, there can be no time."

We shall see in the next chapter that the same is true of space: Without a living subject, there can be neither space nor time. With this observation, biology has once and for all connected with Kant's philosophy, which biology will now utilize through the natural sciences by emphasizing the decisive role of the subject.

ENVIRONMENT SPACES

JUST AS A GOURMET picks only the raisins out of the cake, the tick only distinguishes butyric acid from among the things in its surroundings. We are not interested in what taste sensations the raisins produce in the gourmet but only in the fact that they become perception marks of his environment because they are of special biological significance for him; we also do not ask how the butyric acid tastes or smells to the tick, but rather, we only register the fact that butyric acid, as biologically significant, becomes a perception mark for the tick.

We content ourselves with the observation that perception cells must be present in the perception organ of the tick that send out their perception signs, just as we assume the same for the perception organs of the gourmet. The only difference is that the tick's perception signs transform the butyric acid stimulus into a perception mark of its environment, whereas the gourmet's perception signs in his environment transform the raisin stimulus into a perception mark.

The animal's environment, which we want to investigate now, is only a piece cut out of its surroundings, which we see stretching out on all sides around the animal—and these surroundings are nothing else but our own, human environment. The first task of research on such environments consists in seeking out the animal's perception signs and, with them, to construct the animal's environment. The perception sign of raisins does nothing for the tick, while the perception mark of butyric acid plays an exceptional role in its environment. In the gourmet's environment, on the other hand, the accent of significance falls not on butyric acid, but on the perception mark of raisins.

Every subject spins out, like the spider's threads, its relations to certain qualities of things and weaves them into a solid web, which carries its existence.

The relations of the subject to the objects of its surroundings, whatever the nature of these relations may be, play themselves out outside the subject, in the very place where we have to look for the perception marks. Perception signs are therefore always spatially bound, and, since they take place in a certain sequence, they are also temporally bound.

We comfort ourselves all too easily with the illusion that the relations of another kind of subject to the things of its environment play out in the same space and time as the relations that link us to the things of our human environment. This illusion is fed by the belief in the existence of one and only one world, in which all living beings are encased. From this arises the widely held conviction that there must be one and only one space and time for all living beings. Only recently have physicists raised doubts as to the existence of one universe with one space valid for all beings. That there can be no such space comes already of the fact that every human being lives in three spaces, which interpenetrate and complete but also partially contradict each other.

Effect Space

When we close our eyes and move our limbs, these movements are known exactly by us in their direction and their extension. Using our hand, we find our way in a space that one can designate the free space of our movements, or, in other words, our effect space [*Wirkraum*]. We measure these paths out in the shortest steps, which we will call directional steps, since the direction of each and every step is known exactly to us through the sensation of direction or *directional sign*. We distinguish six directions, in pairs of opposites: to the left and to the right, upward and downward, forward and backward.

Thorough experiments have shown that the smallest step we can execute, as measured by the index finger of the outstretched arm, is approximately two centimeters in length. As one can see, these steps constitute no precise measurement of the space in which they are executed. Anyone can convince himself of this imprecision if he attempts, with closed eyes, to make his fingertips meet. He would see that this generally fails and that the fingertips miss each other by a distance of up to two centimeters.

It is of the utmost significance for us that we can retain these paths, once executed, very easily in our memory, which makes it possible to write in the dark. This skill is called "kinesthesia," which adds nothing new.

However, effect space is not just a space of movement constructed of a thousand crisscrossing directional steps. Rather, it possesses a system by which it is controlled, the well-known coordinate system, consisting of levels that are vertically arranged, one on top of the other. This serves as the basis of all spatial determinations.

It is of fundamental importance that everyone who is concerned with the problem of space persuade himself of this fact. Nothing is simpler. One need only close one's eyes and move one's hand, held perpendicular to the forehead, back and forth in order to establish with certainty where the boundary between right and left lies. This boundary practically coincides with the body's median plane. If one moves one's horizontally held hand up and down in front of one's face, one can easily establish where the boundary between up and down lies. This boundary is located at eye level in most people. Nonetheless, a great number of people place this boundary at the height of the upper lip. The boundary between front and back differs the most; it can be found by moving the forward-facing palm of the hand. A large number of people say that this plane is located at the opening of the ear, while others designate the zygomatic arch as the boundary plane, and others still place it in front of the tip of the nose. Every normal human being carries a coordinate system around with him that is made up of these three planes and is firmly connected to his head (Figure 4) and thereby confers a solid frame upon his effect space, in which these directional steps lurch and reel.

Into the shifting tangle of directional steps, which as elements of movement can give no solidity to the effect space, these resting planes project a firm scaffolding that guarantees the order of the effect space.

It was the great achievement of [Elie von] Cyon[7] to attribute the three-dimensionality of our space to a sense-organ located in the inner ear, the so-called semicircular canals (Figure 5), the location of which corresponds approximately to

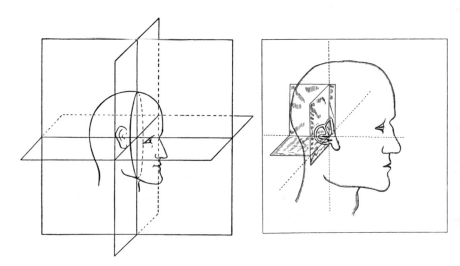

FIGURE 4. Coordinate system of a human being

FIGURE 5. Semicircular canals of a human being

the three planes of the effect space. This connection has been demonstrated so clearly by numerous experiments that we can make the following assertion: All animals that have these three semicircular canals also have available a three-dimensional effect space.

Figure 6 shows the semicircular canals of a fish. It is evident that these must be of great importance for this animal. Their inner structure also supports this conclusion; it presents a system of tubes in which liquid, controlled by nerves, moves

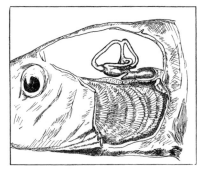

FIGURE 6. Semicircular canals of a fish

in the three spatial directions. The movement of liquid faithfully reflects the movements of the whole body. That indicates to us that, in addition to the task of transposing the three planes into the effect space, another meaning can be assigned to this organ. It seems to be called to play the role of a compass as well—not a compass that only ever points north, but a compass for the "house door." If all the movements of the entire body are analyzed and marked in the semicircular canals, then the animal must be back at its starting point when, in the course of swimming around, it has brought these nerve markings back to zero.

It is beyond all doubt that such a house-door compass is a necessary aid for all animals, whether the house door is a nesting or a spawning place. The establishment of the house door through optical features in visual space is in most cases not adequate, since it must be found even if it has changed its appearance.

The ability to find the house door in effect space can also be demonstrated in insects and mollusks, even though these animals have no semicircular ear canals. The following is a very convincing experiment (Figure 7): When most of the bees have flown out, a beehive is moved two meters. As it happens, the bees gather again at that place in the air where the exit hole—their house door—was previously located. After five minutes, the bees shift course and fly toward the hive.

These experiments have been carried further, with the result that bees whose feelers have been cut off fly immediately toward the relocated hive. This means that, as long as they are in possession of their feelers, they orient themselves

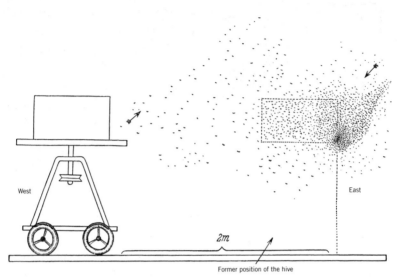

FIGURE 7. Effect space of the bee

foremost in effect space. Without them, they guide themselves by the optical impressions of visual space. The bees' feelers must therefore play in normal life the role of the house-door compass, which shows them the way home more surely than do visual impressions.

Even more conspicuous is the same homing behavior in the case of the common limpet (Figure 8). The limpet lives within the tidal zone on the cliff bottom. The largest individuals dig themselves a bed in the rock with their hard shells, in which they spend the low tide pressed close against the cliff. At high tide, they wander about and graze the cliff rock around themselves bare. When low tide arrives, they return to their beds, but they do not always choose the same path home. The limpet's eyes are so primitive that this snail could never find the house door with their aid alone. The presence of an olfactory perception mark is just as unlikely as that of a visual one. There remains only the supposition of a compass in effect space, of which, however, we can have no conception.

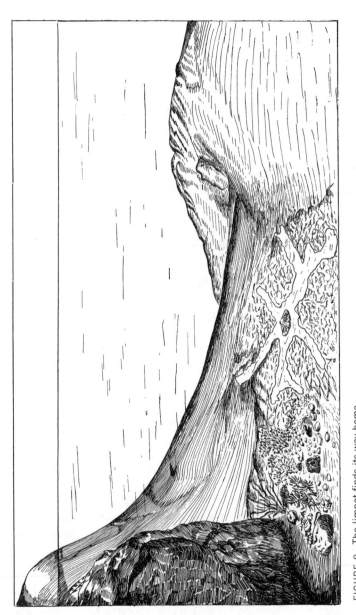

FIGURE 8. The limpet finds its way home

Tactile Space

The basic building block of tactile space is not a unit of movement such as the directional step, but a fixed one, place [*der Ort*]. Place also owes its existence to a perception sign belonging to the subject and is not a configuration dependent upon the

matter of its surroundings. [Ernst Heinrich] Weber provided the proof of this.[8] If one places the points of a compass more than one centimeter apart on the nape of an experimental subject's neck, the subject can clearly distinguish between the two points (Figure 9). Each point is located at another place. If one moves the points down toward the back

FIGURE 9. Weber's compass experiment

without changing the distance between them, they get closer and closer in the tactile space of the experimental subject until they seem to be at the same place.

There results from this that, besides the perception sign for the sense of touch, we also possess a perception sign for the sense of place, which we shall call local signs. Transferred outward, each local sign delivers a place in tactile space. The areas of our skin that produce the same local sign in us when touched change extraordinarily in size according to the meaning that the part of the skin concerned has for touching. After the tip of the tongue, which feels around the inside of the mouth, the tips of our fingers have the smallest areas and are therefore able to differentiate the most places. As we feel out an object, we confer a fine mosaic of place upon its surface with the touch of our finger. The mosaic of place of the objects of the places of

an animal is a gift from the subject to the things in its environment in visual as well as in tactile space, one which is not at all
available in its surroundings.

In feeling out [an object], places connect themselves with
directional steps, and both serve the process of image-formation.

Tactile space plays a very prominent role in some animals. Rats and cats are completely unhindered in their movements even when they have lost the sense of sight—as long as
they have their *vibrissae* [whiskers]. All nocturnal animals and
all animals living in caves live predominantly in tactile space,
which represents a melding of places and directional steps.

Visual Space

Eyeless animals that, like the tick, have skin that is sensitive to
light will most likely possess the same skin areas for the production of local signs for light stimuli as well as for tactile stimuli.
Visual and tactile places coincide in their environments.

Only with animals that have eyes do visual and tactile
places clearly separate. In the eye's retina, the very small elementary areas—the visual elements—close together. To each
sight element there corresponds a place in the environment,
for it so happens that one local sign is assigned to each visual
element. Figure 10 represents the visual space of a flying insect. It is easy to see that, as a consequence of the spherical
construction of the eye, the region of the outside world that
strikes a visual element grows larger as distance increases and
ever more encompassing parts of the outside world are covered
by one place. As a result of this, all the objects that move away
from the eye grow smaller and smaller until they vanish into
one place, for the place represents the smallest spatial vessel
inside of which there are no distinctions.

In tactile space, the objects' growing smaller does not
take place. And that is the point at which visual and tactile
space come into competition. If one reaches out one's arm to

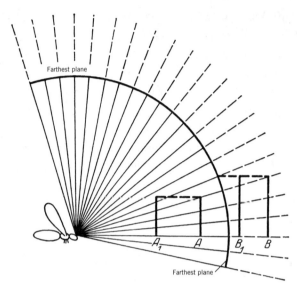

FIGURE 10. The visual space of a flying insect

grasp a cup and bring it to one's mouth, it will become larger in visual space, but its size in tactile space will not change. In this case, tactile space predominates, for the cup's growing in size will not be noticed by an impartial observer.

Like the hand that feels, the eye that glances about spreads a fine mosaic of places over all the things in its environment, the fineness of which depends on the number of visual elements that take in the same segment of the surroundings.

Since the number of visual elements changes extraordinarily in the eyes of different animals, the mosaic of places of their environment must show the same distinctions. The coarser the mosaic, the greater the loss of the details of the things, and the world as seen through a fly's eye must seem significantly coarsened as compared to its being seen through a human eye.

One need only to reduce the same image more and more, photograph it each time against the same grid, and enlarge it again. It will then change itself into an ever more coarse mosaic. Since the grid is too bothersome, we have reproduced here the coarser mosaic images as a watercolor without a grid. Figures 11 a–d were produced with the grid method. They offer the chance to gain an intuition of an animal's environment if one knows the number of visual elements in its eye. Figure 11c corresponds approximately to the image provided by the eye of the housefly. One can easily understand that in an environment that displays so few details, the threads of a spider's web are completely lost to sight, and we may say that the spider weaves a net that remains completely invisible to its prey.

The last figure (11d) corresponds to the image impressed upon the eye of a mollusk. As one can see, the visual space of snails and mussels contains nothing but a number of dark and light surfaces.[9] Just as in tactile space, the connections from place to place in visual space are produced through directional steps. If we prepare an object under the magnifying glass, whose purpose it is to join a large number of places on a small surface, we can realize that not only our eye but also our hand guiding the dissecting pin executes much shorter directional steps that correspond to the places that are now close to each other.

THE FARTHEST PLANE

Unlike effect space and tactile space, visual space is walled about by an impenetrable wall, which we shall call the horizon or farthest plane.

Sun, moon, and stars wander about on the same farthest plane with no difference in depth; this plane includes all visible things. The position of the farthest plane is, however, not firmly fixed. When I took my first steps out of doors after a bad bout of typhus, the farthest plane hung about twenty meters in

a

b

FIGURE 11. a. Photograph of a village street
b. Village street photographed through a screen

FIGURE 11. c. The same village street for a fly's eye
d. Village street for a mollusk's eye

front of me like colorful wallpaper on which all visible things were portrayed. Past twenty meters, objects were neither closer nor farther away, only larger and smaller. Even the coaches that drove past me became not farther away but only smaller as soon as they had reached the farthest plane.

The lens of our eye has the same task as the lens of a photographic camera, namely to focus the objects found in front of the eye on the retina, which corresponds to the photosensitive plate in the camera. The lens of the human eye is elastic and can be bent by special lens muscles (which has the same effect as adjusting the lens on the camera). In contracting the lens muscles, directional signs appear for the direction back to front. As the relaxing muscles of the elastic lens are stretched, there appear directional signs that give the direction from front to back. If the muscles are completely relaxed, the eye is focused on the distance from ten meters to infinity.

Within a radius of ten meters, the things in our environment are known to us through this muscular movement in terms of near and far. Outside this radius, there is originally only an enlargement or shrinking of objects. The infant's visual space ends here with an all-encompassing farthest plane. Only bit by bit do we learn to push the farthest plane ever farther with the help of distance signs, until the adult's visual space ends at a distance of six to eight kilometers and the horizon begins.

The difference between the visual space of a child and that of an adult is explained in Figure 12, which reproduces visually an experience related by [Hermann von] Helmholtz.[10] He reports that, as a small boy, he was walking by the Garrison Church in Potsdam and noticed some workers in the gallery. He then asked his mother if she might take a couple of the little dolls down for him. The church and the workers were already located in his farthest plane and were therefore not far away, only small. He therefore had every reason to assume that his mother, with her long arms, could bring the dolls down from the gallery. He did not know that the church had entirely different

FIGURE 12. The farthest plane of an adult (below) and a child (above)

dimensions in his mother's environment and that the people in the gallery were for her not small but far away. The situation of the farthest plane is difficult to demonstrate in the environments of animals because it is generally not easy to establish experimentally when an object approaching the subject in the latter's environment is becoming not just larger but nearer.

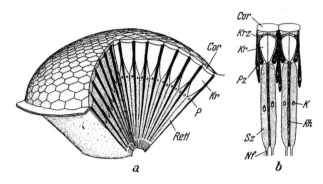

FIGURE 13. Schematic structure of the compound eye of a fly.
a: The whole eye, out of which a piece is cut *(right)* (after Hesse).
b: Two ommatidia. *Cor*: chitin cornea; *K*: nucleus; *Kr*: crystal cone;
Krz: crystal cone cell; *Nf*: nerve fiber; *P*: pigment; *Pz*: pigment cell;
Retl: retinula; *Rh*: Rhabdom; *Sz*: photoreceptor.

Experiments in catching houseflies show that the approaching human hand only causes them to fly away when it is at a distance of about half a meter. By this, one might assume that the farthest plane is to be sought at this distance.

But other observations in the case of the housefly make it seem likely that the farthest plane appears in a still different way. It is well known that flies do not only circle around a hanging lamp or chandelier but always break off their flight suddenly once they are half a meter away from it, in order then to fly away close to or below the light. In this, they behave like a boater in a sailboat who does not want to lose sight of an island.

The eye of a fly (Figure 13) is built in such a way that its visual elements (rhabdoms) present long nerve structures that must catch the image projected by their lenses at varying depths, corresponding to the distance from the perceived object. [Siegmund] Exner[11] has expressed his supposition that this could be a replacement for the muscular lens apparatus of our eye.

If one supposes that the optical apparatus of the visual elements functions like an accessory lens, then the chandelier would disappear at a certain distance and cause the fly to

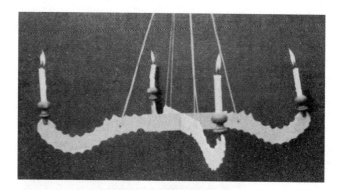

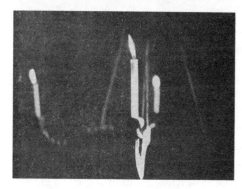

FIGURE 14. *(above)* Chandelier for human beings

FIGURE 15. *(left)* Chandelier for the fly

return. One can compare Figures 14 and 15, which show the chandelier photographed with and without an accessory lens.

Whether the farthest plane closes off visual space in this or in some other way, this plane is always present. We must therefore imagine all the animals that animate Nature around us, be they beetles, butterflies, gnats, or dragonflies who populate a meadow, as having a soap bubble around them, closed on all sides, which closes off their visual space and in which everything visible for the subject is also enclosed. Each bubble shelters other places, and in each are also found the directional planes of effective space, which give a solid scaffolding to space. The birds that flutter about, the squirrels hopping from branch to branch, or the cows grazing in the meadow, all remain permanently enclosed in the bubble that encloses their space.

Only when we can vividly imagine this fact will we recognize in our own world the bubble that encloses each and every one of us on all sides. Then, we will see each of our fellow human beings as being enclosed in bubbles that effortlessly overlap one another because they are made up of subjective perception signs. There is no space independent of subjects. If we still want to cling to the fiction of an all-encompassing world-space, that is only because we can get along with each other more easily with the help of this conventional fable.

PERCEPTION TIME

To Karl Ernst von Baer[12] belongs the merit of making time intuitively understandable as a product of the subject. Time as a sequence of moments changes from environment to environment, according to the number of moments that the subjects experience in the same amount of time. Moments are the smallest indivisible vessels of time because they are the expression of indivisible elementary sensations, so-called moment signs. For the human being, as we already said, the length of a moment is one-eighteenth of a second. And the moment is in fact the same for all areas of sensation, since these are all accompanied by the same moment sign: Eighteen vibrations of the air are no longer perceived distinctly but rather heard as a single note. It has also been shown that human beings perceive eighteen impacts on their skin as an even pressure.

Cinematography offers us the possibility of projecting movements in the outside world onto the screen in the speed to which we are accustomed. Therein, the individual images succeed each other in brief jerks of one-eighteenth of a second.

If we want to follow movements that occur too quickly for us, we use slow motion. Slow motion is the process by which a great number of images is recorded per second in order then to show them at a normal speed. Thereby we stretch the processes of movement over a longer span of time and gain the possibility of making visible processes that are too quick for our human time-speed, such as the beating of a bird's or an insect's wings. Just as slow motion slows down the processes of motion, so does time-lapse photography accelerate them. If we record a process once an hour and then show it at a speed of one-eighteenth of a second, we compress it into a brief span and gain the possibility of making visible for ourselves processes that are too slow for our speed, such as the blooming of a flower.

The question arises as to whether there are animals whose perception time has shorter or longer moments than ours, and in whose environments the motion processes occur more quickly or more slowly than they do in ours.

A young German researcher has conducted the first experiments in this area. Later, in collaboration with another researcher, he used the reaction of a fighting fish to its own mirror image. The fighting fish does not recognize its own image when it is shown to him eighteen times a second; it must be shown at least thirty times a second.

A third researcher trained the fish only to snap at their food when a gray disc was rotated behind it. If, on the other hand, a disc with black-and-white sectors was rotated slowly, this served as a "warning sign," for, in that case, the fish got a light blow when they approached the food. If the black-and-white disc was rotated more rapidly, the reactions of the fish became more unsure at a certain speed until finally they reacted in the opposite manner. That happened only when the black-and-white sectors succeeded each other at a speed greater than one-fiftieth of a second. The black-and-white warning sign then became gray.

One can conclude with certainty that in the case of these fish, which live on fast-moving prey, all processes of motion appear more slowly in their environment, as in slow motion.

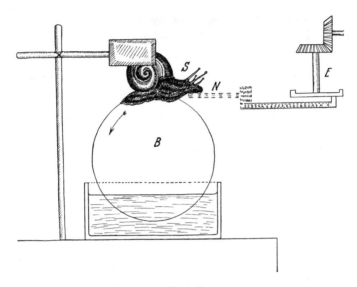

FIGURE 16. The snail's moment. B = ball,
E = eccentric, N = stick, S = snail

An example for fast motion is given in Figure 16, which is taken from the abovementioned research. A snail [*Helix pomatia*] is placed on a rubber ball which, because it is floating on water, can slide freely past beneath the snail. The snail's shell is held in place by a clamp. The snail is thereby free to crawl and also stays in the same place. If one places a small stick at the foot of the snail, it will crawl up on it. But if one strikes the snail from one to three times a second with it, the snail will turn away. However, if the blows are repeated four or more times a second, the snail begins to crawl onto the stick. In the snail's environment, a stick that moves back and forth four or more times a second must be at rest. We can conclude from this that the perception time of the snail takes place at a speed of between three and four moments a second. This has as a result that all processes of motion take place much more quickly in the snail's environment than they do in our own. Even the snail's own movements do not seem slower to it than ours do to us.

SIMPLE ENVIRONMENTS

SPACE AND TIME are of no immediate use to the subject. They only become meaningful when numerous perception marks (features) must be distinguished that would otherwise, without the spatiotemporal framework of the environment, coincide. However, such a framework is not needed in simple environments, which harbor only one perception sign. Figure 17 shows the surroundings of the paramecium. It is covered with thick

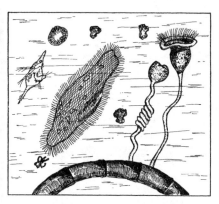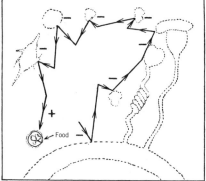

FIGURE 17. Surroundings and environment of the paramecium

rows of cilia, and it moves through the water by the motion of these cilia while rotating constantly on its long axis.

Of all the various things located in its surroundings, its environment only ever notes the same perception mark through which the paramecium, when stimulated, is caused to flee. The same perception mark, hindrance, always brings forth the same movement of flight. This consists in a backward movement with subsequent lateral turning, following which the paramecium resumes swimming forward. The hindrance is thereby placed at a distance. One may say that, in this case, the same perception

FIGURE 18. Deep-sea medusa with peripheral bodies

mark is canceled out by the same effect mark. The little creature can rest only once it arrives at its feed, the putrefactive bacteria, which, alone of all the things in its environment, send out no stimulus. These facts show us how Nature is able to shape life according to a plan even with only one functional cycle.

Even some multicellular animals, like the medusa, Rhizostoma, can manage with only one functional cycle. In this case, the organism consists of a swimming pump which takes in unfiltered seawater full of tiny plankton and pumps out filtered water. Its only vital expression consists in the rhythmical up-and-down motion of its flexible gelatinous umbrella. Through an always constant rhythm, this animal keeps itself swimming on the surface of the sea. At the same time, its fleshy stomach is alternately expanded and contracted, through which motion it pushes seawater in and out through tiny pores. The liquid contents of the stomach are driven through ramified digestive channels, the walls of which take up the nutrients and oxygen. Swimming, eating, and breathing are done through the rhythmic contraction of the muscles on the edge of its umbrella. In order to keep this motion going smoothly, eight bell-shaped organs sit along the edge of the umbrella (represented in Figure 18); their clappers strike a nerve pad with each beat of the disc. The stimulus produced thereby gives rise to the next beat of the umbrella. In this way, the medusa produces its own effect mark, and this produces the same perception mark, which in turn calls forth the same effect mark, and so on *ad infinitum*. In the medusa's environment, the same bell always tolls, and this controls the rhythm of life. All other stimuli are excluded.

Where only one functional cycle is seen, as in the case of Rhizostoma, one can speak of a "reflex animal," since the same reflex runs from each bell to the muscle band on the edge of the umbrella. One may also speak of reflex animals if yet other reflex arcs are present, as in the case of other medusas, as long as these remain completely autonomous. There are also medusas that possess tentacles which also harbor a closed reflex arc. Some medusas also possess a manubrium with its own musculature, connected to the receptors at the edge of the umbrella. All these reflex arcs operate independently of one another and are not directed from a central location.

If an external organ harbors a complete reflex arc, one can properly call this a "reflex person." Sea urchins have a great number of such reflex persons, which perform their reflex tasks without central direction, each on its own. In order to make the contrast of animals of this structure to the higher animals more clear, I have coined the sentence, "When a dog runs, the animal moves its legs. When a sea urchin runs, its legs move the animal."

Like porcupines, sea urchins have a great number of quills, which are, however, developed into autonomous reflex persons. Beyond the hard, pointed quills, which are connected to the calcium carbonate shell by a ball, and are able to point a forest of lances at any stimulus-producing object that approaches the skin, there are also tender, long, muscular tube feet which are used for climbing. Beyond this, many sea urchins possess four kinds of pedicellariae (cleaning pincers, folding pincers, grasping pincers, and venomous pincers), each having its own use, which are scattered over the entire surface of the animal.

Although many reflex persons act together, they work completely independently of one another. In this way, with the same chemical stimulus emitted by the sea urchin's enemy, the starfish, the sea urchin's quills move apart and the venomous pincers leap out and bite into the suction feet of the enemy.

One can therefore speak of a "reflex republic" in which, in spite of the complete autonomy of all reflex persons, a total civil peace reigns, for the tender suction feet of the sea urchin are never fallen upon by the biting, grasping pincers, which would otherwise grab any other approaching object. This civil peace is never dictated from a central location, as is the case with us, since our sharp teeth are always a danger for our tongue, one which is only avoided by the activation of the perception sign of pain in the central organ, for pain inhibits the act that causes pain.

In the reflex republic of the sea urchin, which has no hierarchically superior center, civil peace has to be guaranteed by other means. This occurs through the presence of a substance called autodermin. Undiluted autodermin blocks the receptors of the reflex persons. It is spread throughout the skin in such a dilute form that it has no effect when the skin makes contact with a foreign object. But as soon as two spots on the skin come into contact with each other, its effect is produced and prevents the reflex from occurring.

A reflex republic, such as each sea urchin is, can harbor numerous perception marks in its environment when it consists of numerous reflex persons. These perception marks must, however, remain completely isolated, since all functional cycles work completely isolated from one another.

Even the tick, whose vital expressions, as we saw, consist mainly of three reflexes, represents a higher type of animal because its functional cycles do not make use of these isolated reflex arcs but possess a common perception organ. Therefore, there exists the possibility that, in the tick's environment, the tick's prey can form a single unit even though it consists only of butyric acid stimulus, tactile stimulus, and warmth stimulus. This possibility does not exist for the sea urchin. Its perception marks, composed of separated chemical and pressure stimuli, form completely isolated values.

Many sea urchins respond to any darkening of the horizon with a movement of their quills that, as Figure 19 shows, takes the same form whether against a cloud, a ship, or the real enemy, a fish. But even this presentation of the sea urchin's environment is not simplified enough. It is not a matter of the transfer of the perception sign of darkness to the environment by the sea urchin, since the sea urchin has no visual space. Rather, the shadow acts like the soft passing of a ball of cotton over the light-sensitive skin. It would be technically impossible to represent this.

FIGURE 19. Surroundings *(top)* and
environment *(bottom)* of the sea urchin

FORM AND MOVEMENT AS PERCEPTION MARKS

EVEN IF ONE WANTED TO ASSUME for the environment of the sea urchin that all perception marks of the different reflex persons were provided with a local sign and that each one was therefore located at a different place, there would still be no possibility of connecting these places with each other. This environment would therefore have to lack the perception marks of form and movement that would require the joining together of several places, and this is indeed the case.

Form and movement first appear in higher perception worlds. Now, thanks to experiences in our own environments, we are accustomed to assuming that the form of an object is its originally given perception mark and that movement only comes into play occasionally as an ancillary phenomenon, a secondary perception mark. That is, however, not applicable to many environments of animals. In them, moving form and resting form are not only two perception marks that are entirely independent of each other, but movement even without form can appear independently as a perception sign.

Figure 20 shows the jackdaw hunting for grasshoppers. The jackdaw is completely unable to see a motionless grasshopper and only snaps at it when it hops. Here, we shall first suppose that the jackdaw is well familiar with the form of the grasshopper at rest but cannot recognize it as a single unit due to the blades of grass which crisscross over it, just as we have trouble finding the familiar form in ambiguous picture puzzles.[13] On this account, only in the leap does the form separate itself from the secondary images that are in the way.

But, after further experience, one must assume that the jackdaw is not at all familiar with the resting form of the grasshopper and only searches for the moving form. This would explain the "playing dead" done by many insects. If their resting

FIGURE 20. Jackdaw and grasshopper

form is not at all present in the perception world of the pursuing enemy, then they would certainly drop out of this perception world entirely by playing dead and could not be found even by looking.

I built an angling rod for flies that consists of a little stick on which a pea hangs on a fine thread. The pea is covered with flycatching adhesive. If one makes the pea swing gently back and forth in front of a sunny window sill on which there are many flies, a certain number of flies will always dive at the pea, and some will stick to it. Afterward, one can observe that the caught flies are all males. The whole procedure represents a mating flight gone wrong. In the case of the chandelier, it is also a matter of males who dive upon females as they fly through.

The swinging pea is a convincing imitation of the perception mark of a flying female and is never mistaken for a female fly when it is at rest, from which one can conclude that moving female and resting female are two different perception marks.

That movement without form can also appear as a perception mark is demonstrated by Figure 21, which compares depictions of the scallop in its surroundings and its environment. In the surroundings of the scallop and in sight of its hundred eyes, there is its most dangerous enemy, the *Asterias* starfish. As long as the starfish remains still, it has no effect at all on the scallop. The characteristic form of the starfish is not a perception mark for the scallop. But as soon as the starfish starts to move, the scallop throws out its long tentacles, which serve as olfactory organs. These approach the starfish and receive the new stimulus. The scallop then gets up and swims away.

Experiments have shown that it is completely irrelevant

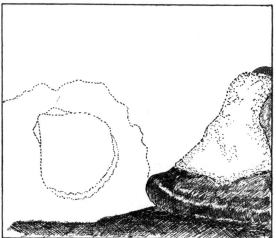

FIGURE 21. Surroundings *(top)* and environment *(bottom)* of the scallop

what form or color a moving object possesses. It will only appear as a perception mark in the scallop's environment if its movement is as slow as that of the starfish. The scallop's eyes are set to pick up neither form nor color, but only a certain speed of movement, which corresponds exactly to that of its enemy. This does not completely describe the enemy, for a certain olfactory perception sign must also come into play in order for the second functional cycle to be activated, which, through flight, brings the scallop out of proximity to its enemy and extinguishes the enemy's perception marks once and for all through this effect mark.

For a long time now, it has been supposed that there is a perception mark for form in the environment of the earthworm. Darwin pointed to the fact that earthworms treat leaves and pine needles differently according to the form of each (Figure 22). The earthworm pulls both leaves and pine needles into its narrow tunnel; they serve as protection as well as nourishment. Most leaves get stuck if they are pulled stem first into a tight tube. On the other hand, they roll up easily and offer no resistance if grasped by the tip. The pine needles, which always fall in pairs, cannot be grasped at the tip, only at the base, if one wants to pull them through a narrow tunnel. From the fact that earthworms handle both leaves and needles correctly with no trouble, it had been concluded that the forms of these objects, which play a decisive role in the effect world of the earthworm, must also be present as perception signs in the perception world.

This assumption has turned out to be false. It was shown that earthworms pulled small sticks of the same shape, which had been dipped in gelatin, into their holes sometimes by one end and sometimes by the other. But as soon as one end had been dusted with powder from the tip section of a dried cherry leaf and the other with powder from the stem section, the earthworms could distinguish the two ends of the sticks just as they were able to distinguish the tip and the stem of the leaf itself.

Although the earthworms had treated the leaves according to their shapes, they went not by the shapes but by the taste of the leaves. This arrangement was obviously arrived at because the perception organs of the worms are still structured too simply to form perception marks based on shape. This

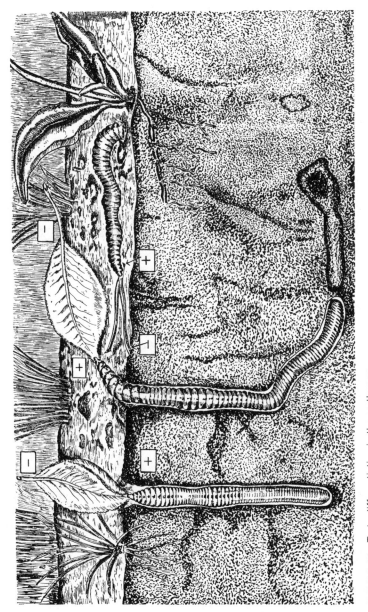

FIGURE 22. Taste differentiation in the earthworm

example shows us that Nature knows how to deal with difficulties that to us seem entirely insuperable.

So there was nothing to the notion of shape perception in earthworms. The question therefore became all the more urgent: Which animals could one assume to have shape as a perception sign in their environments?

This question was only answered later, when it was shown that bees prefer to land on shapes that had a more opened form, such as stars and crosses; they avoid closed forms, such as squares and circles. Figure 23 shows contrasting depictions of the surroundings and the environment of a bee following these observations.

We see the bees in their surroundings, a meadow in bloom, in which blossoming flowers alternate with closed buds. If one places the bees in their environment and transforms the blooms according to their shape into stars or crosses, the buds will take the form of circles. From this, the biological meaning of this newly discovered characteristic of the bees is effortlessly apparent. Only the blooms, not the buds, have meaning for the bees.

Relations of meaning are, however, as we already saw in the case of the ticks, the only certain guides in the investigation of environments. Whether the open forms are physiologically more effective is entirely beside the point.

The *problem of form* is put in these studies in a most simple formula. It suffices to assume that the perception cells for local cells in the perception organ are arranged in two groups, the ones according to the schema "opened," the others according to the pattern "closed." Further distinctions are not present. If these schemata are transposed outward, as wonderful new studies show, they are filled up, in the case of the bees, with colors and odors.

Neither the earthworm nor the scallop nor the tick is in possession of such patterns. They therefore lack any true perception images in their environments.

FIGURE 23. Surroundings *(top)* and
environment *(bottom)* of the bee

GOAL AND PLAN

SINCE WE HUMAN BEINGS are accustomed to dragging our existences wearily from one goal to another, we are convinced that animals live in the same way. That is a fundamental mistake that has led research to this point down the wrong path.

Nobody would ever attribute a goal to earthworms or sea urchins. But, in describing the life of the tick, we already spoke of how they lie in wait for their prey. With this expression, we smuggled our workaday human concerns, even without meaning to, into the life of the tick, which is led purely according to Nature's plan.

It should therefore be our first concern to extinguish the will-o'-the-wisp of the goal in our observation of environments. This can only happen inasmuch as we consider the vital expressions of animals from the point of view of the plan. Perhaps certain acts of the highest mammals will turn out to be goal-oriented actions which themselves are part of Nature's overall plan.

With all other mammals, actions directed at a goal are not at all evident. In order to demonstrate this statement, it will be necessary to give the reader a look at some environments that will leave no doubt that this is indeed the case. Figure 24 is the product of information I was kindly given on the perception of sound in moths. As indicated in the illustration, it makes no difference whether the sound to which the animals are attuned is the sound made by a bat or is produced by rubbing a glass stopper. The effect is the same. Moths that are easily visible because of their bright coloration fly away at the high-pitched sound, while those that have a protective coloration alight at the same sound. The same perception mark has the opposite effect in their case. This cannot be a case of making a distinction or setting a goal, since no moth has ever

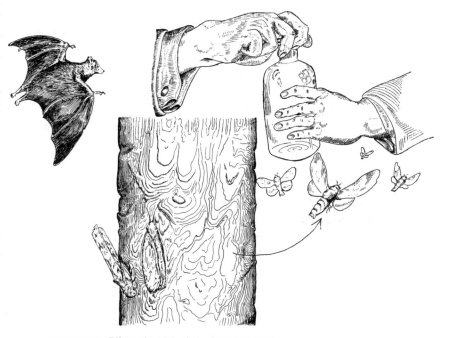

FIGURE 24. Effect of a high-pitched tone on moths

seen its own skin color. Our admiration for the planned character governing both is even greater when we discover that the artful microscopic structure of the moth's hearing organ exists solely for this single high-pitched tone emitted by the bat. These moths are totally deaf to all else.

The opposition between goal and plan is already evident in a wonderful observation by [J. Henri] Fabre.[14] He placed a female emperor moth[15] on a sheet of white paper, on which the moth performed motions with her abdomen. Then, he placed the female under a bell jar next to the paper. At night, whole hordes of males of this very rare species of Lepidoptera came flying through the window and crowded onto the paper. Fabre could not figure out what physical or chemical effect was emitted by the paper.

In this regard, experiments with grasshoppers and crickets have been much more informative; Figure 25 depicts these experiments. In one room, in front of a microphone that serves as a reception device, there sits a lively fiddling individual. In another room, members of the opposite sex gather before a speaker, paying no attention to another individual who fiddles in vain because he is sitting under a bell jar, which his music does not penetrate. The mates cannot come together, since the optical image has no effect whatsoever.

Both experiments prove the same point: it is hardly a case of pursuing a goal. The peculiar-seeming behavior of the males [in the first case; females do not chirp] is readily explained if it is investigated from the point of view of its planlike quality. In both cases, a functional cycle is activated by a perception mark, but, because of the elimination of the normal object, the right effect mark is never produced; this would be necessary in order to cancel out the perception mark. Normally, another perception mark would have to step in as a substitute and trigger another functional cycle. The nature of this second perception mark requires closer examination. In any event, it is a necessary link in the chain of functional cycles that make sexual reproduction possible.

"That's all well and good," one might say. "There's no hope of finding goal-oriented action in insects. They are governed directly by Nature's plan, which, as we already saw in the case of the tick, establishes their perception marks immediately. But anybody who has ever been in a chicken run and seen how a mother hen rushes to the aid of her chicks cannot doubt the existence of truly goal-oriented actions." Some very nice experiments have provided complete certainty precisely in such cases.

Figure 26 explains the results of these experiments. When a chick is bound by one foot, it emits a loud peep, which immediately causes the mother hen to run toward the sound with ruffled feathers, even if the chick is not visible to her. As

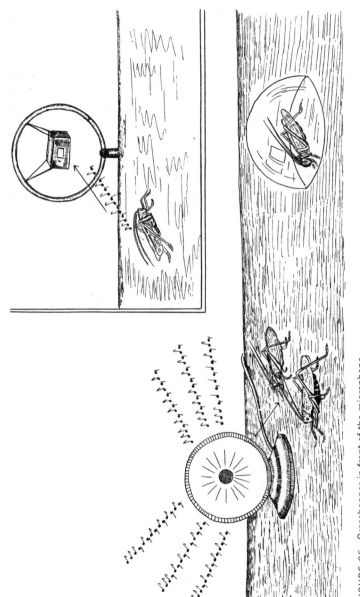

FIGURE 25. Grasshopper in front of the microphone

FIGURE 26. Mother hen and chicks

soon as the mother hen catches sight of the chick, she begins to peck furiously at an imaginary opponent.

However, if one places the fettered chick under a bell jar right before its mother's eyes, so that she can very well see it but not hear its peeping, she is not disturbed in the least by this

FIGURE 27. Mother hen and black chick

sight. Even in this case, it is not a matter of a goal-oriented action but of an interrupted chain of functional cycles. Normally,
the perception mark of peeping emanates indirectly from an
enemy who is attacking the chick. This perception mark is can-
celled out according to plan by the blows of the hen's beak,
which chase off the enemy. The chick that flaps about but does
not peep is not a perception mark that would trigger a particular activity. This would also be completely inappropriate, since
the hen is hardly able to untie a cord.

The hen depicted in Figure 27 behaved in an even more
peculiar and goal-less manner. She had incubated a set of eggs
of another, white variety of chicken along with one egg of her
own, black variety. She behaved in a completely senseless way
toward the black chick, her own flesh and blood. She rushed
toward the black chick's peeping, yet, if she became aware of
its peeping among the white chicks, she hacked away at it. The
acoustic and the optical perception mark of the same object
aroused two contradictory functional cycles in her. The two
perception marks of the chick had not coalesced into one unit
in the hen's environment.

PERCEPTION IMAGE AND EFFECT IMAGE

THE JUXTAPOSITION of the subject's goals and Nature's plan also allows us to get past the question of instinct, which nobody can make any sense of anyway. Does the acorn need an instinct in order to become an oak? Or does a bunch of osteoblasts work instinctively to form a bone? If one denies this and, instead of instinct, takes Nature's plan as an ordering factor, one can recognize the reign of Nature's plans in the weaving of a spider's web or the structure of birds' nests, since, in both cases, one can hardly speak of an individual goal.

Instinct is only a stopgap product that must stand in if people deny the supraindividual plans of Nature. And people deny them because they have no real idea of what a plan is, since it is neither a force nor a material substance.

Yet it is not difficult to have an intuitive understanding of what a plan is if one sticks to a concrete example. Even the most beautiful plan is not enough to pound a nail into the wall if one has no hammer. But even the most beautiful hammer is not enough if one has no plan and leaves things to chance. In that case, one only hits one's own fingers.

Without plans, i.e., without Nature's all-controlling conditions of order, there would be no orderly Nature, only chaos. Every crystal is the product of a natural plan, and, when physicists present Bohr's beautiful atomic model, they explain thereby the plan of inanimate Nature that they were seeking.

Now then, in the study of environments, the rule of living plans of Nature is most clearly expressed. To be on their trail is one of the most interesting pastimes. We therefore do not want to be led astray but rather to continue our course through environments.

The processes depicted in Plate 1 present an overview of the results of studies of the hermit crab. It has been demonstrated that the hermit crab has a very simple spatial schema as a perception image. Each object of a certain magnitude having a cylindrical or conical outline can become significant for it.

As is apparent in the illustrations, the same cylinder-shaped object—in this case a sea anemone—can change its meaning in the environment of the same crab depending upon the mood the crab happens to be in.

We see in each case the same sea anemone and the same crab before us. But, in the first case (pink anemone), the anemones that the crab had carried on its sea-snail shell have been taken from it. In the second case (orange anemone), the snail shell has also been taken from it, and, in the third case (green anemone), a crab carrying a snail shell and a sea anemone was allowed to go hungry for some time. This was enough to put the crab in three different moods.

The anemone changed its meaning for the crab according to each of the three different moods. In the first case, in which the crab's housing must dispense with the protective outer layer of anemones which defends against squid, the perception image of the sea anemone (pink) had a "protective tone." That expresses itself in the action of the crab, which sticks it on top of his housing. If the same crab is deprived of his shell, the perception image of the sea anemone (orange) takes on a "dwelling tone," which expresses itself in the fact that the crab tries to crawl into it, albeit in vain. In the third case, that of the starving crab, the sea anemone (green) takes on a "feeding tone," inasmuch as the crab begins to feed on it.

These experiences are so valuable because they show, already in the environments of the arthropods, that the perception image provided by the sensory organs can be completed and altered by an "effect image," which is dependent on the next action that takes place. The experiments that attempted to illuminate this state of affairs were carried out on dogs. The research question was very simple, and the dogs' responses were clear. A dog had been trained to jump on a chair placed in front of him when he heard the command "chair." Now, the stool was taken away and the command repeated. As it turned out, the dog treated all objects with which he could do the same trick of "sitting" as chairs, and he jumped onto them. A whole series of other objects, such as boxes, shelves, and overturned footstools, acquired a "sitting tone," as we would like to put it, and specifically a "canine sitting tone" and not a "human sitting tone," for many of these "dog chairs" were not proper human seating.

By the same right, it was shown that "table" and "dog basket" acquired for the dog a special tone that had to do with the acts performed by the dog upon them. The problem itself can only be developed in complete relief in the case of human beings. How do we notice the sitting of the chair, the drinking of the cup, the climbing of the ladder, which is not given to the senses in any case? We notice in all objects that we have learned to use the act which we perform with them, with the same assurance with which we notice their shape or color.

I had taken a young, very intelligent, and skillful Negro[16] from the African interior with me to Dar es Salaam. All he lacked was a familiarity with European tools. As I instructed him to climb a short ladder, he asked me, "How am I supposed to do that? All I see are bars and holes." As soon as another Negro had demonstrated climbing up to him, he could imitate him with no problem. From then on, the sensorily given "bars and holes" took on a "climbing tone" for him and were recognized in all cases as a ladder. The perception image of bars and holes had been complemented by the effect image. Through this, it acquired a new meaning, and this meaning expressed itself as a new characteristic, as a performance tone or effect tone.

Through this experiment with the Negro, we become aware that we have worked out an effect image for all the acts we perform on objects in our environment, and that we alloy this effect image so effectively with the perception images we receive from our sense organs that the two acquire a new characteristic, which announces its meaning to us. We will designate this simply its effect tone.

If it serves more than one kind of act, the same object can have multiple effect images, which then give the same perception image another effect tone. A chair can on occasion be used as a weapon and then acquires a different effect image, which expresses itself as a "battering tone." Even in this very human case, just as with the hermit crab, the subject's mood is crucial for which effect image gives a tone to the perception image. Effect images can only be required in cases where central effect organs are present that control animals' actions. All animals that operate in a purely reflective manner, such as the sea urchin, must be excluded from this category. But for other cases, as the hermit crab proves, the influence of mood is felt far down in the animal kingdom.

If we want to use effect images for the portrayal of environments of animals who are farther away from us, we must keep in mind that these images are acts of animals which are projected into environments, which confer meaning upon perception images only through the effect tone. For the presentation of things important for life in the environment of an animal, we shall therefore have to provide their sensuously given perception image with an effect tone in order to fully grasp its meaning. Even in those cases where there is not yet a spatially articulated perception image, as with the tick, we may yet say that, in the case of the only three meaningful stimuli which the tick receives from its prey, the meaning connected to these stimuli—falling off, running around, and boring in—comes from the effect tones. The selecting activity of the receptors, a sort of main gate for the stimuli, certainly plays the leading role, but only the effect tone connected with the stimuli confers infallible certainty upon it.

Since the effect images can be derived from the easily recognizable acts of the animals, the things in the environment of an alien subject take on a high degree of concreteness. When a dragonfly flies toward a branch in order to alight upon it, the branch is not just present in the dragonfly's environment as a perception image but is also distinguished by a sitting tone which makes it recognizable compared to all other branches.

Only when we take the effect tones into account can the environment take on the security for the animals that we admire in it. We may say that an animal is able to distinguish as many objects as it can carry out actions in its environment. If it has only a few actions and a few effect images, its environment will then consist of few objects. The environment is thereby impoverished but is also all the more safe for it, for it is much easier to orient oneself among few objects than among numerous objects. If the paramecium possessed an effect image of its action, its environment would consist of all the same kind of objects, which would all bear the same obstacle tone. In any case, such an environment would not lack at all for security.

With the number of actions available to an animal, the number of objects in its environment also increases. It increases as well in the individual life of any animal capable of accumulating experiences, for each new experience conditions a new attitude toward new impressions. By this means, new perception images with new effect tones are created.

This is especially evident in the case of dogs, which learn to handle certain objects useful to human beings insofar as they make them into things of use to dogs. In spite of this fact, the number of dog objects remains far less than the number of human objects. This should be clear from the three color illustrations (Plates 2, 3, and 4) taken together. In each, the same room is represented. But the objects found therein are reproduced in different colors that correspond to the number of effect tones connected to the room by the human being, the dog, and the housefly respectively. In the human's environment, the effect tones of the objects in the room are represented by the sitting shade (salmon) for the chair, the food shade (pale pink) for the table, and, for the glasses and plates, further cor-

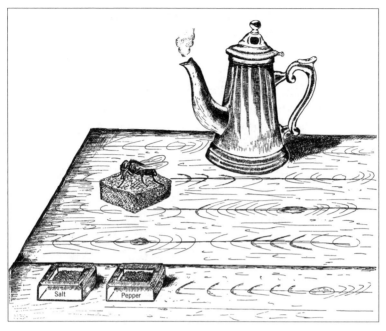

FIGURE 28. The things in the fly's environment

responding effect shades (pink and red: eating and drinking tones). The floor possesses a walking shade, while the book-shelf (purple) has a reading shade, and the secretary shows a writing shade (cream). The wall has an obstacle shade (tur-quoise) and the lamp has a light tone (white).

In the dog's environment, the recurring, similar effect tones are represented by the same colors, but only eating shade, sitting shade, and so on, remain. All else shows an ob-stacle shade. The swivel stool as well has no sitting tone for the dog because of its smoothness.

Finally, we see that, for the fly, everything has only a running tone except for the objects on the table and the lamp, the significance of which we have already indicated.

How surely the fly can orient itself in the room as its surroundings is more precisely explained by Figure 28. As soon as the pot of hot coffee is placed on the table, the flies gather around it because the warmth is a stimulus for them. The tabletop is simply passed through since it has only a running tone. And since flies have taste organs on their feet that, when stimulated, cause their proboscis to protrude, they are captivated by their food source, while all other objects cause them to move on. In this case, it is particularly easy to contrast the fly's environment to its surroundings.

THE FAMILIAR PATH

IT IS EASIEST to be convinced of the differences in human environments when one has a local guide take one through an unfamiliar area. The guide follows a sure path which we ourselves cannot see. Among all the many rocks and trees of the surroundings, there are a few that, placed one after the other, distinguish themselves as path markers from all the other rocks and trees, even though no sign makes this known to anyone not familiar with the path.

The familiar path depends solely on the individual subject and is therefore a typical environment problem. The familiar path is a spatial problem and therefore related to the visual space as well as the effect space of the subject. That is an immediate result of the way in which a familiar path is described—more or less like this: "Past the red house, turn right, then a hundred paces straight ahead, and then left." We use three kinds of perception marks to describe a path: 1. visual, 2. the directional planes of the coordinate system, 3. directional steps. In this case, we do not use the most basic directional step, i.e., the smallest possible unit of motion, but rather the common combination of elementary impulses that we need for the performance of a step in walking.

The walking step, in which a leg moves evenly back and forth, is so fixed in individual human beings and is with so many people approximately the same length that it was used as a common measure of length well into modern times. If I tell someone that he should walk a hundred paces, I mean that he should impart the same movement impulse to his leg one hundred times. The result will be approximately the same measured distance each time even if we pay no attention to visual perception marks. Directional steps therefore play a prominent role in the familiar path.

It would be very interesting to establish how the problem of the familiar path plays itself out in the environment of animals. Different olfactory and tactile perception signs certainly play a defining role in the structure of the familiar path.

For decades now, many American researchers have carried out thousands of series of experiments in which the most different kinds of animals had to find their way through a maze, in an attempt to establish how quickly each animal can learn a certain path. They never saw the problem of the familiar path that is concerned here. They never studied visual, tactile, or olfactory perception marks, nor did they consider the animal's application of the coordinate system; that right and left are a problem in and of themselves never occurred to them. Also, they did not explore the question of counting paces, because they did not see that the pace can also be a measure of distance for animals. In short, the problem of the familiar path must be taken on again from the beginning in spite of the incredible amount of observational material available. Finding out the familiar path in the environment of the dog is, in addition to its theoretical interest, of an eminently practical significance as soon as one takes into account which problems the blind person's guide dog must solve.

Figure 29 shows a blind man being led by his dog. The blind man's environment is very limited; he knows it only insofar as he can feel out his path with his cane and feet. The street

FIGURE 29. Blind man and dog

through which he strolls is for him plunged into darkness, but his dog is supposed to lead him home via a certain path. The difficulty in training the dog consists in introducing perception marks into his environment that do not interest him but, rather, are in the blind person's interest. In this way, the path down which he leads the blind person must be arranged in an arc with obstacles with which the blind person could collide. It is especially difficult to teach the dog the perception sign for a mailbox or an open window, things which the dog would normally pass right under without noticing them. But even the curbstone of the street, over which the blind person would ordinarily stumble, is hard to introduce into the dog's environment, as it is normally hardly noticed by a dog roaming free.

Figure 30 represents an experimental observation of young jackdaws. As one can see, the daw flies around the entire house but then turns around and uses the familiar outbound path for its return flight in order to return to the site from which it flew, which it did not recognize coming from the other side.

FIGURE 30. The familiar path of the jackdaw

We learned recently that rats still use a familiar detour even when the direct path is available to them.

The problem of the familiar path has been approached anew with regard to fighting fish, and the following results were obtained:

One could observe in the case of these fish that the unfamiliar has a repelling effect on them. A glass plate was lowered into the aquarium; the plate had two round holes through which the fish could easily slip. If their food was placed right behind the hole, it took quite a while until the fish slipped hesitantly through the hole to seize the food. Then, the food was

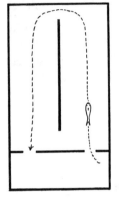

shown to it to one side of the hole; the fish went right through. Then, the food was held behind the second hole. In spite of this, the fish slipped through the familiar hole and avoided using the unfamiliar hole.

Then, as Figure 31 shows, a partition was built on the feeding side of the aquarium, and the fish was lured around the partition with food. If the fish was shown the food on the far side of the partition, the fish swam along the familiar path without fuss, even if the partition was placed in such a way that the fish could have reached the food by swimming past the partition in

FIGURE 31.
The familiar path
of a fish

front. Visual and directional perception marks and perhaps also directional steps were thereby involved.

All in all, one could say that the familiar path works like a streak of a more fluid medium in a more viscous one.

HOME AND TERRITORY

THE PROBLEM of home and territory [*Heimat*] is closely related to that of the familiar path.

As a point of departure, one might best take experiments on sticklebacks. The male stickleback builds himself a nest, the entrance to which is marked by a colored thread—a visual path perception mark for the young? The young grow up in the nest under the father's care. This nest is his home, but his territory extends beyond the nest. Figure 32 shows an aquarium in which two sticklebacks have built their nests in opposite corners. An invisible border stretches through the aquarium and divides it into two areas, each of which belongs to a nest. This area belong-

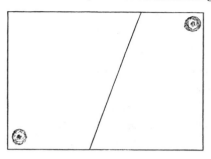

ing to the nest is the territory of one stickleback, and he defends it vigorously and successfully even against larger sticklebacks. In his own territory, the stickleback is always the winner.

FIGURE 32. Home and territory of the stickleback

Territory is purely a problem of the environment because it represents an exclusively subjective product, the presence of which even the most detailed knowledge of the surroundings offers no explanation at all.

One might now ask, "Which animals have a territory, and which do not?" A housefly whose repeated back and forth flight marks a certain segment of space around the chandelier does not have, by that right, a territory. On the other hand, a spider who builds a nest in which it is permanently active has a home which is also its territory.

The same is true of the mole (Figure 33); it, too, has built its home and its territory. A regularly structured tunnel system spreads itself underground like a spider's web. Not only the individual passages, but the whole piece of ground they include are the mole's sovereign territory. In captivity, it lays out these passages so that they resemble a spider's web. We were able to demonstrate that, thanks to its highly developed scent organ, the mole is well able to find its food not only inside the passageway, but, beyond that, that he can smell food objects in solid earth at a distance of five to six meters. In a tightly designed system of passageways such as the mole builds in captivity, the areas of earth between the passageways would also be controlled by the mole's senses, while in nature, where the mole lays out his tunnels farther apart, the animal can still examine the earth around the passageways by smell. Like a spider, the mole goes through this network of tubes several times and collects all the prey that has wandered into it. In the midst of this tube system, the mole builds its own cave, padded with dried leaves—its own home in which it passes its hours of rest. The underground passages are all familiar paths for it, which it can run through with the same speed and agility backward and forward. Its hunting ground, which is also its territory, extends as far as the passages do, and it defends this territory to the death against any and all neighboring moles.

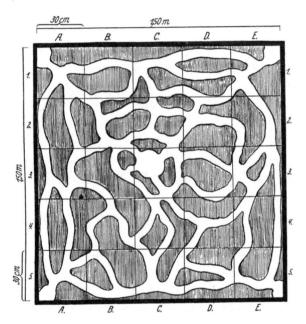

FIGURE 33. Home and territory of the mole

The ability with which the mole, a blind animal, can orient itself without fail in what is for us a completely homogeneous medium is astounding. If it is trained to get its food at a certain spot, it can find this spot again even after all the passages leading to it are completely destroyed. This excludes the possibility that it can be guided by olfactory perception signs.

Its space is purely an effect space. One must assume that the mole is able to find again a path it has been over once already by reproducing directional steps. In this case, the tactile perception marks associated with the directional steps play an important role, as they do with all blind animals. One may assume that the directional steps and directional perception marks are joined in a spatial schema. If its passage system or parts thereof are destroyed, it can produce a new system that resembles the old one with the help of a projected schema.

Bees also build themselves a home, but the area around the hive, while it is their hunting ground, is not an area that is defended against foreign intruders. In the case of the magpie, on the other hand, one may speak of home and territory, for they build their nests in an area in which they tolerate no free-roaming magpies.

With many animals, one would likely experience that they defend their hunting ground against other animals of their own species and thereby make it into their territory. Any piece of land at all would seem to be a political map for all species if one were to inscribe these territorial areas into it, and this demarcation would be established through attack and defense. It would also turn out that, in many cases, no more free land at all is available, and one territory bumps up against another.

All the more remarkable is the observation that a neutral zone insinuates itself between the nest and the hunting ground of many raptors, a zone in which they seize no prey at all. Ornithologists must be correct in their assumption that this organization of the environment was made by Nature in order to keep the raptors from seizing their own young. If, as they say, the nestling becomes a branchling and spends its days hopping from branch to branch near the parental nest, it would easily be in danger of being seized by mistake by its own parents. In this way, it can spend its days free of danger in the neutral zone of the protected area. The protected area is sought out by many songbirds as a nesting and incubation site where

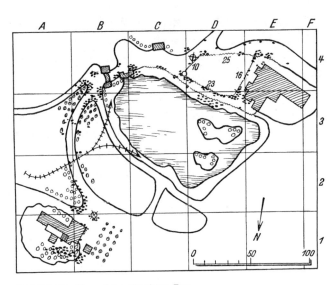

FIGURE 34. Map of the Hamburg Zoo

they can raise their young free of danger under the protection of the big predator.

The way in which dogs make their territory recognizable to other members of their species deserves special attention. Figure 34 represents a map of the Hamburg Zoo, with the paths on which two male dogs who were walked daily urinated on these daily walks. The places where they left their odor marks were the same as those that were easily recognizable to the human eye. Whenever both dogs were walked at the same time, a urinating contest regularly occurred.

As soon as he encounters a strange dog, a spirited dog is always inclined to leave his calling card on the first object he sees. Also, as soon as he enters another dog's territory, which is recognizable by that dog's odor marks, he will seek out the other's marks one after the other and will carefully mark over them. On the other hand, a timid dog would go bashfully past the odor marks of a strange dog in that dog's territory and through no odor sign betray its own presence.

Marking territory is common with the large bears of North America as well, as Figure 35 shows. Standing straight up at his full height, the bear uses his back and muzzle to rub the bark of a lone-standing pine visible from far away. This serves as a signal to other bears to keep well clear of this pine and to avoid the whole area in which a bear of such proportions defends its territory.

FIGURE 35. A bear marks his home

THE COMPANION

I VIVIDLY RECALL a feisty little duckling that had been hatched among turkey chicks and had attached itself so tightly to the turkey family that it never went into the water and strictly avoided the ducklings which emerged fresh and clean from the water.

Soon thereafter, a very young wild duck was brought to me; it followed my every step. I had the impression that it was my boots that attracted it so, since it also ran occasionally after a black dachshund. I concluded from this that a black moving object was sufficient to replace the image of its mother, and I had the duck placed back in the vicinity of its maternal nest so that it could recover the lost family connection.

Today, it seems doubtful to me that this happened, as I have since learned that grey goose hatchlings, freshly taken from the incubator, must be placed in a sack and brought to a goose family so that they willingly attach themselves to others of their species. If they stay any longer in the company of human beings, they reject any association with their own kind.

In all these cases, it is a matter of confusing perception images, which is especially common in the environment of birds. What we know about the perception images of birds is still not sufficient to draw conclusions with certainty.

In Figure 20, we already observed the jackdaw on the hunt for grasshoppers, and we acquired the impression that the jackdaw possesses no perception image for the resting grasshopper and that it is therefore not present in the jackdaw's environment. Another experimental observation concerning the perception images of the jackdaw is given in Figures 36 a and b. Here, one sees a jackdaw in attack position toward a cat that is carrying away a jackdaw in its mouth. A cat with no prey in its mouth is never attacked by a jackdaw. Only when its dangerous teeth are out of action because of the prey between its teeth can it be an object of attack for the jackdaw.

FIGURE 36. a. Jackdaw in fighting position against cat
b. Jackdaw in fighting position against swimming trunks

This seems to a great degree to be a precisely goal-attuned action of the jackdaw. But, in truth, it is a plan-driven reaction which occurs without any insight on the jackdaw's part. For it was observed that the same attack position was assumed when a pair of black swimming trunks was carried past. Also, the cat was not attacked when it carried a white jackdaw by. The perception image of a black object carried past sets off the attack position immediately.

Such a general perception image can always give rise to confusion, as we already observed in the case of the sea urchin, in whose environment clouds and ships were always confused with the enemy, fish, since the sea urchin reacts to any darkening of its horizon in the same way.

With birds, however, we cannot get away with such a simple explanation. With the processes evident in gregarious birds, there are abundant and contradictory experiences concerning the confusion of perception images. Only recently has there been success in working out guiding perspectives in the typical case of a tame jackdaw named Tschock.

FIGURE 37. The jackdaw Tschock and its four companions

Gregarious jackdaws have around them their entire lives a "companion" with whom they undertake all sorts of actions. Even if a jackdaw is brought up alone, it does not go without the companion but, if it cannot find one of its own species, it takes on a "substitute companion," and, in fact, a new substitute companion can fill that gap for each new activity. [Konrad] Lorenz[17] was kind enough to send me Figure 37, in which one can see the companion relations at a glance.

In its youth, the jackdaw Tschock had Lorenz himself as its mother-companion. It followed him all over the place; it called to him when it wanted to be fed. Once it had learned to get its own feed, it chose the maid as its companion and performed the characteristic courtship dance in front of her. Later, it found a young jackdaw which became its adoptive companion and which Tschock fed. Whenever Tschock prepared for a longer flight, it attempted to persuade Lorenz to fly with it in typical jackdaw fashion, by flying straight up just behind his back. When that did not work, it joined flying crows, who then became its flight companions.

As one can see, there is no single perception image available for the companion. This is also not possible, since the role of the companion is constantly changing.

The perception image of the mother-companion seems in most cases not to be fixed at birth as far as its form and color are concerned. To the contrary, this image is often the maternal voice. "One would have to work out on a certain case of mother-companion," writes Lorenz, "which mother-signs are inborn and which are individually acquired. The uncanny thing is that after a few days or even only hours, the acquired mother-signs are so engraved (as with the grey goose in Heinroth) that one would swear, when the young animal is taken from its mother at this early stage, that they are inborn."

The same occurs in the choice of the love companion. Here, too, the acquired signs of the substitute companion are so surely engraved that an unmistakable perception image of

the substitute companion is created—after the first confusion
has occurred. As a consequence of this, even animals of the
same species are rejected as love companions.

This is most clearly illuminated by a delightful experience. In the Amsterdam Zoo, there was a pair of bitterns of
which the male had "fallen in love" with the zoo director. In
order to allow the bitterns to mate, the director had to stay out
of sight for quite some time. This had the positive result that
the male bittern became accustomed to the female. This ended
up in a happy marriage, and, as the female sat brooding over
her eggs, the director dared to show his face once more. And
what happened then? When the male saw his former love companion again, he chased the female off of the nest and seemed
to signal by repeated bows that the director should take his
proper place and carry on the business of incubation.

The perception image of the child companion seems in
general to have more solid contours. Here, the gaping maw
of the young probably plays the leading role. But even in this
case, one sometimes sees in the case of selectively bred varie-
ties of hen, such as Orpingtons, that the mother hen also moth-
ers young kittens and rabbits.

The substitute companion for free flying is viewed in a
slightly broader frame, as the case of Tschock showed.

If one considers that a pair of swimming trunks becomes
an assailable enemy for the jackdaw when the trunks are carried past it, i.e., that it acquires the effect tone "enemy," one
could say that this is a case of a substitute enemy. Since there
are many enemies in the jackdaw's environment, the appearance of the substitute enemy has no effect on the perception
images of the true enemies. This is different in the case of the
companion. The companion occurs only singly in the environment, and the conferral of an effect tone on a substitute companion has to make the later appearance of a true companion
impossible. After the perception image of the chambermaid had

received the exclusive "love tone" in Tschock's environment, all
other perception images became ineffectual.

If one imagines that all living beings, i.e., all moving
things in the jackdaw's environment, fall into one of two categories, jackdaws and non-jackdaws (which is probably analogous to the case of primitive human beings), and if, moreover,
the boundary line is drawn differently in each individual's
experience, then one can perhaps understand how such grotesque mistakes as those described above can occur. It is not
the perception image alone which determines if it is a matter
of a jackdaw or a non-jackdaw, but the effect image of the individual's own attitude. This alone can decide what perception
image the respective companion tones receive.

SEARCH IMAGE AND SEARCH TONE

I SHALL BEGIN once more with two personal experiences that
best explain what we mean by the factor of the search image,
which is so important for the environment. When I spent a
while as a guest at a friend's house, an earthen water pitcher
was placed at my place at the table every day at lunch. One day,
the butler had shattered the clay pitcher and, instead, placed
a glass carafe in front of me. When I looked for the pitcher
during the meal, I did not see the glass carafe. Only when my
friend assured me that the water was in its usual place did
different sparkling lights scattered on knives and plates shoot
through the air and come together to form the carafe. Figure
38 is meant to express this experience: the search image wipes
out the perception image.

The second experience is as follows. One day, I entered a
shop in which I had to pay a rather large bill, and I pulled out

FIGURE 38. The search image wipes out the perception image

a 100-mark note. The banknote was new and slightly creased; it did not lie flat on the counter but stood on edge. I asked the saleswoman for my change, and she told me that I had not paid yet. I attempted in vain to point out that the money was right under her nose. She became irritated and insisted on being paid immediately. I then touched the bill with my index finger in such a way that it fell over and lay down properly. The woman let out a little cry, took the bill and felt it, full of worry that it might vanish again in the air. In this case, too, the search image had evidently eliminated the perception image.

Every reader will surely have had similar experiences, which seem like witchcraft.

In my theory of life, I published what is reproduced here as Figure 39, which explains the different processes that inter-

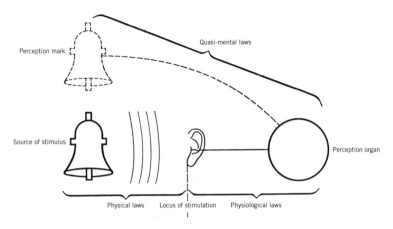

Perception mark

Quasi-mental laws

Source of stimulus

Perception organ

Physical laws   Locus of stimulation   Physiological laws

FIGURE 39. The processes of perception

twine in human perception. If we place a bell in front of a person and make it sound, it will appear in the person's surroundings as a source of stimulus from which airwaves hit the person's ear (a physical process). In the ear, the airwaves are transformed into nerve impulses that encounter the perception organ of the brain (a physiological process). Then, the perception cells and their perception signs take charge and transpose a perception mark into the environment (a quasi-mental process).

If, along with the airwaves that strike the ear, waves also move through the ether to the eye, which also sends impulses to the perception organ, then their perception signs will be formed by sounds and colors into a unit that, transposed into the environment, becomes a perception image. One can use the same visual representation in order to explain the search image. In this case, the bell is supposed to lie outside the field of vision. The perception signs of its sounds are transferred immediately out into the environment. However, an invisible optical perception image is connected to the bell; this serves as a search image. If the bell enters the field of vision after the search, then the perception image then created is united to the search image. If the two differ too greatly from one another,

FIGURE 40. Dog and search image

then it can come to pass that the search image excludes the perception image, as is shown in the preceding examples.

In the dog's environment, there are strictly determined search images. If the dog's master has the dog fetch a stick, the dog has a strictly determined search image of the stick, as Figure 40 shows. Here, we also have the opportunity to investigate how precisely the search image corresponds to the perception image.

The following has been said of the toad: A toad that eats an earthworm after a long period of hunger will also seize upon a matchstick, which bears a certain similarity in shape to the earthworm. One can conclude from this that the worm it just ate serves the toad as a search image, as represented in Figure 41. If, on the other hand, the toad satisfied its initial hunger with a spider, it possesses another search image, for it now snaps at a bit of moss or an ant, which does not agree with it.

Now, we do not by any means always search for a certain object with a unique perception image, but far more often for an object that corresponds to a certain effect image. We do not look around for one particular chair, but for any kind of seating, i.e., for a thing that can be connected with a certain function [*Leistung*] tone. In this case, one cannot speak of a search image but rather, a search tone.

How great a role the search tone plays in the environments of animals is evident in the abovementioned example of the hermit crab and the sea anemone. What we called the different moods of the crab in that case, we can now label much more precisely as the different search tones with which the crab approached the same perception image and conferred upon it a protection tone, or a dwelling tone, or a feeding tone.

The hungry toad goes searching for food at first only with an unspecific feeding tone. Only after it has eaten a worm or a spider is this tone accompanied by a determinate search image.

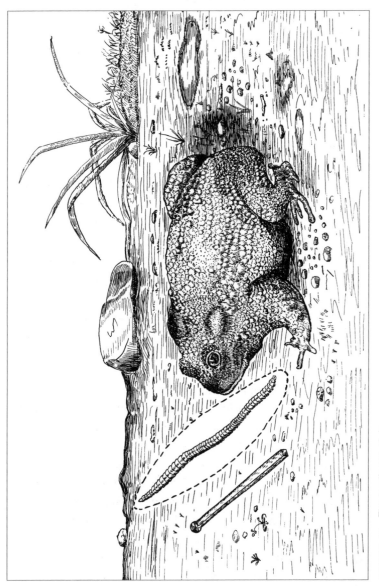

FIGURE 41. The toad's search image

MAGICAL ENVIRONMENTS

WITHOUT A DOUBT, there is always a fundamental opposition between the surroundings that we humans see spread all around animals and the environments which they have built themselves and filled with their perception things. Until now, environments had been the product of the perception signs that were awakened by external stimuli. But the search image, the tracing of the most familiar path, and the demarcation of territory already constitute exceptions to this rule, since they could be ascribed to no sort of external stimuli but represented free productions of the subject. These subjective productions had developed in connection to repeated personal experiences of the subject.

If we now proceed farther, we enter environments in which very effective phenomena appear, visible, however, only to the subject. These phenomena are not bound to experience or, at most, to a singular experience [*Erlebnis*]. We call such environments *magical*.

How deeply immersed in magical environments some children live might be exemplified by the following: [Leo] Frobenius[18] tells in *Paideuma* about a little girl who played the story of Hansel and Gretel, the witch, and the gingerbread house with a matchbox and three wooden matches quietly until she suddenly exclaimed, "Get the witch out of here; I can't stand to see her repulsive face any more!" This typically magical

FIGURE 42. The magical appearance of the witch

experience is indicated in Figure 42. In any case, the evil witch appeared in the flesh in the little girl's environment.

FIGURE 43. Starling and imaginary fly

Such experiences are frequently encountered by traveling researchers in the case of primitive peoples. It is said of primitives that they live in a magical world in which fantastic phenomena blend with the sensually given things of their world. Whoever looks closer, however, will find the same magical formations in the environment of cultivated Europeans.

The question is now raised as to whether animals also live in magical environments. Magical experiences are often reported in the case of dogs. But these reports have not been adequately critically reviewed to this point. By and large, it will have to be admitted that dogs connect their experiences with one another in a way that has a magical character rather than a logical one. The role played by the master in the dog's environment is surely grasped magically and not divided into cause and effect.

A researcher who is a friend of mine reports on a doubtlessly magical phenomenon in the environment of a bird. He had raised a young starling in a room, and the bird had no opportunity ever to see a fly, much less to catch one. Then he observed (Figure 43) that the bird suddenly started after an unseen object, snapped it up in midair, brought it back to its perch and began to hack away at it with its beak, as all starlings do with the flies they catch, and then swallowed the unseen thing.

There was no doubt as to the fact that the starling had had the appearance of an imaginary fly in its environment. His whole environment was evidently so laden with the "feeding tone" that, even without the appearance of a sensory stimulus, the effect image of flycatching, poised to spring, forced the appearance of the perception image, which triggered this whole sequence of actions. This experience indicates to us that we should interpret the otherwise completely puzzling actions of various animals as magical.

Figure 44 explains the manner of action of the pea weevil larva, which bores itself a channel up to the surface in the still-tender flesh of the young pea, a channel that it uses only

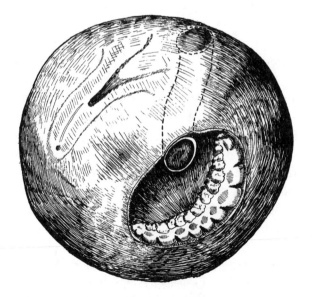

FIGURE 44. The magical path of the pea weevil larva

after its transformation into an adult weevil to slip out of the pea, which has become hard by that time. It is completely certain that this is a matter of a totally planned activity, which is, however, completely meaningless from the point of view of the young weevil, since no sensory stimulus of the future weevil can reach its larva. No perception sign announces to the larva the path which it has never been down and must follow nonetheless, if it is not to waste away miserably after its transformation to a weevil. The path stretches out clearly marked before it as a magical formation. The inborn path takes the place of the familiar path known by experience.

Figures 45 and 46 show two further examples of the inborn path. The female birch-leaf roller begins to cut a curvy line of a prescribed form into the birch leaf at a certain point (which is perhaps known to her by taste). This makes it possible afterward for her to roll the leaf together into a sac in which she will lay her eggs. Even though the beetle has never gone down this path, and the birch leaf gives no indication as to the path, this must still lie before her with full clarity as a magical phenomenon.

The same is true for the flight path of migratory birds. The continents bear the inborn path, one visible only to the birds. This is surely true for young birds, which must make their way without help from their parents, whereas, for the others, the acquisition of a familiar path is not outside the realm of possibility.

As with the familiar path, which we have discussed at length, the inborn path will also lead through visual space as well as effect space. The only difference between the two lies in the fact that, with the familiar path, a series of perception and effect signs that were established through previous experiences follow one after the other, while, with the inborn path, the same series of signs is immediately given as a magical phenomenon.

For the outside observer, the familiar path is just as invisible in a foreign environment as is the inborn one. And if one assumes that the familiar path appears for a foreign subject in

FIGURE 45. The magical path of the birch-leaf roller

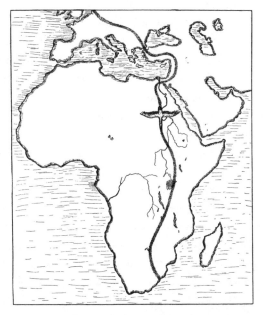

FIGURE 46. The magical path of the migratory bird

its environment—which is not to be doubted—there is no cause to deny the phenomenon of the inborn path, since it is composed of the same elements, the outwardly transposed perception signs and effect signs. In the one case, they are activated by sensory stimuli, and in the other case, they sound one after the other like an inborn melody.

If a certain path were inborn in a human being, this could be described like the familiar path: a hundred paces to the red house, then to the right, and so on.

If one wants to call meaningful only that which is given to the subject through sense experience, then, of course, only the familiar path will be meaningful; the inborn path will not be. The inborn path will for that reason, however, be guided by a plan to the highest degree.

A remarkable experience reported by a young researcher speaks for the fact that magical phenomena play a far greater role in the animal kingdom than we suppose. He fed a hen in a certain stall and, as the hen pecked at the grains, he let a guinea pig into the stall. The hen became furious and flapped all around. From that point on, the hen could not be made to take her feedings in that stall. She would have starved amid the best grain. Evidently, the shadow of that first experience hung over the stall, as Figure 47 expresses. This leads to the supposition that, when the mother hen rushes toward the peeping chick and chases away an imaginary enemy, a magical phenomenon has appeared in her environment.

The deeper we have gone into the study of environments, the more we must have been convinced that potent factors occur in them to which one can attribute no objective reality, beginning with the mosaic of places which the eye impresses upon the things of the environment, and that are so little present in the surroundings as the directional planes that convey environmental space. By the same right, it was impossible to find any factor in the surroundings that corresponds to the subject's familiar path.

FIGURE 47. The magical shadow

There is no division of space into home territory and hunting ground in the surroundings. No traces of the crucial search image are present in the surroundings. Now, in concluding, we have come upon the magical phenomenon of the inborn path, which mocks any and all objectivity and yet intervenes in the environment according to a plan.

There are thus purely subjective realities in environments. But the objective realities of the surroundings never appear as such in the environments. They are always transformed into perception marks or perception images and equipped with an effect tone which only then makes them into real objects even though no part of the effect tone is present in the stimuli.

And finally, the simple functional cycle teaches us that perception marks as well as effect marks are expressions of the subject and that the qualities of the objects included in the functional cycle can only be referred to as their vehicles.

In this way, we then conclude that each and every subject

lives in a world in which there are only subjective realities and that environments themselves represent only subjective realities. Whoever denies the existence of subjective realities has not recognized the foundations of his or her own environment.

THE SAME SUBJECT AS OBJECT

IN DIFFERENT ENVIRONMENTS

THE PRECEDING CHAPTERS described single forays in different directions into the unknown country of the environment. They were arranged according to problems in order to gain a unified manner of observation in each case.

Even though some fundamental problems were addressed, a complete account was neither sought nor attained at all. Many problems still await being grasped intellectually, and others have not yet developed beyond the formulation of the question. We still do not know how much of the subject's own body carries over into its environment. Not even the question of the significance of the subject's own shadow in its environment has been addressed experimentally.

As important as the pursuit of individual problems is for environmental research, it is just as inadequate to provide an overview of the interrelations of environments. One can obtain such an overview in a limited field if one pursues the following question: How does the subject exempt itself as an object in the different environments in which it plays an important role?

I take as an example an oak tree, which is populated by many animal subjects and is called upon to play a different role in each environment. Since the oak also appears in different human environments, I shall begin with these.

Figures 48 and 49 are reproductions of two drawings we

FIGURE 48. Forester and oak

FIGURE 49. Girl and oak

FIGURE 50. Fox and oak

owe to Franz Huth's talented hand. In the thoroughly rational world of the old forester, who must determine which trunks in his forest are ready to be felled, the oak that has fallen to the axe is no more than a few cords of wood, as the forester attempts to establish through precise measurement. In this case, no further attention is paid to the bulging bark which resembles a human face (Figure 48). The next figure (Figure 49) shows the same oak in the magical environment of a little girl whose forest is still filled with gnomes and sprites. The girl is terribly scared as the oak looks at her with its wicked face. The whole oak has become a dangerous demon.

On the grounds of my cousin's estate in Estonia, there stood an old apple tree. A large bracket fungus, which bore a distant resemblance to the face of a clown, was growing on the tree, but no one had noticed it yet. One day, my brother sent for a dozen Russian seasonal workers, who discovered the apple tree and stood before it daily for devotions, murmuring prayers

FIGURE 51. Owl and oak

and crossing themselves. They explained that the fungus must be an image with miraculous powers, since it was not made by human hands. Magical processes in nature seemed to them a self-evident fact.

But let us get back to the oak and its inhabitants. For the fox, who has built its den among the oak's roots, the oak has become a solid roof which protects it and its family from the perils of the weather (Figure 50). The oak possesses neither the use tone from the forester's environment nor the danger tone from the little girl's environment, but only a protection tone. However else it might be configured plays no role in the fox's environment.

The oak also shows a protection tone in the environment of the owl (Figure 51). This time, it is not the roots, which lie entirely outside the owl's environment, but the mighty branches that serve the owl as a protective wall.

For the squirrel, the oak, with its many branches offering

FIGURE 52. Ant and oak

handy springboards, takes on a climbing tone, and for song-birds, which build their nests in the remote twigs, it offers the needed carrying tone.

In accordance with the different effect tones, the perception images of the numerous inhabitants of the oak are configured differently. Each environment cuts out of the oak a certain piece, the characteristics of which are suited to form the

PLATE 1. Sea anemone and hermit crab

PLATE 2. The human being's room

PLATE 3. The dog's room

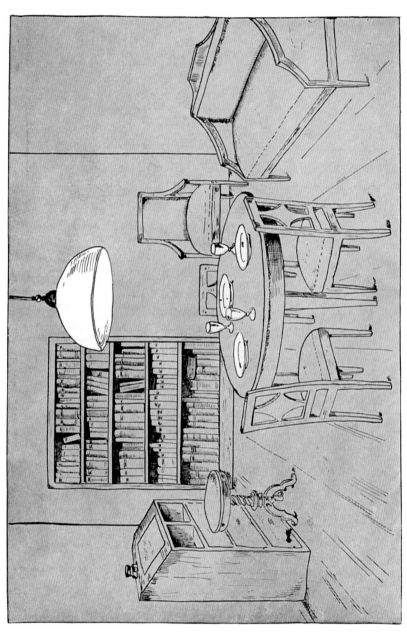

PLATE 4. The fly's room

FIGURE 53. Bark beetle and oak

perception-mark carriers as well as the effect-mark carriers of their functional cycles. In the ant's environment (Figure 52), all the rest of the oak disappears behind its furrowed bark, whose peaks and valleys form the ants' hunting ground.

The bark beetle seeks its food beneath the bark, which it tears away (Figure 53). Here, it lays its eggs. Its larvae drill their tunnels underneath the bark, where they can continue

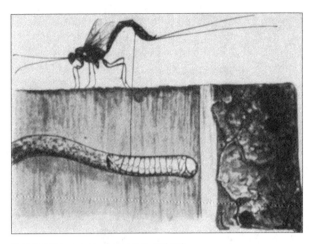

FIGURE 54. Ichneumon wasp and oak

to feed, protected from the dangers of the outside world. But they are not completely protected, for not only the woodpecker, which splits the bark with powerful blows of its beak, is after them. The ichneumon wasp, whose ovipositor penetrates the (in all other environments) hard wood of the oak like butter, also eliminates them by injecting them with its eggs (Figure 54). From these eggs, there emerge larvae, which batten on the flesh of their victims.

In the hundred different environments of its inhabitants, the oak plays an ever-changing role as object, sometimes with some parts, sometimes with others. The same parts are alternately large and small. Its wood is both hard and soft; it serves for attack and for defense.

If one wanted to summarize all the different characteristics shown by the oak as an object, this would only give rise to chaos. Yet these are only parts of a subject that is solidly put together in itself, which carries and shelters all environments—one which is never known by all the subjects of these environments and never knowable for them.

CONCLUSION

W{HAT WE SEE} on a small scale in the oak also plays itself out on a large scale on Nature's tree of life. Of the millions of environments, the number of which would only confound us, we seize upon those that are dedicated to the investigation of Nature—the environments of natural scientists.

Figure 55 shows us the environment of the astronomer, which is the easiest to represent. Atop a high tower, as far as possible from the Earth, there sits a human being who has altered his eyes through gigantic optical aids in such a way that they are capable of penetrating outer space as far as the most distant stars. In its environment, suns and planets circle at a solemn pace. Even swift-footed light takes millions of years to penetrate this environment space. And yet this whole environment is only a tiny excerpt from Nature, tailored to the capacities of the human subject.

With few alterations, one can use the astronomy image to get an idea of the environment of the deep-sea researcher. Not constellations, but fantastic images of deep-sea fish circle his enclosure, with their uncanny maws, their long feelers, and their ray-shaped phosphorescent organs. Here, too, we gaze into a real world that represents a small section of Nature.

The environment of a chemist, who strives to read and write the enigmatic context of Nature's matter-words with the help of the elements and ninety-two letters, is difficult to reproduce concretely.

We would sooner succeed in representing the environment of an atomic physicist, for electrons circle around him just as constellations circle around the astronomer. But here, there is no harmony among the worlds but a frantic hustle and bustle of tiny particles, which the physicist tries to split by a bombardment with the tiniest of projectiles.

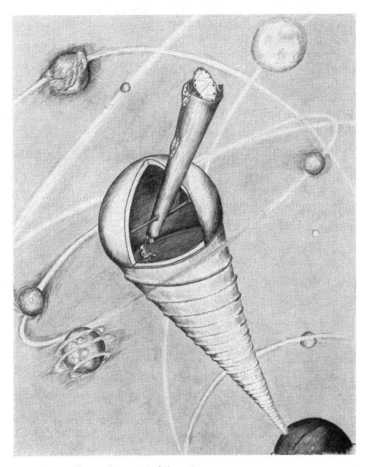

FIGURE 55. The environment of the astronomer

If another physicist researches waves in the ether, he uses other aids entirely, which give him an image of the waves. Then, he can establish that the light waves which hit our eyes also attach themselves to the other waves, showing no distinction. They are only waves, after all, and nothing more.

Light waves play an entirely different role in the environment of the sensory physiologist. Here, they become colors, which have their own laws. Red and green join to become white, and shadows cast on a yellow background turn blue. These processes are unheard of in the case of waves, yet the colors are just as real as the waves in the ether.

The environments of a researcher of airwaves and of a musicologist show the same opposition. In one, there are only waves, in the other, only tones. Both are equally real. And on it goes in this way: In the behaviorist's environment of Nature, the body produces the mind, but, in the psychologist's world, the mind produces the body.

The role Nature plays as an object in the various environments of natural scientists is highly contradictory. If one wanted to sum up its objective characteristics, only chaos would result. And yet, all these different environments are fostered and borne along by the One that is inaccessible to all environments forever. Forever unknowable behind all of the worlds it produces, the subject—Nature—conceals itself.

A THEORY OF MEANING

Commended to the kind attention of my scholarly opponents

CARRIERS OF MEANING

THE SIGHT OF FLITTING INSECTS, such as dragonflies, bees, and bumblebees, which cavort in a meadow full of flowers, always awakens in us the impression that the whole world would be open to these enviable creatures. Even earthbound animals such as frogs, mice, snails, and worms seem to move about freely in a free Nature. This impression is misleading. The truth is that every animal, no matter how free in its movements, is bound to a certain dwelling-world, and it is one task of ecologists to research its limits.

From the beginning, we have no doubt that an enclosing world is present, out of which each animal cuts its dwelling-world. As superficial appearance teaches us, each animal encounters in its dwelling-world certain objects with which it has a closer or more distant relationship. From this state of things, there results apparently automatically for every experimental biologist the task of placing different animals before the same object in order to research the relations between animal and object, a process in which the same object represents the constant measure in all animal experiments. In this way, American researchers have attempted tirelessly, in thousands of experiments, beginning with white rats, to study the most different kinds of animals in their relations to a maze.

The unsatisfying results of these labors, which were conducted with the most precise methods of measurement and the greatest skill in calculation, could have been predicted by anybody who had come to the realization that the tacit assumption that an animal could ever enter into a relationship with an object is false.

The proof of this surprising-sounding assertion can be provided by a simple example. The following case is treated as given: An angry dog barks at me on a country road. In order to get rid of him, I grab a paving stone and chase the attacker away with a skillful throw. In this case, nobody who observed what happened and picked up the stone afterward would doubt that this was the same object, "stone," which initially lay in the street and was then thrown at the dog.

Neither the shape, nor the weight, nor the other physical and chemical properties of the stone have changed. Its color, its hardness, its crystal formations have all stayed the same—and yet it has undergone a fundamental transformation: it has changed its *meaning*. As long as the stone was integrated into the country road, it served as a support for the hiker's foot. Its meaning was in its participation in the function of the path. It had, we could say, a "path tone." That changed fundamentally when I picked up the stone in order to throw it at the dog. The stone became a thrown projectile—a new meaning was impressed upon it. It received a "throwing tone."

The stone, which lies as a relationless object in the hand of the observer, becomes a carrier of meaning as soon as it enters into a relationship with a subject. Since no animal ever appears as an observer, one may assert that no animal ever enters into a relationship with an "object." Only through the relationship is the object transformed into the carrier of a meaning that is impressed upon it by a subject.

What influence the change in meaning exercises upon the properties of the object can be made clear to us by two further examples. I take a curved glass bowl, which can be considered a simple object, since it has entered into no relationship with a human activity. I then insert the glass bowl into the outer wall of my house and transform it thereby into a window, which lets sunlight in but blocks the gazes of passersby through its reflectivity. But I can also put the glass bowl on the table and fill it with water in order to use it as a flower vase.

The properties of the object are not changed thereby. But as soon as it has transformed itself into a carrier of meaning such as "window" or "vase," a distinction of properties according to their rank becomes apparent. For the window, transparency is the "leading" property, whereas curvature represents a supporting property. For the vase, on the contrary, curvature is the leading property and transparency the supporting property.

Through this example, we can gain some understanding of why the Scholastics divided the properties of objects into *essentia* and *accidentia*. They only ever had carriers of meaning in mind, whereas the properties of relationless objects have no gradations. Only the tighter or looser binding of the carrier of meaning to the subject allows for the separation of properties into leading (essential [*wesentliche*] = *essentia*) and supporting (nonessential [*unwesentliche*] = *accidentia*).

As a third example, let an object serve which consists of two long poles and multiple short poles which connect the two long poles to each other at regular intervals. I can confer the "climbing tone" of a ladder on this object if I lean the long poles diagonally against a wall. But I can also confer upon it the function [*Leistung*] tone of a fence if I attach one of the long poles horizontally to the ground. It soon becomes apparent that the distance of the cross poles from each other only plays an incidental role for the fence, but that they must be one step apart in the case of the ladder. In the case of the carrier of meaning "ladder," a simple spatial structure plan is already recognizable that enables the function of climbing.

In an imprecise manner of expression, we designate all our useful things (even though they are one and all carriers of human meaning) simply as objects, as if they were simple, relationless objects. Indeed, we treat a house along with all the things found in it as objectively existent, whereby we leave human beings as dwellers in the house and users of the things completely out of the picture.

How perverse this way of seeing things is becomes apparent immediately if we insert a dog instead of human beings as the dweller in the house and envisage its relation to the things in the house.

We know from [E. G.] Sarris's[1] experiments that a dog which has learned to sit on a chair when he hears the command "chair" will look for another seat, to wit, another dog seat, which needs not at all to be suitable for human use. Seats as carriers of meaning for sitting all have the same sitting tone, for they can be exchanged with one another arbitrarily, and the dog will still use them without distinction at the command "chair."

If we insert a dog as the dweller in the house, we will therefore be able to observe a lot of things which are given a sitting tone. Likewise, a lot of things will be present which exhibit a dog feeding tone or a dog drinking tone. The steps surely have a sort of climbing tone. But most of the furniture only has an obstacle tone for the dog—above all the doors and closets, whether these hold books or clothing. All the small household effects such as spoons, forks, matches, and so on, seem to the dog to be only junk.

No one would doubt that the impression left by the house with its only dog-related things is highly inadequate and hardly corresponds to its real meaning.

Should we not learn the lesson that, for example, the woods, which poets praise as the human being's loveliest abode, is hardly grasped in its true meaning if we relate it only to ourselves?

Before we pursue these thoughts any further, let me place a sentence from the chapter on environments in [Werner] Sombart's[2] book *On the Human Being* at this point: "There is no *forest* as a firmly objectively determined environment, but rather, there is only a forester-, hunter-, botanist-, stroller-, nature-lover–, lumberjack-, berry-collector–, and a fairy-tale–forest, in which Hänsel and Gretel get lost." The meaning of the forest is multiplied a thousandfold if one does not limit oneself to its relations to human subjects but also includes animals.

But there is no point in intoxicating oneself with the excessive number of environments contained in the forest. It is much more instructive to select a typical case in order to take a look at the tissue of relationships among the environments.

Let us examine, for instance, the stem of a blooming meadow flower and ask ourselves which roles are assigned to it in the following four environments: (1) in the environment of a flower-picking girl who is making a bouquet of colorful flowers and sticking it as a decoration on her bodice; (2) in the environment of an ant, which uses the regular pattern of the surface of the stem as the ideal paving to get to its feeding area in the flower's leaves; (3) in the environment of a cicada larva, which bores into the vascular system of the stem and uses it as a tap in order to build the liquid walls of its airy house; (4) in the environment of a cow, which grabs both stem and flower in order to shove them into her wide mouth and consume them as feed. The same flower stem plays the role of an ornament, a path, a spigot, and a clump of food.

This is quite amazing. The flower stem itself, as a part of the living plant, consists of components connected to one another according to a plan; they represent a more thoroughly formed mechanism than any man-made machine. The same components that are subjected to a sure construction plan in the flower stem are ripped apart in the four environments and are inserted into completely different construction plans with the same sureness. As soon as the object appears as a carrier of meaning on the stage of life of an animal subject, each component of an organic or inorganic object is brought into connection with, let us say, a "complement," in the body of the subject, which serves as a consumer of meaning.

This fact calls our attention to a seeming opposition in the fundamental features of living Nature. The planned quality of the bodily structure and the planned quality of the environmental structure stand opposed to and seem to contradict one another.

One should not give in to the illusion that the planned

quality of environmental structure could be less closed than that of the bodily structure.

Each environment forms a self-enclosed unit, which is governed in all its parts by its meaning for the subject. According to its meaning for the animal, the life stage includes a greater or smaller space, in which the places are completely dependent in number and size upon the capacity of the sense organs of respective subjects to draw distinctions. The girl's visual space is like ours; the visual space of the cow still reaches beyond its grazing area, while its diameter in the environment of the ant is no greater than half a meter and in the environment of the cicada no more than a few centimeters.

In each space, the distribution of places is different. The fine street surface which the ant feels in walking on the flower stem is not at all present for the girl's hands and certainly not so for the mouth of the cow.

The structural composition of the flower stem and its chemistry play no part on the life stages of the girl and the ant. On the other hand, the digestion of the stalks is essential for the cow. From the finely structured vascular system of the stem, the cicada taps the juice suited to it. Indeed, as [J. Henri] Fabre showed, it can produce from the poisonous Euphorbia sap a completely harmless juice for its house of foam.

Anything and everything that comes under the spell of an environment is either redirected and re-formed until it becomes a useful carrier of meaning or it is completely neglected. Thereby, the original components are often crudely torn apart without the slightest consideration for the structural plan which controlled them to that point.

As different as the carriers of meaning are in their respective environments according to their contents, they are just as completely similar in their structure. Part of their qualities serves the subject as carriers of perception marks, another part as carriers of effect marks.

The color of the blossom serves as an optical perception

mark in the girl's environment and the grooved surface of the stem as a tactile perception mark in the environment of the ant. The drilling site announces itself, one supposes, as an olfactory perception mark of the cicada. And in the cow's environment, the juice of the stem is the taste perception sign. The effect marks are generally impressed by the subject on other properties of the carrier of meaning. The thinnest spot on the stem is torn through by the little girl in plucking the flower.

Besides producing the tactile perception mark of the ant's feelers, the grooves of the stem's surface serve the ant as a carrier of the effect mark of its feet. The suitable tap, which was made recognizable by its smell, is drilled out by the cicada, and the juice that flows out of it serves as the building material for its airy house. That taste material of the stem makes the grazing cow shove more and more stalks into its chewing mouth.

Since the effect mark imparted to the carrier of meaning cancels out the perception sign that gave rise to the action in every case, every action concludes in this way, no matter how different in kind it might otherwise be.

Plucking the flower transforms the flower into a decoration in the girl-world. Running along the stem transforms the stem into a path in the ant-world, and the cicada larva's sticking it transforms the stem into a source of building material. Being grazed by the cow transforms the flower stem into agreeable cattle feed. In this way, every action impresses its meaning on a meaningless object and makes it thereby into a subject-related carrier of meaning in each respective environment.

Since every action begins with the production of a perception mark and ends with the impression of an effect mark on the same carrier of meaning, one can speak of a functional cycle, which connects the carrier of meaning with the subject. The functional cycles that are most important according to their meaning and are found in most environments are the cycles of the medium, of nourishment, of the enemy, and of sex.

Thanks to its insertion in a functional cycle, every car-

rier of meaning becomes the complement of the animal subject. Thereby, some individual properties play a leading role
as carriers of perception marks or of effect marks, while others
only play a supporting role. Frequently, the greatest part of the
body of a carrier of meaning only serves as an undifferentiated
counterstructure, which is only there in order to hook up the
perception sign–carrying parts with the effect sign–carrying
ones (compare Figure 3).

ENVIRONMENT AND DWELLING-SHELL

ANIMALS AS WELL AS PLANTS build themselves living houses in
their bodies with the help of which they carry on their existence.
Both houses are built according to a plan through and through,
yet they differ from each other in essential points. The animal's
dwelling-house is surrounded by a greater or smaller space in
which the subject's carriers of meaning cavort. Yet they are all
bound to the subject that belongs to them by functional cycles.

The guide-rope of each functional cycle, insofar as it runs
through the animal's body, is the nervous system, which, beginning with receptors (sense organs), guides the current of
stimulation through the central perception and effect organs to
the effectors. The plant's house does without the nervous system; it lacks the perception and effect organs. As a consequence,
there are no carriers of meaning for the plant, no functional
cycles, and no effect marks.

The animal's house is mobile and can move its receptors
anywhere with the help of its muscles. The plant's house does
without its own movement; since it possesses neither receptor
nor effector organs with which it could construct and control its
environment.

The plant possesses no special environment organs but
is immediately immersed in its dwelling-world. The relations

of the plant to its dwelling-world are completely different than those of animals to their environment. Only in one point do the structural plans of animals and plants agree with one another: Both make a precise selection from among the effects of the outside world that press in upon them.

Only a fragment of these external effects is taken in by the sense organs of animals and treated as a stimulus. Stimuli are then transformed into nerve excitations in order to be conducted to the central perception organs. In the perception organs, the corresponding perception signs are heard that, transposed outward as perception marks, become properties of the carriers of meaning. The perception signs in the perception organ induce, one might say, the corresponding impulses in the central effector organ that become sources for the streams of excitations which flow to the effectors. If one can speak of an induction of perception signs to impulses, then it is not at all in the sense of an electrical induction between two parallel switched wires, but rather, the induction which is carried out in the sequence of a melody from note to note.

For plants, too, there are vitally important stimuli that set themselves apart as meaning factors from the effects which press in upon the plants from all sides. The plant encounters these external effects not with the help of receptor or effector organs but, rather, it is capable of making a selection of stimuli from its dwelling-shell thanks to a living layer of cells.

Since Johannes Müller, we know that the idea of the mechanical progression of life processes is not correct. Even the simple reflex of blinking at the approach of a foreign body to the eye is no mere progression of a chain of physical causes and effects, but rather, a simplified functional cycle, which begins with perception and ends with effect. That in this case the functional cycle does not go all the way through to the cerebrum but passes instead through lower centers changes nothing in its character. Even the simplest reflex is in its essence a perception-effect action, even when the reflex arc only represents a chain of individual cells.

We can make this assertion with complete assurance since Johannes Müller showed that each living tissue distinguishes itself from all dead mechanisms in that it possesses a specific "vital energy" alongside its physical energy. If we compare, for the sake of concreteness, a living muscle with a bell, it is shown that one can only cause the bell to perform its activity, tolling, by making it swing back and forth in a certain way. Every attempt to make the bell toll in another way fails. Neither heating nor cooling, neither treatment with acids nor with alkalines, neither magnetic influence nor the production of electrical currents has any effect on the activity of the bell—it remains mute. On the other hand, a living muscle, of which the vital activity is contraction, is caused to contract by any outside influences to the extent that they are at all suited to have an effect. The bell behaves likes a dead object, which only receives effects. The muscle behaves like a living subject that transforms all external effects into the same stimulus, which causes its activity.

If we possessed a quantity of living bells, each of which produced a different tone, we could make a carillon out of them which could be operated mechanically, chemically, or electrically, since each bell would have to respond to any kind of stimulus with its subjective self-tone [*Ich-Ton*]. But the meaning of a living carillon would not consist in this, since it would also be a mere mechanism, provided with useless self-tones, if it were driven electrically or chemically. A carillon made of living bells would have to possess the ability to play its tune not just based on a mechanical drive but also controlled merely by a melody. Thereby, every self-tone would induce the next, according to the sequence of tones established by the melody.

Exactly what is demanded here plays itself out in every living body. One can certainly demonstrate that, in many cases—especially in the transfer of excitation from the nerve to the muscle—the living interplay of the self-tones has been replaced by chemical-mechanical linkage. But this is always only the consequence of a mechanization which appears later.

Originally, all the seeds of living things composed themselves out of free protoplasm cells, which obey only the melodic induction of their self-tones.

The decisive proof of this fact was provided by [Walter] Arndt[3] in his film, which allows the formation of a slime mold to take place before our eyes. The seeds of this mold consist originally of freely mobile amoebas, which feed upon a bacterial flora without paying any attention to each other. In so doing, the amoebas multiply by fission. The more food is available, the faster the reproduction takes place. This has the effect that the food source runs low everywhere at the same time.

And now something amazing happens: All the amoebas mark themselves off from each other in equal zones, and, in each zone, all the amoebas move toward the common center point. Once arrived there, they climb high up, one over the other, a process in which the first to arrive transform themselves into solid supporting points that serve those that follow as a ladder. As soon as the highest point of the hair-thin stalk is reached, the ones that arrive last transform themselves into the fruiting body, the spore-producing structures of which have living spores. The spores are scattered by the wind and carried to new grazing patches.

No one can doubt in this case that the finely worked-out mechanism of the fungal body is a product of free-living cells that obey only a melody which controls their self-tones. Arndt's presentation is also especially important because it is a case of a living being that is active as an animal in the first phase of its existence but, in the second, becomes a plant.

It should not be omitted that we are ascribing to the fungal amoebas an environment that all amoebas have, albeit a limited one, an environment in which the bacteria as meaning carriers separate themselves from the surroundings and are thereby perceived and effectuated. However, the finished fungus is a plant that has no animal environment but only a dwelling-shell which consists of meaning factors. The all-controlling meaning factor of the adult slime mold is the wind, into which the fungus grows with amazing sureness. Even if they are not so cleverly constructed as the blowball of the dandelion, the spore pods of the fungus are an easily carried prey to the wind and sure to be spread widely.

UTILIZATION OF MEANING

THE DWELLING-WORLD OF AN ANIMAL, which we see spread out all around it, transforms itself when observed by the animal subject into the latter's environment, whose space is teeming with the most varied carriers of meaning. The dwelling-world of a plant, which we can demarcate around its location, transforms itself, observed from the standpoint of the subject "plant," into a dwelling-shell that is composed of various meaning factors subject to regular changes. The vital task of animal and plant consists in utilizing the carriers of meaning or meaning factors, respectively, according to their subjective structural plan.

We are accustomed to speak of the utilization of food, only we generally construe this concept too narrowly. The meaning-utilization of food includes not only its being ground up by the teeth and chemically processed in the stomach and intestine, but also the identification of food by eyes, nose, and palate.

For, in the environment of animals, every carrier of meaning is utilized through perception and effectuation. In every functional cycle, the same perception-effect process is repeated. Indeed, one can speak of functional cycles as meaning cycles whose task is determined to be the utilization of carriers of meaning.

In plants, it is not a case of functional cycles, yet the meaning of their organs, also made of living cells, consists in the utilization of the meaning factors of its dwelling-shell.

They master this task thanks to their planned form and the most precisely executed ordering of their materials.

If we look at the play of clouds in the wind, we ascribe changing meanings to the changing forms of the clouds. But this is just the play of fantasy, for the various forms of the clouds are only a product of the changing winds and strictly obey the law of cause and effect.

A completely different image appears to us if we follow the flight of the graceful parachutes of the dandelion in the wind or the corkscrew motion of the maple key or of the light fruit of the linden. In this case, the wind is not a cause of the development of form, as with the clouds, but rather, the forms are adjusted to the meaning factor "wind," which they utilize in different ways for scattering seed. Nonetheless, there are those who want to speak of the wind as the causal agent of these forms because it has affected the object "plant" for millions of years. Yet the wind has affected the clouds for a far longer time without shaping any lasting form.

The meaningful form that lasts is always the product of a subject and never—no matter for how long—of a planlessly worked-on object.

What was true of the wind is also true of the rest of the meaning factors of the plant. The rain is trapped in the drip grooves of leafy foliage and conducted toward the fine tips of the roots underground. Sunlight is captured by the plant cells containing chlorophyll and applied in the execution of a complex chemical process. Chlorophyll is as little synthesized by the sun as the grooves of the foliage are by the rain. All the organs of plants as well as of animals owe their form and their distribution of materials to their meaning as utilizers of the meaning factors which come to them from the outside.

The question as to meaning must therefore have priority in all living beings. Only once it is solved does it make any sense to research causally conditioned processes, since the activity of living cells is directed by their self-tones.

One can speak of a growth melody or a growth order that controls the self-tones of germ cells. As we see from Arndt's film, this growth order is first and foremost a form development order that arranges zones and then creates a technical central point in each zone toward which all cells strive. What becomes of each individual cell depends only on the place it occupies in the form being developed.

The original equality in value of the individual germ cells, which is demonstrated palpably in Arndt's film, had already been arrived at by [Hans] Driesch[4] in his famous experiments on sea urchin germ cells.

Most animals' germ cells first form a mulberry shape and then a hollow ball, which becomes indented at one pole and at the same time becomes three-layered. In this way, the gastrula is created, which, with its three germ layers, comprises the form from which most animals originate. With this simple sequence of tones begins the life of every higher animal. There are animals such as the freshwater polyp that go through their simple lives with the simple gastrula form. As in the case of the slime mold, one has the impression that the execution of the form development order would be sufficient in order to fix their meaning relations.

Until now, we had no occasion to conclude that, in addition to the form development order, there is also a meaning order. But, through the experiments of [Hans] Spemann and his students, we now know better. These experiments were carried out according to the grafting method developed by Spemann, which consists in taking a bit of the body wall from an embryo in the first gastrula stage and implanting in its place a piece of the body wall of the same size from another embryo. It is shown in this case that the new graft does not develop according to its origins but according to its location. In this way, the tissue of the implant placed in the area of the brain became brain even though it would normally have become epidermis.

The form development order conforms to the directives

of a layout that is already recognizable in the gastrula stage. In this stage, it is possible to transplant pieces of tissue from embryos of another race. This remarkable experiment also succeeds when one exchanges pieces of tissue from embryos of another species.

Here, grafts into the mouth area of tadpoles and triton larvae are of specific interest to us. Spemann[5] writes about this: "The triton larva has real teeth in its mouth which are of the same origin and structure as the teeth of all vertebrates; the mouth of the tadpole is, however, occupied by cartilaginous jaws and surrounding tooth rows that arise and are constructed completely differently from real teeth."

He undertook a graft of tadpole tissue into the oral area of a triton larva.

"In one case," reports Spemann, "in which the implantation covered the whole oral area, a typical tadpole mouth with jaw cartilages and surrounding tooth rows arose. In another, perhaps more interesting case, half of the mouth was free of the implantation and had developed into a genuine triton mouth with real teeth." Spemann concludes from this, "In general, we can say with certainty about the inducing stimulus that it is of a very specific nature with regard to *what* arises, but is of a very general nature with regard to *how* it arises. It is just as if, putting it colorfully, the general prompt were 'oral weaponry' and this was then delivered by the ectoderm in the genetic code of its own species."

There would certainly be a great surprise in the theater if, in a performance of the great Kuessnacht scene in *Wilhelm Tell*, the actor playing Tell were replaced by an actor playing Hamlet and the latter, to the prompt "monologue," began not with the words, "Here I'll do it; the opportunity is good,"[6] but with the words, "To be or not to be, that is the question."

Likewise, it must be a great surprise for a carnivore, which is meant to sink its sharp teeth into its writhing prey, if it has a vegetarian's mouth with cartilage-like gums good only for peeling away the soft parts of plants. How is such a mix-up possible? Let us not forget that the implanted cell tissue is a living carillon, whose self-tones were set for the melody "vegetarian mouth" when they received the meaning order "mouth." From this, we see *that meaning order and form development order are not the same.*

In normal development, the originally homogeneous cell material arranges itself in buds that receive their meaning orders according to the primal layout—for the organism is composed of utilizers of meaning. Only then does the specific melody of the buds begin to sound and build up the form of the utilizers of meaning.

If one exchanges the buds of different animal species, each bud receives in its new place a meaning order which matches that place in the layout: "Become a mouth, eye, ear, etc." The transplanted bud will follow the meaning command of the host, even if it had been located at a different spot in its maternal organism and had received accordingly another meaning order. But it then follows the maternal form development melody. It becomes a mouth, not a triton mouth, but rather, a tadpole mouth. The final result is a malformation, for a carnivore with a vegetarian's mouth is an abomination.

We are uncomprehending when faced with such a malformation, which arises from the dissonance between the general meaning order and the specific form development order, because such dissonance is unknown to us in our daily life. It would never occur to anyone to simply order "seating" from a carpenter's workshop, because one would thereby run the risk of getting a milking stool for the living room or a recliner for the cow stall. But here, we are witnesses to a natural occurrence in which the entirely general order "eating apparatus" is imparted to a heterogeneous cell tissue, the meaning of which is not yet fixed and how, following from this, a completely unsuitable eating apparatus arises.

Anyone who has ever asked himself how flatfish, such as

a ray or a plaice, which have analogous living conditions, are built completely differently will admit that, in many cases, the meaning order does not agree with the form order. The goal is the same, but the path is different. Rays are flattened from the back to the belly side. Their eyes remain on the upper side. Plaice are flattened laterally and, as a result, one side takes over the function of the back side. One eye would have to be on the lower side, where there is nothing to see. But it passes through the head and ends up on the upper side as well.

The formal principles applied in order to allow different animals the ability to climb up a smooth wall are highly variable, even though they all lead to the same goal: to utilize the carrier of meaning "smooth wall" as a path. Houseflies have fringes on the soles of their feet that are made erect by their body weight while walking and form vacuum chambers which make the fly stick to the windowpane. Inchworms move, like leeches, with the help of two suction cups. Snails simply stick themselves forward, no matter how great the incline of the surface beneath them. The task is the same everywhere; only its execution is different.

The most striking example for this is provided by the venomous pincers of the short-spined sea urchin, which all have the same task, namely to chase off the meaning carrier "enemy," be it a starfish or a snail. In all these cases, the enemy is characterized by emitting first, on approach, a chemical stimulus and then, at contact, a mechanical stimulus. In response to the chemical stimulus, the venom pincers of all sea urchin species open up. At contact, they close and let their venom escape.

All sea urchin species except only one solve this task by means of a reflex through which they extend a palp toward the enemy upon opening. When the enemy touches the palp, snapping shut occurs reflexively. Only one species of sea urchin proceeds differently. Upon opening, the three jaws of the pincers pull back so far that they are tautened like a crossbow. They therefore need no reflex in order to snap shut at the slightest pressure. Both methods lead to the same goal: In both cases, the carrier of meaning "enemy" is attacked and poisoned by the meaning-utilizing organ. The meaning order is always the same but the form development order is completely different.

Spemann's wonderful discovery is confirmed in all the cases in which animals carry out similar actions with different means of assistance.

Spemann's discovery can further serve to make it easier for us to understand the difference in principle between the construction of a mechanism and that of a living being. The mechanism of any machine at all, for example, a pocket watch, is always structured *centripetally*, i.e., the individual parts of the clock, such as the hands, springs, and gears, must always be made first, then placed in a common central piece. The construction of an animal, for example, of a triton, proceeds, to the contrary, *centrifugally* from a germ outward, which first forms itself into a gastrula and then adds new organ buds. In both cases, a plan is at the root of this change of formation. The clock plan controls a centripetal occurrence, the triton plan a centrifugal occurrence. As it seems, the parts are joined to one another on completely opposed principles.

But now, as we all know but all too easily forget, each living being, unlike all mechanisms, consists not of parts but of organs. An organ is always a formation consisting of living cells which all possess their "self-tone." The organ as a whole has its organ tone, which is its meaning tone. As we should conclude from Spemann's exposition, it is the organ tone which controls the self-tones of the organ's cells—similarly to the meaning plan of Arndt's slime mold, which forces the amoebas to form the fungal body. The meaning tone starts up abruptly and activates the form development order in the self-tones of the previously homogeneous cell elements, which then sort themselves out in different tones attuned to each other and allow the form development to proceed according to a previously established melody.

From Spemann's experiments, we can see that the organs of living beings, in contrast to machine parts, possess a meaning tone all their own and can therefore develop themselves only centrifugally. The three steps of embryonic development must have occurred before the beginning of bud formation, and each bud must have first received its organ tone, before its cells can arrange and reconfigure themselves.

Finally, the entire animal's life tone is composed from the organ tones. The living animal is after all more than its physical mechanism, which the organ cells have built according to the form development order. When the life tone is extinguished, the animal is dead. The physical mechanism might function for a while longer thanks to a few surviving organs.

It goes without saying that the whole account of Nature built on meaning requires thoroughgoing research, for we cannot do very much yet with the brain, which must possess a "thinking tone." But, here too, meaning bridges the gap between physical and nonphysical processes, just as it did between the sheet music and the melody.

THE INTERPRETATION OF THE SPIDER'S WEB

IF I WANT TO ORDER A NEW SUIT, I go to the tailor. He takes measurements in which he fixes the most important stretches of my body in centimeters. Once that has happened, he transfers these onto paper or, if he is very sure of himself, directly onto cloth, which he then cuts according to the copied numbers. Then, he sews the pieces cut from the cloth together. He then conducts the first fitting and, finally, delivers the suit, which represents a more or less accurate portrait of the form of my body.

I would be quite amazed if a tailor could prepare me a suit that fits well without measuring or fitting. I could still always assume that he had taken the right measurements on his own body, since all human bodies look basically similar. One can therefore also manage to wear ready-to-wear suits which reproduce normal human proportions in different sizes. In this way, every tailor's workshop represents a gallery of molds of the human body.

All these preconditions do not apply to the spider—and yet it manages to represent in its web a well-made mold of a fly. It does not use this mold in the interests of the fly but in order to annihilate the fly. The spider's web represents a meaning utilizer of the carrier of meaning "prey" in the spider's environment. This utilizer of meaning is so precisely attuned to the carrier of meaning that one can see the spider's web as a faithful rendering of the fly.

The spider tailor who creates this faithful rendering of the fly has none of the aids of the human tailor. It cannot take measurements on its own body, which has an entirely different shape than the fly's body. In spite of this, it determines the size of the mesh according to the size of the fly's body. It measures the resistance of the threads it spins by the living power of the fly's body in flight. It spins the radial threads of the web tighter than the circular threads, so that the fly is enclosed upon collision by the flexible circular threads and must certainly get stuck on their sticky droplets. The radial threads are not sticky and serve the spider as the shortest path to the prey it has caught, which it then spins a web around and renders defenseless.

Spiders' webs are mostly found in places one could call fly interchanges. The most miraculous thing, however, is the fact that threads of the web are spun so finely that a fly's eye with its crude visual elements cannot spot the web and the fly flies without warning to its doom, just as we, completely off guard, drink water which contains cholera bacilli invisible to our eye. It is indeed a refined picture of the fly which the spider produces in its web.

But wait! The spider does not do that at all. It weaves its

web before it has ever met a physical fly. The web can therefore not be a representation of a physical fly, but rather, it represents the *primal image* [*Urbild*] of the fly, which is physically not at all present.

"Whoa there!" I can hear the mechanicists shout. "The theory of environments is showing its true face here as metaphysics. For anybody who looks for effective factors beyond the physical world is a metaphysician."All right. Then today's physics would be the purest metaphysics after theology.

[Arthur Stanley] Eddington[7] states outright that he has two desks, one that he regularly uses, located in his sensory world. Additionally, he possesses a *physical* desk, the substance of which comprises only the billionth part of the desk seen by the senses, since it is not at all made of wood but of an immeasurably great number of the most minute elements, of which one is not sure whether they are particles or waves, and which spin around each other at an unimaginable speed. These elementary particles are not yet matter, but their effects produce the illusion of the existence of matter in the world of the senses. They get up to their mischief in a four-dimensional space-time magnitude that is supposed to be curved and to be infinite and limited at the same time.

Biology lays no claim to such a far-reaching metaphysics. Biology wants only to point to factors that are present in the subject beyond sensorily given phenomenality and which should serve to clarify the interrelations of the world of the senses. But biology has absolutely no wish to stand the world of the senses on its head, as the new physics does.

Biology takes its point of departure from the fact of planned embryonic development, which begins in all multicellular animals with the three beats of a simple melody: morula, blastula, gastrula. Then, as we know, the development of the buds of the organs begins, which is fixed in advance for every animal species. This proves to us that the sequence of formal development has a musical score which, if not sensorily recognizable, still determines the world of the senses. This score also controls the spatial and temporal extension of its cell material, just as it controls its properties.

There is, therefore, a primal score for the fly just as there is one for the spider. And I now assert that the primal score of the fly (which one can also designate its primal image) affects the primal score of the spider in such a way that the web spun by the latter can be called "fly-like."

Covered by the curtain of appearances, the connection of the various primal images or primal melodies is consummated according to an inclusive *meaning plan*. In individual cases, it is sufficient to search out the meaning utilizers belonging to the carriers of meaning in order to gain insight into the tissue of the environment. Meaning is the pole star by which biology must orient itself, not the impoverished rules of causality which can only see one step in front or behind and to which the great connections remain completely hidden.

Whosoever demands of natural scientists that they follow a new master plan is not only required to convince them that the new plan opens new paths which take our knowledge further than the previous paths. He must also indicate problems unsolved until now that can be solved solely with the help of the new master plan.

The great master of insect biology Jules Fabre has pointed to such a problem in the case of the pea weevil. The female pea weevil lays its eggs on the shoots of the young pea. As they crawl out, the larvae bore into the shoot and penetrate into the still tender pea. The larva that burrows closest to the center of the pea grows the fastest. The others who entered with it give up the race, take in no more nourishment, and die. The sole surviving larva first hollows out the middle of the pea, but then it drills a passage to the surface of the pea and scratches off the skin of the pea at the exit so that a door is created. The larva then goes back into its feeding lair and grows further until the pea, having reached its final size, hardens. This hardening would be the doom of the young weevil, since the pea which has become hard forms a protective shell around it, but, on the other hand, it would become a coffin that the weevil could not leave if the larva had not taken care of the tunnel and the door.

In this case, no experience of trial and error passed on from ancestors can play a role. Any attempt to get out of the hardened pea would turn out to be an error. No, the disposition to make a tunnel and a door must be present in the form development plan of every maturing pea weevil larva in advance. A meaning transfer of the primal image of the pea onto the primal image of the pea weevil must therefore have taken place which brought the pea and the pea weevil into harmony.

The building of the tunnel and the door, vitally necessary to the pea weevil, by its larva is in many cases its doom, for there is a little ichneumon wasp which can hit the door and the channel with deadly accuracy with its fine ovipositor in order to deposit its eggs in the defenseless larva of the pea weevil. A little wasp larva crawls out of this egg and eats its fat host up from the inside, then turns into an ichneumon wasp and gets out into the open through the path worked out by its prey.

Here, one can speak of a trio of meaning connections of these primal scores.

FORM DEVELOPMENT RULE AND MEANING RULE

IT WILL NOT BE EASY to make the just-developed metaphysical notions palatable to contemporary biologists, [especially since] Jacques Loeb's[8] theory of tropism[9] has exercised a very great influence on recent biology. Loeb was a die-hard physicist, who only recognized interactions between objects but knew nothing about any influence of subjects on natural occurrences. According to him, there was only an effect world in which all physical and chemical processes played themselves out. One object affects another like the hammer on the anvil or the spark in the powder keg. The reaction occurs according to the energy input by the affecting object and the potential energy stored up in the effectuated object.

With plants, the reaction occurs according to the form and the order of the substances in its organs. We need only think of the drip grooves of the leaves or the starchy grains in the wheat kernel, which one can also include under the heading of potential energy. Of course, one leaves out the total figure of the plant, which owes its structure to the planned effects of the impulses of living cellular subjects. There are certainly no nerves or sense organs in plants, so that their whole existence seems to play itself out in an effect world.

Loeb's theory consisted in only recognizing an effect world even in the case of animals and paying no attention whatsoever to the perception world. This occurred by means of a simple trick. Whatever complicated action an animal might perform, the animal will always either approach or move away from the effectuating object. Loeb declared these simple spatial components of each action to be the action itself and therefore divided all actions into actions turning toward and actions turning away from. The place of actions was taken by tropisms. By this means, he transformed all living animal subjects into dead machines, which must thus confront each other spatially. Even the simple magnet which attracts iron behaves positively ferrotropically and the magnet needle either positively or negatively polartropically. This theory was decisive for the total worldview of an entire generation of biologists.

If we stand before a meadow covered in flowers, full of buzzing bees, in which butterflies pantomime and dragonflies whir, over whose blades of grass grasshoppers make their great leaps, where mice scurry and snails crawl slowly onward—then, we are forced to ask ourselves, "Does the meadow present the same impression to the eyes of such different animals as it does to our eyes?"

The naïve person will answer without further ado, "Of course, it is always the same meadow which is looked upon by all."

The answer of a convinced follower of Loeb is completely different: Since all animals are mere mechanisms which are steered here and there by physical and chemical effects, the meadow consists of a tangle of ether waves and air vibrations, of finely distributed clouds of chemical substances and mechanical contacts which have their effect from object to object.

The theory of environments directs itself against both of these versions of the meadow, for—to take only one example—the bee collecting honey does not see the meadow with human eyes, nor is it without feeling like a machine.

Colors are ether waves which have become perceptible, i.e., they are not electric excitations of the cells of our cerebrum but are the self-tones of these cells themselves. Sensory physiology provides proof of this. Since Goethe and [Ewald] Hering,[10] we know that colors follow their own laws, which are entirely different from the physical laws of ether waves. Ether waves forced by a prism to order themselves according to wavelength form thereby a sort of ladder with rungs of diminishing lengths. The shortest rungs are found at one end of the ladder, the longest at the opposite end.

From this ladder, our eye extracts a short stretch, which the cells of our cerebrum transform into a ribbon that consists of color perceptions which we transpose outward. In this ribbon, the pure colors follow each other, red-yellow-green-blue, with the mixed colors located between them.

In contrast to the linearly structured ether wave spectrum, the color ribbon forms a circle closed on itself, since violet, the mixed color between red and blue, joins one end of the color ribbon with the other. Even in other regards, the color ribbon displays remarkable regularities which are lacking in ether waves. For instance, the colors opposite one another in the color circle do not mix with each other but instead make white. These opposing colors produce each other mutually, which is not rare in opposing perceptions but flouts all mechanical experiences. Again, with colors, it is not a matter of physical effects of living cerebral cells on one another, but of the relations in sensitivity of their self-tones.

Just as the colors are the specific energies (self-tones) of those cerebral cells which are under the influence of the eye, which sorts the ether waves and, transformed into nerve excitations, sends them to the cerebrum, the tones are the specific energies of those brain cells that are under the influence of the ear, which takes in certain air vibrations.

The laws of tones are set down in music theory. Consonance, dissonance, eighths, fourths, fifths, and so forth, owe their existence to the sense of tone and dispense with embodiment—just try to reduce the sequence of tones in a melody to the laws of causality valid for all physical processes.

Our sensory organs of the eye, ear, nose, palate, and skin are built according to the principle of a Swedish box of matches, in which the matches only respond to certain effects of the outside world. These produce waves of excitation in the nerves, which are conducted to the cerebrum. To this extent, everything proceeds according to the law of cause and effect. But here, the inner front of the sensory organs is located in the form of a living carillon whose individual cell bells sound in different self-tones.

To what extent is this kind of structure of the sensory organs also valid for animals? No one doubts the analogy of the human part of the sensory organs in animals. They are therefore designated reception organs. But how is it with the inner front?

Although we are not familiar with the sensations of our fellow human beings, we do not doubt that they receive seeing signs by means of their eyes which we call colors, and we doubt just as little that they receive hearing signs by means of their ears which we call tones. By the same right, we ascribe to their noses the ability to awaken smelling tones, to their palate to awaken tasting signs, and to their skin to awaken touching signs, which, one and all, consist of self-tones. We summarize all these qualitatively different sense signs under the name "perception signs," which, transposed outward, become perception marks of things.

Now we ask ourselves the following: Do perception signs corresponding to the specific sensory energies of the central brain cells appear in animals, which they also transpose outward and use as a perception mark for building up of the properties of all the things on their life stage? The pure mechanicists deny this and assert that the reception organs of animals possess no inner front at all, but instead serve only to bring together the various stimuli of the outside world in a way corresponding to their own nature and to connect them to the corresponding parts of the brain.

Are the sensory organs the expression of different sensory circles, or are they, as reception organs, merely the expression of different physicochemical kinds of effects of the outside world? Was the eye constructed by ether waves or by colors? Is the ear structured by air vibrations or by tones? Is the nose a product of air saturated with gases or with smell corpuscles, or is it a product of the olfactory signs of the animal subject? Does the taste organ owe its creation to chemical substances dissolved in water or to the taste signs of the subject?

Are animals' reception organs products of the outer, physical front or the inner, nonphysical front? Since the sensory organs in us human beings represent organs that connect the outer form with the inner, it is likely that they have to fulfill the same task in animals and therefore owe their structure to the inner as well as the outer front.

That one cannot consider the reception organs of animals only as a product of the outer front is proven beyond a doubt by the fish that have a tasting organ alongside what is clearly an olfactory organ even though they only come into contact with substances that are soluble in water. Birds, on the other hand, which would have the best opportunity to develop both organs, do without an olfactory organ.

Only when we have clearly recognized the task of the sensory organs will the structure of the whole organism be comprehensible to us. In relation to the outer front, they serve as a sieve for the physicochemical effects of the outside world. Only such effects as are meaningful for the animal subject are transformed into nerve excitations. For their part, the nerve excitations in the brain draw out the perception signs of the inner front. In this way, the outer front also affects the inner front and determines what quantity of seeing signs, hearing signs, olfactory signs, tactile signs, and tasting signs can appear in the circuits of sensation of the respective animal subjects. The kind of structure of the environments is also decided thereby, for every subject can only transform the perception signs that are at his disposition into the perception marks of his environment.

On regarding a number of pictures by the same painter, one speaks of "his palette" and means by this the number of those colors at his disposition in the execution of his pictures.

These relationships become perhaps clearer still if one imagines that a perception cell in the brain lets a certain perception sign sound owing to the cell's self-tone. Each of these living bells is then connected to the outer front through a nervous bell cord, and here it is decided which outer stimuli are allowed to ring the bell and which are not. The self-tones of the living cellular bells are connected with each other through rhythms and melodies, and these are what allow them to sound in the environment.

After Mathilde Hertz's experiments, we can assume that, in bees, the colorful perception-sign ribbon of the spectrum related to the same ether-wave ladder as in human beings is displaced one step toward the violet side. The outer front of the bee's eye does not correspond to the outer front of the human eye, while the inner fronts of both do seem to correspond to each other. Until now, one has only been able to make suppositions about the meaning of this displacement.

On the other hand, the meaning of the perception-sign palette in moths is known without a doubt. As Eggers showed, these animals possess only two taut bands as resonators in their hearing organ. With these aids, they are able to respond to air vibrations which are at the upper audible limit for our human ear. These tones correspond to the peeping sound of the bat, which is the main enemy of the moth. Only the sounds emitted by their specific enemy are picked up by the moths. Otherwise, the world is silent to them. In the bats' environment, the peeping serves as a sign of recognition in the darkness. The same sound strikes the ear of a bat at one time and the ear of a moth at another. Both times, the peeping bat appears as a carrier of meaning—one time as friend, the next as enemy—depending on the meaning utilizer with which it is confronted.

Since the bat's perception-sign palette is large, the higher tone it hears remains one among many. The perception-sign palette of the moth is very limited, and there is only one sound in its world—an enemy sound. The peep is a simple product of the bat, and the spider's web is a very artful product. But both have one thing in common: Neither of them is only meant for one, physically present subject, but for all animals of the same structure.

How, then, does an apparatus for hearing bats come about in the structure of a moth? The form development rule of moths contains in advance the direction to develop a hearing organ which is set for the peep of the bat. Beyond any doubt, it is here the meaning rule which works on the form development rule, so that the carrier of meaning is faced by its meaning utilizer and vice versa.

As we saw, the form development rule creates a cartilage mouth for the vegetarian tadpole and a mouth with real teeth for the carnivorous triton. The meaning rule everywhere intervenes decisively in embryonic development and makes sure of the formation of a food utilization organ which grows at the right spot for the right carrier of meaning of vegetable or animal food. But if the form development rule is taken down the false track by grafting, no rule of meaning can call it back.

It is thereby not active form development itself that is influenced by meaning, but rather, it is only the rule of form development as a whole which comes to be dependent upon the meaning rule.

THE MEANING RULE AS THE BRIDGING

OF TWO ELEMENTARY RULES

WHEN, ON A WALK THROUGH THE WOODS, we pick up an acorn that comes from a mighty oak and was perhaps carried off by a squirrel, we know that diverse tissues will emerge from this plant germ, part of which will form the underground root system, part the aboveground trunk with its roof of leaves, according to a form development rule characteristic of the oak. We know that the rudiments of the organs that will make it possible for the oak to take up the struggle for life against hundreds of outside effects are in the acorn. We see in our minds the future oak in its struggle with future rain, future storm, and future sunshine. We see it endure future summers and future winters.

In order to be capable of meeting all the influences of the outside world, the multiplying tissue cells of the oak will have to organize themselves into organs—in roots, trunk, and leaf canopy, which captures the sunshine and the leaves of which yield like light banners to the wind that the gnarled branches resist. At the same time, the canopy serves as an umbrella that carries the precious moisture from the sky to the fine roots under the earth. The leaves contain the miraculous substance chlorophyll, which uses the rays of light in order to transform energy into matter. The canopy is lost in winter, when the frozen ground prevents the stream of liquid saturated with groundwater salt from rising up to the leaves. All these future effects on the future oak are in no condition to influence the form development of the oak causally. Just as incapable of this are the same effects of the outside world, which once affected the mother oak, since the acorn was not present at all at that time. With regard to the acorn, we stand before the same riddle as we did in observing every plant germ and every animal egg. In no case will we be able to speak of a causal linkage of external effects upon an object in its pre-existence or post-existence; only when cause and effect meet at the same place at the same time can we speak of a causal link. There is also no chance of finding the solution to the problem if one looks for it in the remote past. An acorn of a million years ago presents the same problems to our understanding as it will a hundred thousand years from now.

From this, it follows that we had run into a blind alley with our questions when we counted on producing with the help of artificial constructions a causal chain between our seedling, the acorn, and physicochemical outside effects. This case presents no mechanically solvable problem to which phylogeny could offer a key. Therefore, we must attempt to deal with the problem from another angle.

If we regard the effects of the outside world on the oak as human observers from the location of the oak, then we will soon discover that they are subject to a common rule of Nature. Sun, moon, and stars travel in fixed paths across the sky above the oak. Under their influence, the seasons change. Calm, storms, rain, and snow alternate in the course of the seasons. Sometimes the air is full of spring scents, other times with the bitter odors of the fall. Every spring, the woods are full of birdsong. The oak itself offers a changing shelter for hundreds of guests, feathered and not, in its canopy and bark, sometimes for summer guests and sometimes for winter guests.

The oak is also bound to this rule of Nature, known already to Noah, even if many of the natural factors familiar to us do not get as far as the oak's dwelling-shell. Neither sun nor moon nor stars are found in the number of meaning factors that form the dwelling-shell of the oak. On the other hand, certain chemically efficacious rays of light do penetrate to the chlorophyll of the leaves, and rays of warmth of diverse kinds affect the young energies of the tree to encourage growth. The falling drops of rain are usefully diverted, and the greatest resistance is offered to the storm. Nonetheless, neither odors nor sounds have any effect on the oak.

It is the same meaning rule that, today just as one million years ago, made this selection from among the elementary natural factors and allowed it to sound in the living carillon of the oak cells as its own melody, finally making the organs of the oak emerge from the protoplasmic germ cells.

Thanks to Arndt's film, we are not dependent here on mere suppositions. We can observe how numerous independent amoebas emerge by fission from the first germ cell. Like their free-living sisters, these amoebas adapt themselves to the nutrients available to them. Only after the nutrition is consumed does a new subject formation begin. The amoebas that come together to form a new, unified subject are no longer oriented to the meaning factor "food" but to the meaning factor "wind," toward which they grow together. The carillon of the amoeba stage, which occupied itself with a rule-less, confused cacophony of the cell bells, is followed suddenly by a unified melody, a new meaning rule, which bridges the two elementary rules of the wind, on the one hand, and the free formation of cells, on the other, and leads them to a new subjective unity. The direct effect of wind pressure on the freely mobile amoebas, no matter how finely dosed, will never succeed in producing a slime mold.

Unlike the slime mold, which unifies its mobile protoplasm cells to a single bud, which represents after the completed development of its shape an individual that consists of a single organ subject, the acorn forms numerous buds, from every one of which emerges an organ subject that is adjusted to one or several meaning factors. In this way, the oak leaf serves not just as a drip groove for the rain but also as a receiver of light rays thanks to its chlorophyll cells.

All organ subjects with their organ melodies join together to form the symphony of the organism of the oak, a symphony which one can also describe as the primal image of the oak. The process of heightened subjectification of cell tone to organ melody to organism symphony stands in direct contradiction to any mechanical process that represents the effect of one object on another object.

On the contrary, it is on the same level as every musical composition. The behavior of meaning factor in plants and of carriers of meaning in animals toward their meaning utilizers shows this especially clearly. As, in the composition of a duet, the two voices have to be composed for each other note for note, point for point, the meaning factors in Nature stand in a contrapuntal relation to the meaning utilizers. We will be closer to understanding the form development of living beings when we succeed in deriving a *composition theory of Nature* from it.

THE COMPOSITION THEORY OF NATURE

THE IMPRESSION "composition theory [*Lehre*] of Nature" can be misleading, since Nature teaches no lessons at all. One should understand theory, therefore, only as a generalization of the rules that we think we discover in the study of the composition of Nature. It is therefore called for to proceed based on individual examples and establish their rules in order to get to a theory of the composition of Nature in this way.

Musical composition theory can serve as a model that takes its point of departure from the fact that at least two tones are necessary in order to form a harmony. In the composition of a duet, the two voices that are supposed to melt into a harmony should be composed for each other, note for note, point for point. The theory of counterpoint in music rests on this.

In all examples from Nature, we must also look for two factors that together form a unit. We begin, therefore, with a subject located in its environment and research its harmonious relationships to the individual objects that present themselves to the subject as carriers of meaning. The subject's organism forms the utilizer of meaning or at least the receiver of meaning. If these two factors join together in the same meaning, then they have been composed together by Nature. Which rules come to the surface thereby—this forms the content of the composition theory of Nature.

When two living beings enter into a harmonious relationship to each other, it is necessary first to make the decision as to which of the two organisms we want to speak of as the subject and utilizer of meaning and to which we assign the role of the carrier of meaning. Then, we shall search for the mutual properties that behave toward each other as point and counterpoint. If, in a given case, we possess enough knowledge of the functional cycles that connect the respective subjects with their carriers of meaning and which can count as circuits of meaning, then we are enabled to search for the counterpoints on the perception side as well as on the effect side, in order to establish finally according to which specific meaning rule the composition was done.

To refer to the aforementioned example of the acorn, I place the schema of the question of the composition of the oak and one of its meaning factors, the rain, at the top:

Canopy of the Oak	Rain
meaning recipient	*meaning factor*
POINTS	COUNTERPOINTS
Roof tile arrangement of the leaves with drop groove	Raindrops rolling down
Form development rule of the oak	Physical rule of drop formation

Common meaning rule:
capturing and distributing the liquid to the root tips

The canopy of the oak operates mechanically upon the distribution of the raindrops, while the rule of drop formation intervenes compositionally in the melody of the living carillon of the oak cells.

If we turn to animals and seek to feel out the individual circuits of meaning, we will find similar relations in the circle of the medium as with the oak and the rain.

If we take as a first example the *octopus as subject* in relation to the *seawater as carrier of meaning,* we will come upon contrapuntal relationships immediately. The incompressibility of the water is the precondition for the construction of a muscular swimming sac. The pumping movements of the swimming sac operate mechanically upon the incompressible water and drive the animal backward. The rule of constitution of the seawater intervenes compositionally upon the living carillon of the protoplasm cells of the octopus embryo and forces the counterpoints corresponding to the properties of the water upon the form development melody; first and foremost, the organism is produced, the muscular walls of which will drive the incompressible water in and out. The meaning rule that connects point and counterpoint with each other here is provided by swimming.

The same meaning rule in numerous variations controls the development of all swimming animals. They swim forward or backward or sideways; the waving motion of the tail or the fins or the legs propels the animal through the water, but the properties of the organism always relate to the properties of the water as point to counterpoint. A composition that aims at a common meaning is demonstrable everywhere.

The same is true of all the different circles of the medium, whether it is a matter of water, land, or air animals. Everywhere, the effector organs for running, jumping, climbing, flapping, flying, or sailing are built contrapuntally to the properties of the respective medium. Indeed, in many insects that live in their youth in the water and when they are older in the air, one can observe with what lightness the constitutive rule of the new medium wipes away the old organs in the second larval stage and makes new ones arise.

But the investigation of the receptorial relations between subject and medium teaches the same lesson. For the obstacle that stands in the subject's way, a contrapuntally built sensory organ is always present. In the light, this is the eye; in the dark, it is tactile organs or the ear.

From the beginning, the bat is adjusted to perceive the obstacles in its flight path by means of completely different aids than the sparrow.

"That," people will reply, "is just a bunch of banalities. These are surely everyday experiences one can have everywhere." But why has it been neglected to draw the one possible conclusion from these experiences, that, in Nature, nothing is left to chance, but rather, that the animal and its medium are everywhere connected by an intimate meaning rule which binds the two in a duet in which the properties of both partners are composed contrapuntally to one another?

Only extreme deniers of meaning as a natural factor will

want to deny that, in the functional cycle of gender, males and females are composed for each other according to meaning, and assert that the love duet which permeates the entire living world in a thousand variations arose without a plan. In the love duet of animals and human beings, two partners of equal status face each other, each of which rules as a subject and appears as a recipient of meaning in his environment, while the role of carrier of meaning is given to the other partner. The perception organs as well as the effect organs are contrapuntally arranged toward one another in both partners.

The first demand one must make of a successful natural composition is that the carrier of meaning clearly emphasizes itself in the environment of the recipient of meaning. To this end, the most varied perception marks can be used.

Fabre reports of the emperor moth that the female makes pumping motions with her hindquarters while pressing her scent glands to the ground. The scent that streams from the ground after this is so effective in the males' environment that they fly toward the odoriferous spot and are distracted by no other smells, all of which sink below their threshold of perception. The attraction of this scent perception mark is so strong that even the sight of the female, which has been placed in the path of the males in a glass housing impermeable to scent but where she is still visible, does not confuse them in their efforts to get to the fragrant ground as a carrier of meaning. Unfortunately, the whole experiment has not yet been done with a running female dog. Perhaps the male dogs would behave just like the male butterflies.

In a very interesting case reported by [W.] Wunder,[11] the sexual partner serves not as an immediate carrier of meaning, but rather, a second carrier of meaning is inserted into the sexual circle. At breeding time, the male of the bitterling, a small freshwater fish, puts on a glowing wedding dress. This happens not upon seeing the female, but upon seeing the pond mussel and especially upon feeling the in and out flow of the mussel's water breathing. The female lets her long ovipositors grow out in response to the same stimulus. While the male lets his sperm out into the water, the female fastens the fertilized egg to the gills of the mussel, where the young larva can grow in the middle of the food stream and be protected from all dangers. The meaning of the male's wedding dress is naturally not related to the mussel, but rather, it serves to scare off the other male bitterlings.

That we have in meaning the true key to comprehending gendered natural compositions in our hand is proven by those examples in which the carrier of meaning does not change in the least but, in spite of that, experiences the opposite treatment from the subject, because the latter has switched itself to receive another meaning.

Fabre reports on the life of brown ground beetles, which, in the beginning, go hunting male and female together, but then connect sexually. Once the coupling is consummated, the behavior of the males toward the females does not change at all, but the latter throw themselves on the males ravenously and tear them limb from limb, against which the males defend themselves only feebly. In the females' environment, the carrier of meaning "friend" has changed to "food" without changing its constitution in the least, just as when the curbstone, without changing, gives up its meaning as an element of the path in order to transform itself into a projectile when the mood of the subject "human being" changes and impresses a different meaning upon the stone.

The puzzling behavior of young grey geese, reported by [Konrad] Lorenz, also consists in imprinting meaning. The grey gosling imprints—as Lorenz puts it—as its "mother companion" the first living being it sees upon hatching and follows that creature permanently. Even the human being can acquire the meaning "mother" for the grey goose in this case. "How does the human being imprinted as mother companion look to the grey goose?" is the question which particularly occupies

Lorenz. I think we should not forget that we appear in the environment of our puppies not as "mother" but indeed as "milk bearer" and are sucked on without, by that right, assuming the shape of a dog for the puppies.

Von Korff reports on an eagle [or horned] owl that hatched two duck eggs, treated the ducklings as young owls, attempting to feed them with raw meat—which did not work— and observed them by day sitting on a branch over the duck pond. In the evening, it returned with them to its cage. If other young ducks joined them, they were immediately struck and eaten by the owl. In this regard, the owl's fosterlings differed from the others of their species only in the meaning conferred upon them by the owl. While all other young ducks entered the owl's environment only as carriers of the meaning "prey," the two ducks hatched by the owl played the role of young owls.

The span of the meaning rule which has to bridge the gap between the carrier and the recipient of meaning is short in the areas of sex and offspring, since it is mostly a case of individuals of the same species. On the other hand, the consideration of the functional cycles of the enemy and of food shows us that there are no limits to this span and that the properties of the most distant things can be connected to one another contrapuntally.

I have already discussed the bridging of the constitutive rule of the bat to the constitutive rule of the moth by the meaning rule. On the one side is the bat as carrier of meaning that only produces one tone; on the other is the moth that, as a consequence of his very specialized hearing organ, can only receive one tone. This tone is the same in both animals. The meaning rule that has produced this agreement lies in the relationship between attack by the enemy and its being defended against by the prey. The tone, which is built in as a recognition signal from bat to bat, also serves the moths as a signal to flee. In the bat's environment, it is a friend tone, in the moth's, an enemy tone. The same tone becomes, according to its different meanings, the producer of two thoroughly different hearing organs.

Since the bat is able to hear many different tones, its hearing organ is set up for expanded resonance, but it can produce only this one tone.

It is just as interesting to follow the bridging of the gap between tick and mammal by the meaning rule.

Tick *recipient of meaning* POINTS	**Any mammal** *carrier of meaning* COUNTERPOINTS
1. The olfactory organ is set for only one smell, that of butyric acid.	1. The only smell common to all mammals is the butyric acid in their perspiration.
2. A tactile organ is present that secures the tick's exit from the hairs of its prey.	2. All mammals are hairy.
3. A temperature organ is present that lets a perception sign for warmth sound.	3. All mammals have warm skin.
4. A stinger suited for boring through the skin of any mammal is present that also serves as a pump for liquid.	4. All mammals have soft skin well supplied with blood.

Common meaning rule:
recognizing and attacking the prey,
taking blood on the part of the tick.

The tick sits motionless on the tip of a branch until a mammal runs past beneath it, then it is awakened by the smell of the butyric acid and lets itself fall. It falls on the hairy coat of its prey, through which it must then work its way in order to get to the warm skin into which it drives its stinger, and pumps the blood liquid into itself. It has no taste organ. The progress of this simple meaning rule includes almost the entire life of the tick.

The constitution of the tick, which is blind and deaf, is composed only to the end of allowing every mammal to appear in its environment as the same carrier of meaning. One can describe this carrier of meaning as a radically simplified mammal, which has neither the visible nor the audible properties by which species of mammal are differentiated from each other. This carrier of meaning for the tick has only one smell, which comes from mammals' perspiration and is common to all. Furthermore, this carrier of meaning is touchable and warm and can be bored into for blood withdrawal. In this way, it is possible to find a common denominator for all these animals, so different in shape, color, emission of noises, and scent expression, such as we have before us in our environment. The properties of this common denominator fill in contrapuntally and activate the vital rule of the tick at the approach of any mammal, be it human, dog, deer, or mouse.

In our human environment, there is no mammal-in-itself as intuitable object, only as a notional abstraction, as a concept which we use as a means of analysis but never encounter in life. With the tick, this is completely different. In its environment, there is a mammal that is composed of few properties but thoroughly intuitable, one which corresponds exactly to the tick's needs, since these few properties serve the tick's abilities as counterpoints.

For as long as one searches for mechanical causes, the adaptation of the hermit crab to the snail shell must seem especially mysterious, since it cannot be interpreted through any kind of anatomical transition as a gradual adaptation. But as soon as one abandons such fruitless experiments and simply observes that the hermit crab does not use its tail like other long-tailed crabs, as a swimming organ, but as a gripping organ for snail shells, its gripping tail is not less enigmatic than the rowing tail of the crawfish. The gripping tail is just as contrapuntally composed to the snail shell as the rowing tail is to the water.

Mathilde Hertz made the interesting discovery that honey-gathering bees can only distinguish two shapes: open and closed. Ray shapes and many-sided shapes of all kinds attract the bees, while circles and rectangles repel it. Gestalt theorists chalk this up to the idea that the open shape has a higher attraction value. One might admit that. But what is that supposed to mean? As soon as one asks this question, the answer is apparent: All the inaccessible buds, which the bees avoid, have closed shapes. On the other hand, the open blossoms, which offer their honey, have open shapes. In the design rule of the bees, two spatial perception schemata for blossoms and buds are included thanks to the interpretation rule which controls honey-gathering. The two schemata are contrapuntally in a fixed relation to the two principal shapes of the flowers.

How does Nature manage, though, when an animal subject is required in its actions to distinguish shapes but, at the same time, has a wholly primitive nervous system incapable of creating shape schemata? The earthworm, which pulls linden or cherry leaves into its hole (which serve as food and at the same time as protection), has to grasp the leaves by their tips so that they can be rolled up easily. If the worm tried to grasp them at their base, they would block the way and not follow being pulled. Now, the worm is in no condition, by its constitution, to develop shape schemata, but it does possess an especially fine-honed organ for tasting.

We owe to [Otto August] Mangold[12] the discovery that, even with finely torn-up leaves, the worm can still distinguish the pieces that belong to the base from those that belong to the tip. The tips of the leaves taste different to the worms than the bases do. That is sufficient in order to treat them separately.

Here, the taste perception marks fill in instead of the shape schemata in order to make possible the action of pulling in the leaves, which is so important for the life of the worm.

One would be justified in speaking here of a refined natural composition.

Experience has taught the human fisherman that it is not necessary to use an exact image of their prey when angling for predatory fish, but rather, that it is sufficient to offer a simple silver disc, i.e., a very general imitation of a whitefish, to the pike as bait. Nature does not need these experiences. *Lophius piscatorius*, the anglerfish, is a wide-mouthed fish that has a long, mobile, bony filament on which a silver lappet flaps back and forth. This is enough to lure smaller predatory fish. These are sucked down into the wide mouth by a sudden vortex when they snap at the bait. Here, the span of the meaning rule is stretched further still, for it connects the design rule of the *Lophius* not with the figure of the prey pursued by the predatory fish, but rather, with the very simplified imitation of this prey in the environment of the predatory fish for which the *Lophius* fishes.

A similar example is offered by the butterflies decorated with eyespots, which, by opening their wings, scare away the small birds which hunt them because the birds take flight before the suddenly appearing eyes of a small predator. *Lophius* does not know what prey looks like in the environment of the predatory fish it catches, nor does the butterfly know that the sparrow is running away from a cat's eyes. But the composer of these environment compositions must know.

This is no human knowledge that could be gained through experiences. The tunnel digging of the pea weevil larva, which carries out an action conditioned by a supersensory knowledge not bound to time, taught us this already. Thanks to this knowledge, it is possible for the composer to turn the vital necessity of a not yet present weevil into the cause of the action of the weevil larva.

THE SUFFERANCE OF MEANING

IN THE EXAMPLE of a flower's stalk, with whose transformation we became familiar in the four environments of the girl, the ant, the cicada larva, and the cow, the flower's stalk as a carrier of meaning came up each time against a new recipient of meaning, to which one could also refer as a utilizer of meaning, for it utilized the stalk as an ornament, or as a path, or as a supplier of material for building a house, or as a hunk of food.

This example has another side, though, which is shown if, instead of the stalk, we take the whole plant to which it belongs as a subject and join to it the earlier four subjects as meaning factors. Then, one cannot speak of a utilization of meaning by the plant. The reception of meaning can only be equated any longer to the sufferance of meaning. This sufferance demonstrates different gradations. The transformation of the stalk into an ant path is easy to bear. Even the removal of juice for the cicada larva's housebuilding means only slight damage. On the other hand, the plucking of the blossom on the part of the girl and grazing by the cow can be ruinous for the plant. In none of the four cases can one discover a meaning rule in the interests of the plant.

Even the meaningful role played by the spider's web in the life of the fly is by no means to be valued in the interests of the fly, but rather, it contradicts that interest. The fly that is caught in the spider's web cannot utilize this carrier of meaning in its environment at all but only suffer it. The pea weevil larva, too, which, preparing for the future, has drilled its hole in the pea at the right time, before the pea hardens, is defenseless against the carrier of meaning "ichneumon wasp" and can only suffer the bringer of death.

The meaning of these things apparently contrary to meaning becomes immediately clear to us when we turn our gaze away from the single individual and contemplate the higher unity of the species. The insertion of the short-lived individual into the long-lived species forms the foundation of all life. In pairs, the individuals of every generation reach into one another to produce the new generation. The number of children always exceeds the number of parents. In order to maintain the species at the same number of individuals, the surplus ones must go under. Then, the same number of parents comes together in the younger generation for the reproduction of the species. The elimination of the surplus individuals happens in very different ways. In most species, the life span of individuals is set by the change of seasons. It is clear that all one-year individuals must make room every year for the new generation.

In this way, the wasp states with their thousands upon thousands of individuals die off completely every fall, and only a few female individuals hibernate, in order to found the same number of states in the next year. So many of our houseflies die each year that one could suppose them to be extinct, yet they come back in the same numbers in the following spring. The number of flies that find an untimely end in the web of their enemy, the spider, plays but a small role in the population balance of flies.

The flights of migratory birds eliminate year after year the surplus individuals who are not equal to this enormous exertion. It is not the number of individuals alone that is important for the species, but also their stamina. Herein, we recognize the great significance of the sufferance of harmful factors which exclude the weaker individuals again and again from the production of weak offspring.

Hawks and foxes become benefactors of the species they hunt by snatching away the weak prey animals. Where foxes are eliminated, hares go under due to epidemics, because the sick animals were not culled at the right time. In this way, the lapwing whose clutch of eggs is threatened by the approach of an enemy will not simply fly away but will distract it by playing lame, luring the enemy toward it by its apparent inability to fly, until it is far enough away from the nest to fly away safely. The ichneumon wasp, which preys upon the pea weevil larva, is the protector of the peas, which would otherwise be delivered over to the greater numbers of their enemies.

Australia provides a considerable example of how important the introduction of such specific enemies can be for the entire plant and animal life of a landscape. One hundred years ago, a peasant woman who emigrated from South America to Australia brought with her a shoot of the prickly pear, which flourished wonderfully in its new homeland. Soon, it became apparent how useful the prickly plant was in order to fence in gardens and farmyards. After this, the prickly pear was planted everywhere.

However, the useful plant transformed itself into a plague on the countryside. It grew wild over the gardens and fields it was supposed to protect. It encroached on the woods and smothered all plant growth wherever it spread. When vast stretches of land succumbed to the devastation, the authorities intervened. With axes and fire, they grappled with the new enemy. When that did not help, they had poison scattered from airplanes onto the woods overgrown with cactus. However, the result was that, while all other plants went under, the prickly pear kept on flourishing.

In their desperation, the authorities turned to the botanical departments of the universities. These departments sent a number of diligent researchers to South America, the *ur*-homeland of the prickly pear. These practiced observers succeeded in locating a small caterpillar belonging to a moth species that fed solely on the flesh of the prickly pear. After many years of experimentation, millions of eggs of this enemy of the prickly pear were raised and scattered over the areas devastated by the prickly pear. And behold—in a couple of years, they managed to annihilate the forests of prickly pear and regain land for cultivation.

It is very appealing to pursue natural compositions and to establish which meaning goes with each sufferance of meaning. Two points of view have to be considered thereby: The sufferance of meaning wipes out the excess of individuals in the interests of the species, whereby all unhealthy and poorly resistant individuals are cast off; or the removal of the excess individuals happens in the interests of Nature's economy. In this way, according to K. E. von Baer, the surplus of fly larvae serves fish as nourishment, and the same seems to be true of the surplus of tadpoles.

It was a fundamental error on the part of Herbert Spencer[13] to interpret the annihilation of surplus offspring as a "survival of the fittest" in order to predicate progress in the development of living beings on that. It is hardly a matter of the survival of the fittest, but rather, of the survival of the normal in the interests of an unchanging further existence of the species.

THE TECHNIQUE OF NATURE

As BEST I RECALL, it was a symphony by Mahler, which was movingly conducted by Mengelberg in the Amsterdam Conzertgebouw. The large orchestra, backed by men's and women's choirs, swept upward in splendor and fullness.

Next to me sat a young man who was totally absorbed in the score and who closed the book of music with a sigh of contentment as the final chord faded away. In my musical ignorance, I asked him what pleasure he could take from following in musical notation with his eyes that which his ear heard directly in sounds. He assured me fervently that only someone who follows the score can obtain the full vision of a musical artwork. Each voice of a person or instrument is a being for itself, but one which melts into a higher form through point and counterpoint with other voices, which form then grows further, gaining richness and beauty in order to bring forward to us the composer's soul. Reading the score, he said, one can follow the growth and branching off of the individual voices that, like the columns of a cathedral, bear the weight of the all-encompassing dome. Only in this way does one get a glance into the many-membered form of the performed artwork.

This speech, delivered with great power of persuasion, gave rise in me to the question as to whether it is the task of biology to write the score of Nature. Back then, I was already well familiar with the contrapuntal relationships in Nature from one environment to another, and I began to follow the example of the flower stalk further in its relationships to the four environments.

The girl gave her boyfriend a bouquet of flowers that she was using as decoration, and so the flower stalk entered a love duet. The ant, which used the stalk as a path, hurried along it to the ovary of the flower in order to milk its milk cows, the aphids, there, while the cow converted the green feed, to which the stalk belonged, into milk. The cicada larva grew up in the foam house that the juice of the stalk had provided for it and soon filled the meadow with its soft love chirps.

Other environments came along. The bees, which were contrapuntally linked to the scent, the color, and the shape of the leaves, hurried hence and, after they had satiated themselves on the honey, communicated their new find to their hive mates through impressive dances—which [Karl] von Frisch[14] relates in detail. The color of the flowers is not the same for the bees as for us, but it serves the bees nonetheless as a certain perception feature, since the flower and the bee are composed contrapuntally to each other.

That is indeed a humble beginning, but a beginning nonetheless in order to solve the problem posed to us by a natural score.

One can reduce all musical instruments to a common denominator if one places the tones they produce next to one another as in a carillon. Then, for the violin, one gets a very rich carillon, which consists entirely of violin tones; for harp tones, one must use another, simpler carillon; and the one for triangle tones sinks to the smallest possible measure. That task is assigned to every musical composition to seek out in the carillon of one instrument those tones that form a melodic sequence and to connect them harmoniously to the tones from the carillons of other instruments. This occurs according to the theory of counterpoint, which makes the rules according to which the tones of different voices in a score can be unified. But it is up to the composer to connect the tones of each instrument contrapuntally with the tones of every other instrument.

In order to find a common denominator between animals and musical instruments, it is sufficient to speak of their central nervous system as a carillon and to call the perception signs of its living cells, which are transposed outward as perception marks, "perception tones," while the impulses that cause the execution of movements become "effect tones." Like every instrument, every animal harbors a certain number of tones, which enter into contrapuntal relationships to the tones of other animals.

It is not enough to treat musical instruments as mere producers of airwaves, as the mechanicists do. Nobody can create either a melody or a harmony from airwaves, or write a score with their help. Only the relationships of the airwaves to the human hearing organ, where they are transformed into tones, creates the possibility to produce melodies and harmonies and to write scores.

It is also not enough if one assigns to the plants in the meadow the spatial extension of their colors, tones, and scents as their only task. These must first be taken up into the environments of other animals and transformed into perception signs. Then, one can transpose the relationships of living beings into the musical sphere and speak of the perception and effect tones of the various animal subjects, which belong to each other contrapuntally. Only then can one arrive at a score of Nature.

In Nature, the perception tones of different animals can be applied contrapuntally; the luring tone of the bat in the bat environment is at the same time a warning tone in the environment of the moth. The house that the snail carries has a dwelling tone for it—but once it has died and the empty house remains, this takes on for the hermit crab a dwelling tone suitable to it. And this consonance is exploited in the snail–hermit crab composition.

Just as the composer of a symphony knows no limits in the choice of instruments he wants to use for his composition, Nature is completely free in the choice of animals it wishes to connect contrapuntally. The rod of the anglerfish is structured contrapuntally to the catching tone of the schema that is supposed to attract his fish prey. The designations "catching tone" and "dwelling tone" prove that, in applying the musical simile to animals, we have abandoned pure music theory, since, on that basis, one can speak of a violin tone or a harp tone, but never of the prey's catching tone or the dwelling tone of a house—just as little as of the drinking tone of a cup or the sitting tone of a chair. And yet the great applicability of the musical simile in the field of biology lies in this very expansion of the concept of tone from a mere heard tone to the meaning tone of objects which appear in a subject's environment as carriers of meaning.

If one says that the dwelling tone of a shell in the snail's environment can be represented contrapuntally with the dwelling tone in the hermit crab's environment, then this refers to the fact that each of the two tones, without being identical to the other, can nonetheless be taken from one natural composition over into the other, because both have the same meaning.

Meaning in the natural score takes the place of harmony

in the musical score, which works as a conjunction or, more precisely put, a bridge in order to unify two natural factors with each other. For, as any bridge has its feet on both sides of the river, which it connects as point and counterpoint with each other, these are linked to each other in music through harmony and in Nature through the same meaning. With examples numerous enough to wear the reader out, I have demonstrated that this is a matter of real natural factors and not merely of logical concepts.

We are now at the point where we can refer to the meaning score as a description of Nature that can be placed beside a musical description done through a score set down in notes.

If we take a glance at an orchestra, we see on each individual rostrum in musical notation the voice-leading[15] for the instrument to which it belongs, while the whole score is on the conductor's rostrum. But we also see the instruments themselves and wonder if these are possibly adapted to each other not just in their respective tonalities, but in their entire structure, i.e., if they form a unit not just musically but also technically. Since most instruments in the orchestra are capable of producing music by themselves, this question cannot be answered in the affirmative as simply as that.

Whoever has listened to the production of musical clowns, who work with instruments that otherwise serve for making noise, such as hair combs, cow bells, and other such things, will have been convinced that one can very well play a cacophony, but not a symphony, with such an orchestra. Upon closer examination, the instruments of a real orchestra demonstrate a contrapuntal behavior already in their structure.

This is even more readily apparent already in a natural orchestra. We need only to think of the flower in the four environments. This relation reveals itself most strikingly in that of the structure of the flower to the structure of the bee, of which one can say:

Were the flower not beelike
And were the bee not flowerlike,
The consonance could never work.

Therein, the fundamental principle of the whole technology of Nature is enunciated. We recognize in it Goethe's wise saying:

Were the eye not sunlike,
It could never gaze upon the sun.[16]

But we can also complete Goethe's pronouncement by saying,

Were the sun not eyelike,
It could not shine in any sky.

The sun is a light in the sky. The sky is, however, a product of the eye, which constructs here its farthest plane, which includes all of environmental space. Eyeless living beings know neither a sky nor a sun.

COUNTERPOINT AS A MOTIF/MOTIVE

OF FORM DEVELOPMENT

WE CAN NOW APPLY the basic technical rule expressed by the bee-likeness of the flower and the flower-likeness of the bee to the other abovementioned examples. Surely, the spider's web is configured in a fly-like way, because the spider is also fly-like. To be fly-like means that the spider has taken up certain elements of the fly in its constitution: not from a particular fly but from the primal image of the fly. Better expressed, the fly-likeness of the spider means that it has taken up certain motifs[17] of the fly melody in its bodily composition. What is very clear is the penetration of individual mammalian motifs into the body-plan of the tick. And most clear are the effects of the bat motif in the configuration of the hearing organ of the moth.

Everywhere, it is the counterpoint which expresses itself as a motif in such configurations. We should already be aware of this from the structure of human use-objects. A coffee cup with a handle shows immediately the contrapuntal relation to coffee, on the one hand, and to the human hand, on the other. First of all, these counterpoints influence the motifs in the production of the cup. Indeed, they are even more important than the material from which the cup is formed.

It sounds like a banal commonplace if one were to pronounce the sentence "The coffee cup is coffee-like." Yet this sentence signifies more than it seems to. It signifies that the function of the coffee cup is to shelter the coffee, but, beyond this, that this function is also the motive for its production.

The theory of meaning culminates in the uncovering of this connection. The meaning of our use-object for us lies in its function, and this function can always be brought back to a bridging of the counterpoint in the object to the human being, which at the same time forms the motive of the bridging. In its meaning as seating that rises above the floor, the chair consists entirely of bridges to different counterpoints. The seat, the back, and the arms find their counterpoints in the human body, to which they build the bridges, while the legs of the chair build clear bridges to the counterpoint "ground." All these counterpoints are at the same time motives for the carpenter in his production of the chair.

It would go too far to adduce yet other, evident examples. The indication that we have built bridges between ourselves and Nature with all of our use-objects, but that we have not

thereby come closer to Nature, but rather, have detached ourselves from it, must suffice. But then, we began at an ever
hastier rate, to build bridges to the bridge, of which the man
living close to Nature has no overview even in the structure of
simple machines. In the big city, we are surrounded any more
only by artificial things, for even the trees and flowers of our
parks, which we plant and uproot however we wish, we have
taken out of the whole of Nature and have made into human
use-objects. Much-lauded human technology has lost all sense
of Nature; indeed, it boldly presumed to solve the deepest
questions of life, such as the relation of human beings to God-
Nature, with its wholly inadequate mathematics.

All this is beside the point. It is much more important to
get an idea of what paths Nature takes in order to draw forth
its creatures (which it, unlike us, does not put together of individual parts) from the undifferentiated germ cell.

Arndt's film of the slime mold showed us as the first
phase of life an increasing rate of growth of free-living amoebas, which are constructed contrapuntally to their bacterial
food. Once the food is consumed, a new counterpoint intervenes
abruptly as a motif and transforms the amoebas, which are
pushing themselves one on top of the other, into the tissue cells
of a plant that points into the wind.

If we take a look into the little dwelling-world of the
slime mold that erects itself as a light, hairy layer on top of a
pile of old horse dung, we discover the spore-spreading wind as
the only other effective natural factor in addition to the spore-
bearing mold. Spore-bearers and spore-spreaders are melted
into a duet. First are the free amoebas, which form a living
carillon with their like-sounding self-tones. Nature plays with
them and transforms them into tissue cells according to a new
motif and builds out of them a spore-bearing figure which presents itself to the wind.

This process is as inconceivable for us as the change of

motifs in one of Beethoven's sonatas. But our task is not to compose a natural sonata, only to transcribe the score.

Our knowledge of vertebrates is still very rudimentary where technical questions are concerned. One can connect the bud-like emergence of the organs, which are bound to an elementary model, to the fact that the meaning of each bud is fixed through its relation to the whole, so that there is no loss of meaning and no double formation. This fixation is so secure that, as Spemann showed, a graft of tadpole epidermis, implanted into the germ cell of the triton at the site of the future triton mouth, becomes a mouth, but a tadpole mouth, since the frog's mouth-formation score was transferred along with the frog cells. If one ripped a page out of the sheet music for the first violin and inserted it at the same spot in the music for the cello, a similar discrepancy would result.

The tunnel drilling of the pea weevil larva is informative for these morphogenetic scores. In this case, the counterpoint, which becomes the motif for the tunnel drilling, is the form [*Gestalt*] of the fully developed weevil, which appears only in the future, and which would have to go under without the tunnel exit created by the larva. The future form can play a role as a motif in the becoming of that form.

This opens up further possibilities. If the future form, which represents the goal of formation, can itself become a motif, then K. E. von Baer is right when he speaks of a goal-pursuing quality in the emergence of living beings. Only he does not grasp all the facts.

When the spider builds its web, the different stages of web-formation, such as the frame built in the form of rays, can be referred to as both goal and motive for the formation of the frame. The web—but never the fly—can be called the goal of forming the web. But the fly does indeed serve as the counter-point as the motive for the formation of the web.

The function of the birch-leaf roller is a striking example

of how many riddles the technology of Nature will yet pose to us. The contrapuntally composed partners facing each other here are the little snout beetle with its fretsaw of a snout and the large birch leaf which is to be sawed up. The path of the saw has to be directed in such a way that the beetle can roll the bottom part of the leaf together afterward without difficulty into a sack into which it will lay its eggs. This path, which has a characteristic curvature, is a constant for all birch-leaf rollers, even though no trace of any disposition to this path is present in the birch leaf. Is the "constant path" itself the motive for its own emergence? This belongs to Nature's compositional secrets, which we encounter at every turn in researching the technology of Nature.

The first researcher who occupied himself with the technology of Nature seems to have been [Jean-Baptiste] Lamarck.[18] In any case, the experiment he undertook, to bring the long neck of the giraffe into consonance with the tall trunk of the palm tree, contains the first indication of a contrapuntal behavior.

Later, all interest in the technology of Nature was lost, and [Ernst] Haeckel,[19] first and foremost, replaced it with speculations about ancestors' influence. No one will be able to recognize a technical function in the assertion that amphibians descended from fish. Especially the fantasy image of the so-called "rudimentary" organs saw to it that our gaze was diverted from the true technical problems.

Only with the demonstration provided by Driesch that a sea urchin germ cell cut in half became not two half, but two whole sea urchins of half the size, opened the way for a deeper understanding of the technology of Nature. Everything physical can be cut with a knife—but not a melody. The melody of a song played on a free carillon of living bells remains unchanged, even if it only controls half the number of bells.

PROGRESS

THIS TIME, the biological parallel forced itself upon me as I listened to the St. Matthew Passion in St. Michael's Church in Hamburg. This noble work, interwoven with the most beautiful songs, advanced with the iron step of destiny. But this was certainly not the progress that researchers fantasize into the temporal succession of natural events.

Why should the powerful drama of Nature, which unfolded since the appearance of life on our Earth, not be one single composition in its heights and depths, just like the Passion? Was the much-lauded progress, which was to lead living beings from imperfect beginnings to ever-greater perfection, really, after all, only a petty bourgeois speculation on the increasing utility of business?

At least to me, no imperfection was apparent even in the simplest animals. As far as I could judge, the material available for construction was always used in the best possible way. Every animal had its own life stage, populated with all the things and all the fellow players that were meaningful for its life. The characteristics of the animal and those of its fellow players harmonized everywhere with assurance, like the points and counterpoints of a many-voiced chorus. It was as if the same masterful hand were gliding across the keys of life since time immemorial. One composition followed the other, endlessly many, serious and light, majestic and terrible.

In the waves of the primordial sea, simple yet fully formed crustaceans cavorted. Long stretches of time went by; then, the age of the rule of the cephalopods came, to which the sharks put an end. From the warm swamps of the solid land emerged the dinosaurs, which, with their gigantic bodies, exaggerated life to the point of the grotesque. But the masterful hand glided on. From the old trunk, new figures unfolded in new life-melodies, living out hundreds of variations, but never showing any transitions from the imperfect to the perfect.

Environments were certainly simpler at the beginning of the world-drama than they were later. But, in them, each carrier of meaning faced a recipient of meaning. Meaning ruled them all. Meaning bound changing organs to the changing medium. Meaning bound food and the consumers of food, predator and prey, and, first and foremost, males and females in amazing variety. Everywhere there was a progression, but nowhere progress in the sense of the survival of the fittest, never a selection of the better by a planlessly raging battle for existence. Instead, a melody reigned which entwined life and death.

I decided to lay the question before our greatest historian: Is there progress in human history?

Leopold von Ranke writes in his *Epochen der neueren Geschichte*: "If one wanted . . . to assume that this progress consisted in that, in every age, the life of humanity grows exponentially, that each generation entirely surpasses the one before it, in which the latest one would always be preferred, and the preceding one only the bearer of the ones following it, then this would be an injustice on the part of the Deity. Such an intermediary (separate) generation would have no meaning in and for itself; it would only mean something if it were the stepping stone for the next generation and would not stand in immediate relation to God. But I assert: Every age is immediate to God, and its value consists not in that which comes of it later, but in its own existence—in its own self."

Ranke rejects progress in human history because all ages have to do immediately with God and, therefore, none can be more perfect than any other. What should we understand as an age in Ranke's sense but a group of human environments that belong together within a limited period of time? One can conclude from this that each environment in this group has to do immediately with God because all environments belong to the same composition, the composer of which Ranke designates as God.

Now, the word "God" is for every materialist like a red

rag for a bull, while the materialist would recognize a composition that arises by chance in the course of enormous stretches of time if one would only concede to him that matter and energy have been the same since the beginning of the world and that the law of conservation of energy has a general and eternal validity.

At the beginning of my discussion, I showed that research on environments proves first and foremost the inconstancy of objects, which change their form as well as their meaning in every environment. The same flower stalk became four different objects in four different environments.

It remains only to show by the already adduced examples that even the constancy of matter is an illusion. The properties of the matter of an object are dependent on the sensory spectrums of that subject which is the object of our present investigation.

Given the case that we are examining, the yellow color of a flower on which a bee lands, we can say with certainty that the flower is not yellow in the bee's environment (it is probably red), because the color spectrum of the bee's eye has a different scale of lightwaves than does the color spectrum of our eye. We know just as well that the tone spectrum of a moth, the odor spectrum of a tick, the taste spectrum of an earthworm, and the shape spectrum of most invertebrates are completely different from those of human beings. Even the hardness spectrum must be completely different for the ichneumon wasp, who can drill through the hardest fir wood as if it were butter.

No single property of matter remains constant as we course through the series of environments. Each object observed by us changes not only its meaning tone but also the structure of all of its properties, in form as well as content, from environment to environment. In this human environment, matter is the *rocher de bronze*[20] on which the universe seems to rest, yet this very matter volatilizes from one environment to another. No, the constancy of matter on which the materialists insist is no solid basis for an encompassing worldview.

Much better founded than the constancy of objects is the constancy of subjects. "But," the materialists will object, "subjects also consist of matter!" That is correct, but the matter of the bodies proper to subjects must be built anew from generation to generation.

The quantity of matter that the single individual receives from its parents is extremely small: a germ cell capable of splitting and a clavier of stimulus corpuscles, the so-called genes, which is taken over in each cell division by the daughter cells, for this clavier makes it possible for the formative melodies to play on it as on the keys of a piano and thus to complete the form development. Every corpuscle put into action intervenes as a differentiated impulse in the protoplasm of its cell in a way that is formative of structure.

The formative melodies that take on a structure in this way take their motifs from the formative melodies of other subjects which they will encounter on their life's stage.

If the flower were not bee-like,
If the bee were not flower-like,
The harmony would never succeed.

These motifs are taken from the areas of food, or of the enemy, or of sex, among others. The formative melody takes most of its motifs from the area of the medium; the structure of our eye is sun-like, and that of the maple leaf with its drip channels rain-like.

Thanks to its taking on foreign motifs, the body of any and every subject is formed into a recipient of meaning from those carriers of meaning whose formative melodies have taken shape in its body as motifs. The flower therefore affects the bee as a bundle of counterpoints, since its formative melody, rich in motifs, has had an effect in the form development of the bee and vice versa.

The sun only shines on me from my sky because it, our

most important natural component, entered into the composition of my eye as the principal motif. However great as the influence of the sun is upon the eye formation of an animal, it appears just as great and shining or just as small and unimportant in the environment-sky of an eye (such as the mole's) in the formation of which it took little part. If we take the moon instead of the sun, we can still say here that, as great as the meaning of the moon is for the eye of an animal, so great also will be its meaning as a motif in the formation of the eye.

However great the meaning of mammals is in the tick's environment, the formative melody of mammals takes part to the same extent in the formation of the tick, to wit, as the odor of butyric acid, as the resistance of hair, as warmth, and as penetrability of the skin. It is completely indifferent to the tick that mammals possess thousands of other properties. Only those properties common to all mammals appear as motifs in the formation of the tick, where its perception organs as well as its effect organs are concerned.

We are always led astray when we want to introduce the measure of our world into the judgment of animal worlds. But I could argue that all of Nature takes part as a motif in the development of my personality, concerning my body as well as my mind. If that were not the case, I would lack the organs with which to know Nature. I could also express this more humbly and say: I will be a part of Nature to the extent that Nature takes me up into one of its compositions. Then, I am not a product of all of Nature but only the product of human nature, beyond which no knowledge is afforded me. Just as the tick is only a product of tick nature, the human being remains bound to its human nature, from which each individual always emerges anew.

Our advantage over animals consists in our being able to broaden the compass of inborn human nature. While we cannot create new organs, we can provide our organs with aids. We have created perception tools [*Merkzeuge*] as well as [effect] tools [*Werkzeuge*],[21] which offer each of us who knows how to use them the possibility of deepening and broadening his environment. None leads out of the compass of the environment.

Only the knowledge that everything in Nature is created according to its meaning and that all environments are composed into the world-score opens up a path leading out of the confines of one's own environment. Blowing up our environmental space by millions of light-years does not lift us beyond ourselves, but what certainly does is the knowledge that, beyond our personal environment, the environments of our human and animal brethren are secured in an all-encompassing plan.

SUMMARY AND CONCLUSION

IF WE COMPARE an animal's body with a house, then the anatomists have studied closely the way it is built and the physiologists have studied closely the mechanical appliances located in the house. Ecologists, too, have demarcated and investigated the garden in which the house is located. But the garden has always been depicted as it offers itself to our human eye, and it has therefore been neglected to take into account how the garden changes when looked at by the subject who lives in the house.

This view is extremely surprising. The garden does not demarcate itself from a surrounding world of which it represents only a section, as it seems to our eye. Rather, it is surrounded by a horizon which has the house as its center. Each house is covered by its own canopy on which the sun, moon, and stars, which belong directly to the house, wander along.

Each house has a number of windows, which open onto a garden: a light window, a sound window, an olfactory window, a taste window, and a great number of tactile windows. Depending on the manner in which these windows are built, the garden changes as it is seen from the house. By no means does it appear as a section of a larger world. Rather, it is the only world that belongs to the house—its environment.

The garden that appears to our eye is fundamentally different from that which presents itself to the inhabitants of the house, especially with regard to the things filling it. While we discover a thousand different plants, stones, and animals in the garden, the eye of the homeowner perceives only a very limited number of things in his garden—and only such as are of importance to the subject who lives in the house. Their number can be reduced to a minimum, as in the tick's environment, in which only the same mammal with a very limited number of properties appears. Of all the things we discover around the tick—the colorful, scented flowers, the rustling leaves, the singing birds—none enters the tick's environment.

I have shown how the same object, placed in four different environments, takes on four different meanings and, each time, changes its properties fundamentally. This can only be explained by the fact that all the properties of things are nothing other than the perception signs imprinted upon them by the subject with which they enter into a relation.

In order to understand this, one must recall that the body of each living being is built from living cells that together form a living carillon. The living cell possesses a specific energy that makes it possible for it to respond to any effect which approaches it from outside with a "self-tone." Self-tones can be combined with one another into melodies and do not require the mechanical interrelation of their cell bodies in order to have an effect on each other.

In their basic features, the bodies of most animals are similar in that they possess as a basis organs, which carry out metabolism and provide the energy gained from food for their vital functioning. The vital functioning of the animal subject as a carrier of meaning consists in perceiving and affecting.

They perceive with the help of the sensory organs, which

serve to sort the stimuli pressing in from all sides, to block out the unnecessary ones and to transform the ones useful to the body into nerve excitations that, once they arrive in the center, make the living carillon of the brain cells sound. The self-tones that respond serve as perception signs of external events. According to whether they are auditory signs, visual signs, olfactory signs, etc., they are stamped as perception marks corresponding to the respective source of stimulus.

At the same time, the cellular bells sounding in the perception organ induce the bells in the central effect organ, which send out their self-tones as impulses, in order to set off and conduct the movement of the effector's muscles. It is therefore a sort of musical process that, starting from the properties of the carrier of meaning, leads back to it. It is therefore permissible to treat the receptor as well as the effector organs of the recipient of meaning along with the corresponding properties of the carrier of meaning as counterpoints.

As one can see over and over again, a very complicated physical structure is required in most animals in order to connect the subject smoothly with its carrier of meaning. Physical structure is never present from the beginning, but rather, each body begins its construction as a single cellular bell, which divides itself and arranges itself into a resounding carillon according to a certain formative melody.

How is it possible that two things of such different origin as, for instance, the bumblebee and the snapdragon blossom, are constructed so that they suit each other in every detail? Only by the fact that these two formative melodies influence each other mutually—that the snapdragon's melody intervenes as a motif in the bumblebee's melody and vice versa. What was true of the bee is also true of the bumblebee: if its body were not flowerlike, its structure would never work.

With the recognition of this cardinal principle of natural technology, the question of whether there is progress from the imperfect to the more perfect is already decided negatively.

For, if foreign meaning-motifs intervening from all sides shape the structure of animals, then one cannot foresee what a succession of generations, however long it might be, could change.

If we leave behind all speculation about ancestry, we step onto the solid ground of natural technology. But a great disappointment awaits us here. The successes of natural technology are plain for us to see, but their melody formation is inscrutable. Natural technology has this in common with the creation of every work of art. We can very well see how the painter's hand put one spot of color after another onto the canvas, until the painting stands finished before us, but the formative melody that moved the hand remains completely unknowable for us.

We can certainly understand how a music box makes its melodies sound, but we shall never understand how a melody constructs its music box. That is precisely the question in the creation of every living being. The material is there in each germ cell; the clavier is also present in the genes. Only the melody is lacking in order to complete the formative process. Where does the melody come from?

In every music box, there is a cylinder with pins on it. When the cylinder turns, the pins strike metal reeds of different lengths and produce vibrations in the air which our ear perceives as tones. Every musician would easily be able to recognize the melody played by the music box based on the position of the pins on the cylinder.

Let us forget for a moment about the human builder of the music box, and let us suppose that it is a natural product. Then, we shall be able to say that this is a matter of a score developed physically in three dimensions, one which has evidently been crystallized out of the melody itself, since the melody represents the *meaning-germ* of the music box itself, from which all its parts come, given that sufficient pliable material is present.

In the National Museum in Stockholm, there is a small picture by Ivar Arosenius dubbed *Jul* (Christmas), which shows a tender young mother with her child on her lap. Over the mother hovers a delicate, light halo. It is a simple mansard room in which this touching little Madonna is sitting. Everything around her is completely ordinary, but all the objects in front of her on the table, the lamp, the curtain, the dresser with its utensils, are atmospheric motifs which augment the touching sacredness. The picture is so perfectly through-composed that one forgets the painter and believes one is seeing a little natural wonder. Here, the meaning-germ is "Madonna." From it, all other things result automatically, as in the melodic formation of a crystal. At the same time, one seems to be looking into a pure environment, in which there are no foreign ingredients. Everything fits together like point and counterpoint.

Only a little bit of material, but pliable—a bit of canvas and a couple of muted colors—was necessary in order to make this little artwork crystallize out. The amount of material plays an entirely secondary role. With more or less material on a larger or smaller scale, the artist would have been able to achieve the same result. But, with the same amount of material, another artist would have created an entirely different painting of the Madonna out of the same meaning-germ "Madonna."

Now, we want to use the creation of the artwork in order to show to what degree the creation of a living being proceeds in the same way.

There is no doubt that we may refer to the acorn as the meaning-germ of the oak and to the egg as the meaning-germ of the chicken. The material is in each case the most pliable Nature possesses, namely, living protoplasm, which yields to any form development if it comes from self-tones and is able to hold any form. Departing from the meaning-germ of the acorn, the oak crystallizes out just as surely as does the chicken from the egg—but how does this happen?

As was already discussed, new organ buds are constantly being added that develop completely independently. In each organ bud, there is a meaning-germ that makes the finished

organ crystallize out of the material available to it. If one re-
moves part of this building material, the organ will be well
developed in all details, but it will be smaller in size than the
normal organs. [Hermann] Braus[22] has shown that the ball
of the shoulder joint no longer fits the scapula and glenoid if
they have not reached normal size because of lack of formative
material. And Spemann, as we have seen, has proven that a
newly implanted organ bud from another species contains the
meaning-germ corresponding to the position in the body but
makes another organ emerge that might be useful to the donor
animal but not to the host, since each animal carries out this
function in a completely different way. In both cases, the eating
function was the meaning-germ, but the frog eats in a different
way than the triton does. And so, two paintings of the Madonna,
if they were done by two different painters, would have the same
meaning function but would not resemble each other.

As soon as the organs have come together for a common
bodily function, malformations from lack of material, such as
Braus observed, no longer occur. Wessely was able to show that
in young rabbits, which regenerate their ocular lenses to an en-
larged or reduced scale, all the organs taking part in the act of
seeing enlarge or reduce themselves at the same scale, so that,
in every case, the function of vision goes on undisturbed. Here,
too, it is meaning which directs reconstruction.

That it is really meaning which controls regeneration follows strikingly from an experiment by [Franz] Nissl.[23] Without
a doubt, the cranium in mammals has the meaning of a solid
protective covering for the cerebrum which lies beneath it. In
young rabbits, the cranium is also regenerated without problems, as long as the cerebrum is not damaged. On the other
hand, if half of the cerebrum is surgically removed, the cranium above it does not regenerate. It has lost its meaning. In
this case, a simple scarring is sufficient. As one can see, meaning appears everywhere as a decisive natural factor in always
new and surprising forms.

If we let the environments pass once more before our mind's eye, then we find in the gardens that surround subjects' bodily houses the most incredible figures serving as carriers of meaning, the interpretation of which often causes great difficulty. From this, one gets the impression that the carriers of meaning represent secret signs or symbols, which can only be understood by individuals of the same species and remain completely incomprehensible for members of other species.

The silhouette and the water streams of the pond mussel provide the bitterling its love symbol. The change in taste between the tip and the stem of the leaf become a form symbol for the earthworm. The same tone is a friend symbol for the bat and an enemy symbol for the moth, and so on in an endless series.

If we have finally convinced ourselves, based on the overwhelming number of examples, that every environment is in principle only filled with meaning symbols, then a second, even more surprising fact will impose itself upon us: that every meaning symbol of the subject is at the same time a meaning motive/motif for the physical formation of that subject.

The house of the body is, on the one hand, the producer of the meaning symbols that populate its garden and, on the other hand, the product of the same symbols, which intervene as motifs in the construction of the house.

The sun owes its light and its image in the sky above, which forms a vault over the garden, to the house's eye-window. At the same time, it is the motive/motif for the construction of the eye-window. That is true of animals and human beings and can only be caused by the fact that the same natural factor appears in both cases.

Let us suppose that moths have become extinct because of some natural event and we were faced with the task of replacing this loss on the clavier of life with the help of natural technology. How would we proceed in this case? We would probably take a butterfly and retrain it for nocturnally blooming flowers, in which case the development of the olfactory feelers would have to take priority over the development of the eyes. Since the new moths would be delivered over defenselessly to the bats, which are agile flyers, a sign of recognition must be invented for this enemy that makes it possible for the majority of butterflies to escape their enemy in time. The peeping sound of the bat can be used best as an enemy symbol, since the bat always uses it as a friend symbol. In order to perceive this peeping tone, the butterfly must be reconstructed and receive a hearing organ that can place it in relation to the enemy symbol. This means that the symbol enters the construction plan as a motif:

If the moth were not batlike,
Its life would soon be over.

One can well imagine that the tick arose in order to fill a gap in the clavier of life. In this case, the carrier of meaning which consists of the general properties of mammals would be at once a symbol for the prey and a motif in the structural plan of the tick.

Let us now attempt, in concluding, to regard our own body-house with its garden from the outside. We now know that our sun in our sky, along with the garden which is filled with plants, animals, and people, are only symbols in an all-encompassing natural composition, which orders everything according to rank and meaning.

Through this overview, we also gain knowledge of the limits of our world. We can certainly get closer to all things through the use of increasingly precise apparatuses, but we do not gain any more sensory organs thereby, and all the properties of things, even when we analyze them down to the smallest details—atoms and electrons—will always remain only perception marks of our senses and ideas.

We know that this sun, this sky, and this earth will disappear upon our death; they will survive in similar forms in the environment of coming generations.

There are not only the manifolds of space and time in which things can be spread out. There is also the manifold of environments, in which things repeat themselves in always new forms. All these countless environments provide, in the third manifold, the clavier on which Nature plays her symphony of meaning beyond time and space.

In our lifetime, the task is given to us to form with our environment a key in the gigantic clavier over which an invisible hand glides, playing.

BUBBLES AND WEBS: A BACKDOOR STROLL

THROUGH THE READINGS OF UEXKÜLL

Geoffrey Winthrop-Young

Darwin at Stalingrad

Jakob von Uexküll was a prolific writer. Between 1892 and his death in 1944 he published more than a dozen books and well over twelve dozen papers. The latter range from reports on pioneering experiments to stimulate octopus skin to rambling demands that biologists should abstain from participating in general elections, from suggestions for a new terminology in the life sciences to analyses of Kant's influence on biology. From paramecia and peanut worms to Platonic dialogues, Uexküll had a lot to say, and he said it well. *A Foray into the Worlds of Animals and Humans* is Uexküll at his best: a happy blend of observational skills and literary talent delivered with an equally engaging mix of boyish enthusiasm and avuncular bonhomie. Now and then, however, you can sense the frustration of a very self-assured man who is convinced that he has something vitally important to tell the world but who realizes that he is not being listened to. Uexküll was prepared to cross many boundaries, and none more so than the one that separates popularizing from proselytizing.

Take, for instance, the last text Uexküll published during his lifetime, an essay entitled "Darwin's Guilt" that appeared on January 14, 1943, on the front page of the *Deutsche Allgemeine Zeitung*. At first glance it stands far apart from the momentous news items of the day. The lead story, not surprisingly, is Stalingrad. Though under constant attack and bereft of all initiative, the German Sixth Army appears to be doing well: Russian advances invariably fail as tanks are vanquished by hand grenades. Other front-page stories deal with the growing rift among the British, French, and Americans in North Africa (January 14 marked the beginning of the Casablanca Conference) and the recent declaration of war on the Allies by Japan's Nanking-based Chinese puppet state, a momentous tiding that is heralded as a "turning point." In the face of such global drama Uexküll withdraws into a bygone scholarly idyll. He recounts how upon first arriving in Naples half a century earlier to join the famous *Stazione Zoologica* he had dinner with an unnamed philosopher in a *trattoria* facing Mount Vesuvius. During their animated conversation the philosopher managed to convince Uexküll that Darwin's theory was fundamentally flawed. The most incontrovertible piece of evidence was right in front of them on the table: an egg. Had it not been thrown into boiling water, the philosopher expounded, it would have turned into a chicken, for like all eggs it was endowed with a formative impulse, a score, as it were, that guides developmental processes much like a melody organizes tones into harmonious sequences. Indeed all of nature "was borne by meaningful instructions indicative of a spirit that had created this methodical unity."[1] But by reducing evolution to variations of a material structure mindlessly acted upon by outside pressures, Darwin deprived nature of score and spirit. *Darwin mundum stultitiat*, the philosopher decreed, Darwin dumbed down the world. Such was the force of this argument with its structure-score antithesis and ovarian exhibits that Uexküll could not but agree. But what starts out as a conventional critique reminiscent of today's intelligent design turns into a double-barreled indictment of Darwin's nefarious influence on culture and mores: "First, he [Darwin] is to blame that the wider public's former veneration of nature has turned into contempt; second, the very close relationship established by Darwin between humans and apes has thrown the religious sentiments of the educated classes into such disarray that the effect will last for decades."[2]

A pleasant story, and no doubt one that was easier to stomach than the increasingly transparent fairy tales of German superiority at Stalingrad. But it, too, is a contrived yarn. Uexküll had distanced himself from Darwin long before he arrived in Naples. His objections were rooted as much in the distinct German reception of Darwinian theory as in the fact that Darwin had become an ally, as it were, of the Tsarist government's increasingly hostile attempts to silence Estonian independence and oust all German influence. Whether it was a matter of Russian Darwinists attacking the vitalism of their German and Estonian colleagues, or of the more blatant attempts by Panslavists to justify the Russification of the Baltics with Darwinist arguments, "for Uexküll . . . this instrumentalization of Darwin's teaching, which up until then he had held in high regard, represented a dangerous threat to which he reacted with a renunciation of Darwin."[3] Throughout his life Uexküll never veered from his belief that Darwin had wrecked "his own science, biology"[4] and that his teachings were fundamentally un-German, a conviction clearly on display in the more vigorous patriotic essays he wrote during the First World War.[5] Indeed, the struggle against Darwinism came to be part of the grand war waged between biology and physics, two competing worldviews "that are destined to combat each other as mortal enemies."[6] Given Uexküll's martial metaphors, readers of "Darwin's Guilt" must have drawn analogies to the ongoing military conflict. But the exact correspondence remains unclear. Is the essay a reminder that the soldiers of the German Sixth Army are the endangered spearhead in a metaphysical struggle against Darwin? But given the esteem that Darwinism—primitively refashioned into a doctrine of eternal struggle—enjoyed in the Third Reich, the essay can just as well be read as a tacit admission that Germany, too, has succumbed to its tooth-and-claw philosophy by invading the East. Are German troops fighting Darwin at Stalingrad or did Darwin drive them there in the first place?

In any case things were coming to an end. Two and a half weeks after the appearance of the essay, the Sixth Army surrendered at Stalingrad; two and a half years later the Third Reich ceased to exist. Uexküll did not live to witness Germany's defeat; he was also spared a harsh critique that originated in the remote northwestern regions of Poland. Living out the war as an army doctor in the barracks of Landsberg (now Gorzów Wielkopolski) on the Warta River, the poet Gottfried Benn took aim at Uexküll. Benn was familiar with Uexküll's work, he shared some of his anti-Darwinian sentiments and had excerpted him for some of his earlier essays, but now he offered a distinctly unflattering assessment. Uexküll's Umwelt, Benn proclaimed, goes beyond Darwin and in fact supersedes the latter's "moral and political doctrine of struggle," yet when it comes to the question of what it means to be human "it represents a far greater nihilism than Darwin's theory." For all his insistence on random mechanics, Darwin had appreciated man as the "in principle highest result of a long descent" and was thus still willing to grant him a special place, but Uexküll saw him as nothing more than one of the many keys of a giant clavier on which nature plays its "symphonies of meaning." By placing the human Umwelt on the same level as the many animal Umwelten, the human mind turns out to be just another note of nature, equivalent to the bat's sonar or the tick's responsiveness to butyric acid. Debunking the musical metaphors so precious to Uexküll (and later to Deleuze), Benn scoffed that the whole idea amounted to "general musical promiscuity." In short, Uexküll's Umwelt is "a grandiose vision, but with regard to man a kind of orphic cynicism bordering on the jovial."[7]

Promiscuity, cynicism, nihilism—Uexküll would have been infuriated. As we shall see, Benn's critique is informed by the first major philosophical engagement with Uexküll's work, yet his indictment must also be understood as a Stalingrad symptom. To draw on Helmut Lethen's recent account, Stalingrad confirmed Benn's profound historical pessimism.[8] The battle not only put an end to Germany's eastern conquest, it was a traumatic contraction that seemed to terminate the very notion of linear progress. Benn only needed to peer over the shoulder of his superiors at increasingly unsettling maps: The planned movement forward into Russian space was replaced by ever-tightening inescapable circles, from the cutoff of the Sixth Army salient and the encirclement of Stalingrad to the containment of isolated pockets of German resistance and from there to the last fading image of a soldier cowering in a foxhole waiting to be crushed by a tank. Uexküll's Umwelt suggested itself as an apposite metaphor, since its isolating encirclement in combination with an indifference to teleology or progress seemed to correspond to a notion of history as static and circular.[9] At the same time it had a welcome aesthetic dimension. The subject enmeshed in its Umwelt comes to resemble Edgar Allan Poe's shipwrecked observer in the gyrating maelstrom: it is possible to study in relative peace the surrounding catastrophe.

Uexküll's Theory Meadow
The abyss that separates Uexküll's Neapolitan idyll from Benn's nihilist Stalingrad Umwelt is indicative of the widely disparate appropriations, adaptations, and speculations that characterize the reception history of Uexküll, in particular, of his Umwelt concept.[10] Uexküll's reemergence over the last decades—be it his promotion to a pioneer of biosemiotics, his puckish cameo performances in the works of Gilles Deleuze and Giorgio Agamben, or his growing prominence in post-humanism and critical animal studies—is at first glance a sequence of loosely connected stories, of frequently unrelated, if not downright incompatible discoveries and appropriations in the course of which very different approaches perceive and act upon those particular features of Uexküll's work that strike them as significant. The analogy is as gratuitous as it is irresistible: Uexküll's oeuvre is much like the flowery meadow placed before the reader at the beginning of *A Foray*, and the

numerous anthropological, philosophical, cybernetic, or semiotic engagements with Uexküll resemble the ways in which the many bubble-bound creatures, each apprehending the meadow in its own species-specific way, happily frolic in, above, and underneath the grass.

And yet there is an underlying logic to this checkered engagement. Or, to employ Uexküll's second guiding metaphor, these bubbles are connected and woven together into a web. In ways that need to be explored, Uexküll's reception is linked to the tension between the metaphors. Uexküll talks of webs *and* bubbles as complementary, but what is of greater interest—and of greater importance to his reception history—is the inherent polarity. Webs *versus* bubbles, contact versus boundary, connection versus isolation, communication between versus representation within—the tension between these poles will resonate throughout Uexküll and beyond. Guided by this metaphorical tension, the following remarks will attempt an eclectic stroll through that meadow and its inhabitants. It will neither amount to a comprehensive reception history nor provide a full account of Uexküll's Umwelt theory.[11] Instead I have two more modest goals in mind. First, to point out to interested readers a set of back doors that lead to certain ideas that—be it by chance or by design—tend to be absent from many English discussions. Second, to illustrate the considerable impact and fecundity of Uexküll's work by presenting a few noteworthy *literary* encounters. The latter are an integral part of the meadow. Just as Uexküll did not grant any objective superiority to the human Umwelt over its nonhuman counterparts, these literary takes must be taken as seriously as the more sober academic encounters. As we shall see, the literary worms and moles tend to focus on some of the darker, less idyllic aspects of the meadow that frequently are not part of the loftier Umwelten of the scholarly birds and bees. The latter are more interested in the gains that may come from resurrecting Uexküll, while the literary engagements tend to reveal the costs.

Lonely Danish Worlds (Part I): The Poet's Hell

Uexküll did not invent Umwelt; he attempted to redefine the meaning of an already existing word. Such semantic purification ventures are fraught with difficulties because they never take place in a semantic vacuum. Words have undercurrents of meaning that no cleansing can completely suppress. So what was Umwelt before Uexküll? When and why did it emerge?

Its first recorded use occurred in an ode entitled "To Napoleon" written in 1800 in German by the Danish writer Jens Immanuel Baggesen (1764–1826):

> Und es verwandelt die Fluth in Feuer sich,
>   Nebel in Nordlicht,
> Regen in Strahlenerguß, daß von fern erscheinet
>   der Umwelt
> Ein' ätherische Feste die Schicksalshölle des Dichters.[12]

> And floods turn into fire, mist into northern lights,
> Rain into radiant outpour, so that to the surrounding world
> The poet's hellish fate appears as an ethereal castle.

According to conventional wisdom Baggesen first conceived of the poem in his native tongue, in which case *Umwelt* would have been a second-order German neologism derived from the Danish neologism *omverde*. The latter, however, did not appear in print until later. In order to explain how the German copy could have preceded the Danish original, the latter was assumed to have been present inside Baggesen's Danish mind all along. In his essay "Milieu and Ambiance" Leo Spitzer claimed that the Danish detour was misleading. For one, the multilingual Baggesen produced copious amounts of German poetry without having to rely on mental Danish drafts. More importantly, the combination of intonation and placing of Umwelt in the quote above pointed to a specifically German origin. Baggesen, Spitzer argued, was trying to live up to the stylistic guidelines of his friend Johann Heinrich Voss (1751–1826), the famed German translator of Homer, who had a marked preference for ending Homeric hexameters with a spondee. Semantically, Umwelt appeared to offer nothing new—according to Spitzer, Baggesen could just as well have used *Welt* or *Aussenwelt* ("outer world")—but to satisfy metrical requirements he fashioned Umwelt.[13]

Umwelt, then, came about due to stylistic exigencies, but it was soon refunctionalized to act as the German equivalent of French *milieu*, a term that came with determinist implications. Milieu, be it that of Taine or Zola, is something that acts upon and shapes the subject. Uexküll's Umwelt, however, excludes such one-way causalities. "Nobody is the product of their milieu—each is the master of his Umwelt."[14] His usage, then, represents a further refunctionalization. It is a scientific semantic neologism, that is, an attempt to redefine the meaning of a widely used word in accordance with a scientific theory. A difficult task; it is easier to launch a formal scientific neologism (Lavoisier's *oxygen*) or respecify a scientific term (the switch from thermodynamic to information-theoretical *entropy*). The best one can hope for is that the semantic neologism, protected and supported by specialized discourse networks, will come to coexist with the common usage (as in the case of *noise*). Uexküll wasn't very successful. Unless they happen to be versed in ethological arcana, native speakers of German do not think of perception marks, effect signs, and functional cycles when hearing Umwelt. Ironically, Darwin's language—which according to Uexküll's grumpy assessment "enforces simplification"[15]—has kept faith with the neologism: English umwelt (*sic*) is much closer to Uexküll's Umwelt than the commonly used German Umwelt.

But why? On a very general level Uexküll's theories are no doubt related to a distinctly German discourse on nature. It is no coincidence that his semantic reform coincided with the rise of what has been called *naturism*, that is, the widespread attempt to offset the ills of industrial modernism by reorienting the German people toward nature (see Williams[16]); just as it is no coincidence that the reemergence of Uexküll in Germany occurred in tandem with the rise of the new ecological movements. But it is precisely the importance of Umwelt in German political and ecological thought that precluded the widespread acceptance of Uexküll's redefinition. Today, Umwelt—as evident in the compound nouns *Umweltschutz, Umweltverschmutzung, Umweltbewusstsein* (environmental protection, pollution, and environmental awareness)—is a term of concern, indeed of such concern that it routinely sabotages efficient political discourse (Luhmann).[17] The nineteenth century is inverted: If milieu posited the environment as something that acts upon humans, Umwelt is seen as something humans need to act upon in a constructive and protective manner because less informed earlier humans have been mistreating it for centuries. Yet while Uexküll himself may have applauded increased environment awareness, his theory—and with it his usage of Umwelt—remains in a neutral zone devoid of collective political concern. Somehow the reconnect with nature appears to be linked to a social disconnect.

At this point we have to return to Baggesen's ode. Have another look at the quote above. Observers located in the Umwelt are looking "from afar" *at* the world of the poet.[18] The prefix *um* connotes apprehension from a center. By deploying the neologism Umwelt the observing world is briefly seen from the point of view of the observed—and misunderstood—poet; and the momentary change of perspective renders the observers' misperception all the more striking. This is the crucial semantic point that Spitzer's focus on stylistics failed to see. Whenever Baggesen uses Umwelt it connotes lack of comprehension, if not downright hostility on the part of the surrounding world.[19] The term, then, comes with a semantic bias originating in the grand hermeneutic dilemma of Romanticism: The price for the increased ability to express subjective inwardness is the growing inability to successfully communicate it to others. No account of Umwelt is complete without taking account of this undercurrent. Notions of isolation, incommunicability, and even hostility reverberate and ricochet through its history.

Human Bubbles (Part I):
The Open Excentricality of Deficient Beings

Judging by Anglophone scholarship the most noteworthy appropriations of Uexküll are those written or available in English. This is unfortunate because it misses out on Ucxküll's reception at the hand of German Philosophical Anthropology, which was not only the first major engagement with his work to take place outside of biology, but also set the stage for many subsequent appropriations. Yet although some of the work by leading representatives such as Max Scheler, Helmut Plessner, and Arnold Gehlen were translated, *Philosophische Anthropologie* never made it outside of Germany.

Philosophical Anthropology—to provide a caricature as a shortcut—is the bastard offspring of a distinctly German union of high-flying early-nineteenth-century idealism and hard-core late-nineteenth-century naturalism. Its most basic move is to play off the parents against each other. Too informed by insights into the natural and physical (pre)conditions of human existence to succumb to idealist temptations to place mind, spirit, or consciousness at the center of analysis, it is also too steeped in idealist philosophy to submit to the reduction of mind to materiality. It is too involved in bodies and embodiment to buy into the phenomenological proposals of mind and intentionality as put forward by Edmund Husserl, and yet it is too hostile to paradigms of external determination (especially when it appears in tandem with Darwinian mechanics) to view the development of the mind as a random coda to the grand parade of evolution. This precarious balancing act is particularly apparent in the way Philosophical Anthropology proceeds. As

Joachim Fischer has analyzed in great detail, its characteristic opening move is to start neither at the top (mind, subject) nor at the bottom (basic material or physical processes) but in the middle, in an intermediate realm in which organisms are always already mediated in and by their environment. This allows for lateral moves from subject to object and back, vertical moves from organic base to conscious concepts, and movements along the evolutionary axis from plants to animals to humans.[20] No wonder Uexküll became so important: Not only does he offer a biology that is as committed to philosophical inquiries as the philosophical inquiries by Plessner, Gehlen, and others are to biological research,[21] his Umwelt concept with its *Einpassung* or "fitting-into" of organisms into their specific environments is precisely what Philosophical Anthropology needed as a point of departure. But the initial adoption is followed by an equally determined rejection that hinges on the question: Can we speak of a *human* Umwelt? Three possible answers are put forward.

1. Yes, there is a human Umwelt. It may be more complex and differentiated because unlike ticks we don't spend our lives hanging from twigs waiting for something warm and woolly to come lumbering by, but at rock bottom we are just as enclosed in our bubble. This is essentially Uexküll's position (more of which in the next section).

2. Yes, humans have an Umwelt but we can escape or transcend it. The philosopher Theodor Litt, for instance, posited that the difference between the animal and the human Umwelt is that the former encloses the organism while the latter also acts as a summons to exit:

> Compared to the human Umwelt the animal Umwelt appears to be of such fixed immobility primarily because it does not in any way refer beyond itself. It is closed and hardened

into a self-sufficiency that does not suggest, let alone permit any movement beyond. The human Umwelt, however, is not only that which it contains, it is also open in the direction toward that which it not yet is. Its peculiar mixture of fullness and lack demands that it be transcended.[22]

The species-specific boundaries of the animal Umwelt, then, are insurpassable limits, while those of the human Umwelt are more like an American frontier that invites transgression. Uexküll's pincers turn into spreaders that force and enlarge Umwelt openings.

3. No, humans do not have an Umwelt. On the contrary, what characterizes us is the absence of a stabilizing, species-specific enclosure bubble. Plessner (who started out as a biologist and had been in contact with Uexküll since 1913) spoke of man's excentricality, that is, his location on the border between body and corresponding environment—a move off-center, as it were, that represents a clear contrast, and in fact only makes sense in contrast to Uexküll's Umwelt. Gehlen, in turn, invoked man's status as a *Mängelwesen*, a deficient being no longer secured by instincts and neatly interlocking functional cycles, the absence of which requires the creation of a functionally equivalent guiding edifice in the shape of culture. Man is by nature a cultural being. And then, of course, there is the more famous take by Martin Heidegger that Sagan touched on in his introduction. Heidegger was neither an upper- nor lower-case philosophical anthropologist (he would have been as irritated by that label as he was by the moniker "existentialist"), but his initial steps are quite similar: He, too, accepts the animal portions of Uexküll's analysis, claiming that animals are "benumbed" in and by a disinhibitory ring. He, too, interjects that animals do not have a double vision that allows humans to see objects of their environments as things-in-themselves beyond their integration into the cycles. But then the analysis heads

off in a different direction. For Philosophical Anthropology the importance of the man/animal Umwelt distinction lies in how it is able to address the question what *man* is; for Heidegger, the importance of that distinction lies in how it is able to address the question—to borrow a quote from a less philosophical context—what the meaning of *is* is when we claim that man "is" this or the other.

This was the background for Benn's harsh objections. Versed in the arguments put forward by Philosophical Anthropology, Benn was anything but a concerned humanist; he was not irritated by the denial of man's higher status but by Uexküll's putative blindness to man's fundamentally problematic nature. This critique of Uexküll (which will resurface time and again) is a kind of speciesism in a minor key that tries to reclaim a special place for humans not as the masters but as the misfits of creation. There are always faint echoes of Kierkegaard: somehow, we are special because we are broken, lost, abandoned, or derelict incomplete beings. (Alternately, "unfinished" humans may be labeled as evolutionary to-do projects that await completion.) Uexküll's "jovial" theory appears to be devoid of tragedy. There is—to span the extremes of the German pantheon—too much Goethe and too little Nietzsche. Heaping insult upon insult, Benn acknowledged the similarity between Uexküll and Goethe but then added that in Goethe's time this type of harmonious leveling of differences may have been "worthy of a great man," but nowadays it revealed nothing other than the "primary joviality of the biologist and insect specialist."[23]

Human Bubbles (Part II): Jobs and Jews
This allows us to briefly address the question why Uexküll is of such promise to current studies in posthumanism, especially its animal side. No matter how sophisticated and self-critical, humanism (so the argument goes) is ultimately based on speciesism; speciesism, in turn, is based on the assumption

that humans alone are thinkers and makers of culture and nature, which implies that we are autonomous subjects operating at a certain remove from that which we contemplate and/or engineer. Animals, too, may make and think but they do not do so as subjects, that is, as self-reflexive agents. It is precisely this suppression of nonhuman subjectivity that, in turn, is denied by Uexküll, who instead furnishes a notion of a human subject as always already enmeshed in its environment on the basis of operating principles that are similar to those of animals. The abyss between animals and humans (an abyss that Heidegger and Philosophical Anthropology tried to reinscribe even after accepting Uexküll's basic premises) is narrowed and bridged. Animals are promoted by virtue of their human-like ability to construct their own environment; humans are demoted by virtue of our animal-like inability to transcend our Umwelt.

Let us enter this philosophically fraught debate by a somewhat flimsy back door (though with the caveat that one of the most elementary rules for reading Uexküll is to be on guard when he tries to be funny, folksy, or flimsy).

> In the dog world there are only dog things, in the dragonfly world there are only dragonfly things, and in the human world there are only human things. Even more so, Mr. Schulz will only encounter Schulz things and never Meyer things, just as Mr. Meyer will not encounter Schulz things.[24]

There appears to be no need to individuate canine or anisopteran Umwelten. Once you grasp Lassie's functional cycles you also gain access to the Umwelt of Rin Tin Tin, Benji, and Cujo—but Messieurs Schulz and Meyer live in very different soap bubbles. Ultimately, the focus on internal differentiation within the human species results in an external leveling. The more Uexküll distinguishes individual human Umwelten, the less importance accrues to the distinction between human and animal Umwelten. In addition (and here matters get both entertaining and dangerous), human Umwelten are frequently located on interim levels between species and individual. To name a few:

1. *Nations.* Especially during wartime, Umwelten can be differentiated according to nations. As the essay "Darwin and English Morals" indicates, the internal moral organization of the German bubble differs significantly from that of its English counterpart. As a result, the receptor organs of those fitted into an English Umwelt react differently—that is, more positively—to the perception marks on display in Darwin's morally dubious texts.

2. *Regions.* Uexküll's beloved Neapolitans live in their own Umwelt, which (as we shall see in the next section) is the best of all bubbles. Fortunately, you do not have to be born and bred in Naples to share it. Probably the greatest compliment Uexküll received in his lifetime was the acknowledgment by Neapolitans, *"Il signore non e un forestiere, il signore e di qua*—The gentleman is not a foreigner, the gentleman is from here."[25]

3. *Gender.* Women, Uexküll divined, are not like men. The crucial difference is that women are far more aware of the fact that people live in their respective bubbles. *"Umwelten* are natural to them. Every woman knows that her neighbors live in a different world."[26] Hence women—who don't need to read Uexküll—make ideal readers of Freud and Heidegger, for they instinctively ward off the "two impersonal powers, the Id (*Es*) and the One (*Man*)" that endeavor to impose abstract rules on individual Umwelten. This gender differentiation reveals two aspects: In line with traditional gender roles that relegate women to home and hearth (and which Uexküll was not the man to challenge), the strong association between women and the "natural" awareness of environment points to the rooted,

homebound, even domestic quality of the Umwelt concept. Second, while women have the great advantage of natural Umwelt awareness, its scientific study, which requires a temporary distancing into objectivity, is a predominantly male domain.

4. *Professions*. Toward the end of *A Foray*, Uexküll refers to the worlds of astronomers, chemists, and physicists; in his popular essays from the 1920s there are numerous references to the specific Umwelten of cobblers, tailors, smiths, and so on. This may seem the most flimsy collective level of all, yet it points toward one of the most serious aspects of Uexküll's writings that is especially on display in his study *State Biology*. First published in 1920, it has all the hallmarks of a standard exercise in reactionary organicism: The state is a body ruled by the brain, its central organ, i.e., a monarch or somebody in an equivalent position. Democracy represents a dysfunctional power distribution, as if the brain were to share its tasks with spleen, liver, and kidneys. A national community, then, is an organism composed of cells performing different tasks, and it is the duty of the state to supervise and coordinate functionally differentiated elements.

Needless to say, *State Biology* and the related papers that Uexküll placed in conservative journals rarely appear in many of his reception bubbles. Those eager to establish him as a pioneer in their particular field are understandably not too keen on tarnishing his image. It comes in handy that the crudity of Uexküll's argument with its standard right-wing collapse of politics into biology makes it easy to dismiss: *State Biology* can be neglected because it is too dumb to be dangerous. Roberto Esposito, however, has drawn attention to certain features of the text that are anything but irrelevant. The first is the fact that Uexküll is no longer talking, as nineteenth-century organicists were prone to do, in general terms, but is specifically addressing "the German state with its peculiar characteristics and vital demands that arise in response to specific challenges of modernization."[27] In this particular regard Uexküll is to the origin of biopolitics what Edmund Burke is to the origins of conservatism: just as Burke tried to immunize his audience against the threat arising from the universalism of the French Revolution by emphasizing the specific organic growth of England's political structure, Uexküll is trying to ward off the challenges of modernization with its bubble-bursting universalism by mobilizing the specific biopolitical circumstances of Germany after the lost war.

The special Uexküllian twist is linked to the distinction between people (*Volk*) and state (*Staat*). The constituent elements of a people are families (Uexküll is a family-values fundamentalist) while that of the state are the various professions. But how are we to combine the two in the most effective and beneficial manner? Once again, it is a question of Umwelt coordination. Families and professions each have their own Umwelten, and while that of a family is a great deal more complex than that of a profession, "these two Umwelten must be aligned in such a way that they complement rather than disturb each other. To place an architect in the position of a gardener and vice versa would immediately result in utter confusion."[28] Underlying all this is the idea that individuals are destined for a certain profession based on their longtime exposure to the Umwelt of that particular profession. In other words, in the interest of the harmonious relationship between *Volk* and state the sons of cobblers should become cobblers because from a very early age on they were fitted into the cobbler-specific Umwelt. Uexküll frequently emphasizes that somebody who watches his father following a certain profession will be much better at it than somebody who switches jobs as an adult—a position made easier by Uexküll's marked preference (which he shares with Heidegger) for time-honored artisanal occupations that traditionally were passed on from father to son.[29] Political biology appears to merge with the medieval notion of *ordo*: Each profession has its preordained place in a hierarchical grid, and their coordination is managed by a higher authority—be it God, the priests, or the biologists as quasi-divine lawmakers.

However, to label this medieval is a misnomer (and an insult to the Middle Ages). Uexküll was not medieval, he was Estonian. In this instance the latter does not refer to the country itself but to a peculiar social makeup that characterized regions like Estonia in the nineteenth century. On the one hand, there was still an almost Russian division between a powerful landed nobility and the peasant class. When Uexküll deals with Estonian farmers in his memoirs he is in a very patronizing fashion depicting a very different, self-enclosed world. On the other hand, there was a strong Western orientation with the attendant modernization especially of the urban regions. The tensions arising from these horizontal distinctions were compounded by vertical boundaries that pitted native Estonians, Germans, and Russians against each other. Contained in a fairly small area, then, was a highly diverse social, linguistic, and ethnic mixture, a precarious balance that required that none of the component elements arrogated a hegemonic position. In a word, the distinct mixture of autonomous bubbles and overriding web-like integration that characterizes Uexküll's meadow and his ideal state is, among other things, a projection of the idealized Estonia of his youth into nature and politics.

But just as the Estonian equilibrium was unsustainable and broke down—from Uexküll's point of view—due to Panslavist ambitions, the modern biological state is under threat from self-aggrandizing components no longer willing to follow the central authority. In the 1920 edition Uexküll spends a lot of time detailing the "pathology" of the state; this etiology of the various diseases reappears in the second edition of 1933 though with the assurance that in Germany many of the dangers have been averted thanks to "Adolf Hitler and his movement."[30] One great danger, however, survives: parasites. Self-serving members of a foreign race may invade the state, monopolize key functions, weaken its immunity, and especially in times of war threaten its very integrity. Esposito has emphasized that this represents a far more serious concretization than the specific reference to Germany mentioned above. "Uexküll's threateningly prophetic conclusion is that one needs to create a class of state doctors to fight the parasites, or to confer on the state a medical competency that is capable of bringing it back to health by removing the causes of the disease and by expelling the carriers of the germ."[31] Uexküll is not only a pioneer of biopolitics and state-enforced immunization initiatives, he is also one of the very first to argue and demand that medical and biological experts be acknowledged as the resident experts and unquestioned leaders in the attempt to cleanse the national, ethnic, or racial biomass. Only a decade after the publication of the second edition of *State Politics* this collapse of philosophy and politics into biology reached its zenith in the "*therapia magna auschwitzciense*."[32] The essence of modern biopower—to be more precise, of Nazi zoopolitics directed against human animals—is the doctor on the selection ramp indicating with a flick of his finger whether arrivals are to be sent straight to the gas chamber.[33]

Yet while Uexküll puts all the key words of modern racism on parade one is conspicuously absent: Jews. Instead, Jews turn up in his memoirs. The ninth chapter is entitled "The Russians Jews in Their Umwelt," and it begins with a scene that recalls a similar racial *ur*-scene in Hitler's *Mein Kampf*. In the small city of Tuckum in Courland the young Uexküll had his first encounters with Jews:

> Who were these people, what were they doing, what did they want in the green garden of Courland whose soil they did not plough, whose meadows they did not mow, and whose

orchards they did not tend? . . . An utterly alien people was living here, disseminated across a country otherwise inhabited by Germans and Latvians. A tightly congested urban people rigorously cut off from the rural population, connected only by loose economic ties. They could all be extracted and moved away without changing the face of the country.[34]

Note the standard—and in 1936: official—view of Jews as rootless and essentially unproductive (that is, exclusively focused on trade and finance with no sense of soil). Jews have no natural Umwelt based on any physical interaction with their immediate surroundings; instead it is produced by social exclusion and the subsequent feeling of solidarity. But modern reform movements are undermining Jewish identity, for the emancipation of the Jews is eroding their cultural ties and letting them loose on the world. Young Russian Jews in particular are "increasingly turning toward nihilism."[35] This ambiguous assessment is captured in the chapter's final paragraph when Uexküll recounts a walk with a Jewish student:

During our walk . . . we passed a flock of sheep circled and held together by a dog. Suddenly he stopped, turned around and pointed at the flock: "You see," he cried, "that's what we need, and I daily pray to God that he may send us the implacable (*unerbitterlichen*) anti-Semitism that will round up the lost sheep of Judah."[36]

Containment produces identity. Following this logic, ghetto walls and concentration camp watchtowers will resurrect the Jewish Umwelt that was destroyed by their emancipation.

To be sure, Uexküll was not an eliminationist racist. A lot of what he says about the necessity to maintain and respect racial diversity, not to mention his critique of the belief that racial mixing produces inferior offspring, is clearly at odds with Nazi doctrines. The problem is that for reactionary modernists like Uexküll, who strove to reconcile their preference for premodern societal structures with up-to-date developments in technology and the sciences, Jews represented the most irritating incarnation of the ills of modernity: rootlessness, the dissolution of time-honored communities and traditional belief systems, and the apotheosis of money. So strong was the association that Jews came to be seen as operators rather than mere carriers of the overall decline. Especially in the immediate aftermath of the First World War, and in his intimate correspondence with England's most toxic export to Germany, the master racist Houston Stewart Chamberlain, Uexküll appeared to be "tortured by an image of the Jews, especially of secularized Jews, as ruthless, state-destroying parasites."[37]

However, the diagnosis needs to be more specific. To coin a Uexküllian-Heideggerian neologism, Jews were to Uexküll the epitome of *Umweltvergessenheit* or the "forgetfulness of Umwelt"—an inability to grasp and experience one's own preordained environment that is both brought about and glossed over by vague appeals to universal liberty and justice. But this was nothing specifically or uniquely Jewish; historical circumstances conspired to make the Jews the avant-garde of modern decline universal, a portent of what was to come if the world succumbed to newfangled notions of absolute time, absolute space, absolute symbolic exchange in the shape of money and mathematics, and the abstractions of modern science. This "regrettable laying-waste of the worlds-as-sensed [that] has arisen from the superstition started by the physicists"[38] could be averted if people—or rather, the elites—were to accept his new biology, but while Uexküll could pass on the *knowledge* of what it means to inhabit and shape one's own Umwelt next to all the myriads of other human and animal Umwelten, he was not able to impart the *experience*. That is the business of artists.

The Estrangement of Panthers

> *With all its eyes the natural world looks out*
> *into the Open. Only our eyes are turned*
> *backward, and surround plant, animal, child*
> *like traps, as they emerge into their freedom.*
> *We know what is really out there only from*
> *the animal's gaze; for we take the very young*
> *child and force it around, so that it sees*
> *objects—not the Open, which is so*
> *deep in animals' faces.*[39]
>
> —RILKE, *The Selected Poetry of Rainer Maria Rilke*

The Rilke admirer Heidegger was at pains to point out that the ability of animals to gaze into the "open" referred to in the opening lines of the Eighth Duino Elegy is not the openness to unconcealment he attributed to humans. Yet while Heidegger's discussion of Rilke's recapitulates the salient points first presented in the Uexküll-inspired sections of *The Fundamental Concepts of Metaphysics*, it is not known to what extent Heidegger was aware of the personal connection between Rilke and Uexküll.[40]

The two first met in 1905 on the estate of Luise von Schwerin, Uexküll's mother-in-law and one of Rilke's many aristocratic patronesses. They went for long walks (Uexküll, no doubt, the boisterous talker, and Rilke the attentive listener) and together studied Kant's *Critique of Pure Reason*. A fortuitous encounter, one might think, for Rilke was keen on expanding his philosophical horizon and Uexküll kept reiterating that his insights were rooted in Kantian epistemology. But it may have been a case of the blind leading the lame. It is questionable whether Rilke gained a lot from discussing transcendental idealism and synthetic apriori judgments, and closer inspection reveals that Uexküll's frequent invocations of Kant (uncritically rehashed by many scholars) stand on shaky ground.[41] With his straightforward claim—often dressed up as an appeal to Kant—that all reality is subjective in appearance, Uexküll is less a proponent of Kant than of a Kantian vulgate that breezily ignores fundamental distinctions between the transcendental and the empirical which were essential to Kant's epistemological housecleaning exercise. If idealist philosophy is to be mobilized as a precursor of Uexküll's biophilosophy, Schelling and Hegel are more appropriate forerunners.[42]

What truly linked the two was the question of seeing and significance. Uexküll's basic objection against the physiology of his day was that it rigorously denied any kind of animal subjectivity. It posited one objective environment for all life forms and, subsequently, proceeded to analyze animals from the outside in, that is, by torturing them with selected stimuli in order to elicit mechanical responses. The new (and true) biology required a radical reorientation on the part of the researcher. The blind reliance on an indifferent environment had to be replaced by the recognition of species-specific Umwelten, a shift in perspective which required that human researchers forego what is of significance to them for what is significant to the animal. This enterprise had more than a passing resemblance to Rilke's quest to master perception without projection, to apprehend things—as opposed to mere objects—beyond the significance or use value they may have for the observer. Both Rilke and Uexküll agree that to observe things is to observe the creation of the thing within the observer (in this particular regard, Uexküll's Umwelt is close to Rilke's *Weltinnenraum* or "inner world space"). While the grand goal expressed in the Ninth Duino Elegy of saying "them more intensely than the Things themselves / ever dreamed of existing"[43] is beyond Uexküll (and, for that matter, far beyond Kant), the two projects met when it to came to the *vision of animals*. How can we in our world see how animals see their world? Here is Rilke's most famous answer:

THE PANTHER

In the Jardin des Plantes, Paris

His gaze has been so worn by the procession
Of bars that it no longer makes a bond.
Around, a thousand bars seem to be flashing,
And in their flashing show no world beyond.

The lissom steps which round out and re-enter
That tightest circuit of their turning drill
Are like a dance of strength about a center
Wherein there stands benumbed a mighty will.

Only from time to time the pupil's shutter
Will draw apart: an image enters then,
To travel through the tautened body's utter
Stillness—and in the heart end.[44]

Were it not for the title the poem could be about any caged
being with any number of feet, a lack of specificity that stands
in marked contrast to the specific location, the Jardin des
Plantes, which happened to be one of Rilke's favorite visual
hunting grounds. The text depicts an act of observation (Rilke's
animals, we should note in passing, are almost always *eyeni-
mals*), more precisely, a situation in which the dearth of significant objects outside ("no world beyond") is linked to internal
nonreceptiveness.[45] Images end in the heart because there is
no contrapuntal relationship between the web of marks and
the web of perceptive faculties. Read along these lines, "The
Panther" is an *ex negativo* depiction of Uexküll's Umwelt: a
snapshot of a defunct Umwelt destroyed by the removal of
the animal from the habitat that contained all the perceptual
markers it had been "fitted into." Though Rilke wrote the poem
prior to their encounter, it was later singled out by Uexküll in

response to Rilke's request for further instruction in biology: "[Y]our poem 'The Panther' proves that you possess an outstanding talent for biology and for comparative psychology in particular. The observation that you develop [in the poem] is masterful. . . . I believe that you are already too much of a master to still be a disciple."[46]

While Uexküll came to harbor certain reservations about Rilke's increasingly complex poetry and his lackluster support of the German war effort in the First World War, his memoirs praise him as the greatest poet since Tasso. And it is here that one of the most interesting references occurs. Luise von Schwerin had died in 1906; it was one of the first of many deaths that Rilke's poetry, with its refined ghoulishness, came to thrive on. His farewell poem "Death Experienced" contains the stanza:

> *When, though, you went, there broke upon this scene*
> *a shining segment of realities*
> *in the crack you disappeared through: green*
> *of real green, real sunshine, real trees.*[47]

Uexküll, in turn, recounts a strange experience he had following the burial of his mother-in-law: "My thoughts were with her—when suddenly the landscape changed not its shape but its essence. All the colors that on that gloomy day had appeared subdued gained a wonderful luminous power. Leaves, trees, the sky, and the clouds were ablaze in undreamed-of splendor. The apparition lasted for a quarter of an hour until it gradually faded."[48] Upon reading "Death Experienced" he realized that Rilke had described a similar experience and concluded: "Maybe it had been granted to us both to cast a glance into her real Umwelt."

Here we arrive at arguably one of the most tantalizing and certainly one of the most overlooked qualities of Uexküll's theory. It would no doubt be possible to trace basic similarities between

Uexküll's Umwelt and Husserl's cotemporaneous *Lebenswelt*, or life-world, with its intentionality of consciousness. There are equally striking parallels between Uexküll's epistemology of perceptual significance—that the subject encounters and is affected by its projections—and the basic epistemology of early quantum theory with its assurance that "modern man confronts only himself," so that "even in science the object of research is no longer nature itself, but man's investigation of nature."[49] But the most interesting affinity is that to the Russian Formalists' concept of *ostranenie* or defamiliarization: the ability—indeed the need—of art to invigorate perception by presenting the familiar in unfamiliar ways. Uexküll's writings have an aesthetic thrust: his new biology implores us not to succumb to ingrained perception habits, to be constantly aware of the way in which we see—and project—our world. His romanticized view of the Neapolitan Umwelt was based not on the city's natural beauty but on the Neapolitan ability never to get used to it:

> [C]an people who experience this wonder with such fervor ever become philistines?
>
> A philistine is someone who worships the everyday and who wants to perpetuate his petty bourgeois well-being.
>
> The Neapolitan doesn't know the everyday. To him, every day is a new beginning, for it can be the last. Which is why it has to be experienced in all its depth, in love and hatred, in admiration and happiness, in ecstasy and beauty.[50]

Neapolitans are natural artists. To retrieve a pun from bygone psychedelic days, they real-eyes what they in-habit. The rest of us, who are neither born at the feet of Mount Vesuvius nor equipped with Rilke's poetic sensibilities, are forced to rely on artistic support to keep us from descending into philistine monotony. Art complements biology, it provides the direct experience of alternate sense islands that biology investigates.[51] To borrow Sagan's apt metaphor, a poet like Rilke is as much a shaman as Uexküll by virtue of his ability to sneak into and ventriloquize an animal Umwelt. But whether it is your mother-in-law or an imprisoned feline, experiencing another bubble will make you see and appreciate your own bubble in new ways. The always present danger, of course, is that this may entail a reification of other Umwelten. The question *How can we in our world see how animals see their world?* may easily turn into the more self-interested inquiry *How can we see how animals see their world in such a way that it will change and enrich the way in which we see ours?*

Sleuthy Ticks:
The World as Media-technological Crime Scene
Ixodes ricinus: What would Uexküll be without his tick? Following its memorable cameo performance in *A Foray* it outgrew its original textual habitat to join Maturana's frog, Nadel's bat, and Flusser's vampire squid in an exclusive animal menagerie located at the intersection of biology, philosophy, and literature. It repeatedly crops up in (or drops into) Philosophical Anthropology; Deleuze and Guattari have a special fondness for it; and Agamben considers its bare-life travails "a high point of modern anti-humanism."[52] But the most widely-read reference occurs in a literary text:

> [T]he tick, stubborn, sullen and loathsome, huddles there and lives and waits, Waits, for that most improbable of chances that will bring blood, in animal form, directly beneath its tree. And only then does it abandon caution and drop, and scratch and bore and bite into that alien flesh.[53]

On several occasions Uexküll's tick is invoked to describe the serial killer Jean-Baptiste Grenouille in Patrick Süskind's bestseller *Perfume*. Grenouille is an olfactory prodigy with a sense of smell so developed that he relates to the world primarily through his nose, which, of course, dramatically changes his world. To the dismay of many critics the depraved, stench-based eighteenth-century Umwelt Grenouille is fitted into is a far cry from enlightened *siècle des lumières* on display in Western tales of progress. Tick analogies abound: Grenouille's first, premammalian host is a reptilian (the cold-blooded, unfeeling Madame Gaillard who only tolerates Grenouille because she has lost the sense of smell); he spends years withdrawn into barest life waiting for the right stimulus to awaken him; and once he has vampirized the body he craves there is nothing left to live for. But as in the case of Rilke there is a more revealing hidden dimension that sheds light on the fascination exerted by Uexküll.

Perfume recycles entire genres such as the *Bildungsroman* and—in the third, final section—the detective novel. Antoine Richis, father of the beautiful Laure Richis, has deduced that his daughter will be the serial killer's next victim and proceeds to take the necessary precautions. But his profiling skills are no match for Grenouille's talent to evade detection by concocting an artificial body odor that renders him so insignificant as to be invisible. Nothing can move about and kill more freely than that which is outside the subjective world-construction of its victims and enemies. Richis's ability to interpret signs is inferior to Grenouille's ability to turn himself into a nonsign. And here, by way of a novel that turns the conventional sense of hierarchy on its head, we arrive at another interesting but frequently overlooked back door to Uexküll's oeuvre that leads into a world of clues, markers, and indices. The notion that subjects are *constant interpreters*, always already reacting to and acting upon environmental markers, is a fundamental prerequisite for Uexküll's posthumous rise to prominence as a "cryptosemiotician" whose work provides the basis for the concept of the "semiosphere."[54] Thomas Sebeok, John Deely, Jesper Hoffmeyer, and Kalevi Kull, among others, have furnished indispensable accounts of this promotion; what is missing are a few remarks on the preconditions that enabled this promotion.

"Uexkull's theory provides *signs* and *rules*; it thus aspires to become the kind of life science as well as the kind of sign science that Peirce called nomological and that Piaget calls nomothetic."[55] The enabling condition for this astonishing aspiration is less the fusion of signs and rules than that of *signs* and *machines*. Uexküll's world is one in which signs are always already connected to the subject's data-processing facilities. Ultimately, it belongs to the paradigm of detection described in Carlo Ginzburg's essay "Clues and Scientific Method" on the similarities between the clue-based analytical techniques of Sherlock Holmes, Sigmund Freud, and Giovanni Morelli.[56] Ginzburg offers a precise account of the way in which the attention to revealing details rules widely disparate scientific inquiries, but he gives no indication why this increased semiotic sensitivity became particularly important in the Freudo-Holmesian period of the late nineteenth and early twentieth centuries. For Friedrich Kittler, the matter is clear. The rule of clues, tracks, and traces is due to the dethronement of symbolic media—in the first instance, writing—by new "technological"—read: analog—media:

> With technological media, a knowledge assumes power that is no longer satisfied with the individual universals of its subjects, their self-images and self-representations—these imaginary formations—but instead registers distinguishing particulars. As Carlo Ginzburg has shown . . . , this new knowledge rules . . . aesthetics, psychoanalysis, and criminology. However, Ginzburg fails to see that the shift in technologies of power simply follows the switch from writing to media. Books had been able to store and convey the imaginary corporeal self-images entertained by individuals. But unconsciously treacherous signs like fingerprints, pitch, and foot tracks fall into the purview of media without which they could neither be stored nor evaluated.[57]

For all his "messianic drive to save man from the spiritual devastation of materialism"[58] incurred by the abstractions of modern physics and a misguided physiology that turns living beings into dead machines, Uexküll's own work is part of the "Discourse Network 1900" in which according to Kittler subjects are revealed to be information machines whose skulls are full of phonographs, cinematographs, projection screens, typewriters, and so on. Much as Plato had denounced writing as unworthy of philosophy only to resort to writing metaphors to show how truth is inscribed into the human soul, Uexküll constantly denounces machines but then resorts to a Helmholtz world of cycles, couplings, and feedback routines to describe the subject's Umwelt wiring. He keeps emphasizing that ticks and humans are not machines, but he leaves unmentioned that it took the arrival of data-processing machines to conceive of ticks and humans as machinists instead. This neglected medial apriori is the basis for the semiotic appropriation of Uexküll. To concentrate on the semiotic dimension it appears necessary to remove the technologies that provided the model for conceiving subjects as receivers, processors, and emitters of signs in the first place.

This abstraction from the media-technological apriori underlying Uexküll's theory is closely related to a specific feature of his theories that already in the early days had drawn criticism both from biologists and philosophers. In his critique of Uexküll Gehlen, among others, had drawn on a widely circulated definition offered in 1939 by the biologist Herman Weber: Umwelt should be understood as "the totality of conditions contained in an entire complex of surroundings which permit a certain organism, by virtue of its specific organization, to survive."[59] Note that this definition pays no attention to signs, meaning, or internal or external representation; it is a far cry from Uexküll's pithy description of Umwelt as a "sense island" or allegedly correct translations such as "significant environment" or "cognitive map."[60] Following Weber, Gehlen was highlighting Uexküll's questionable distinction between Umwelt and *Umgebung.* Critics argued that the term Umwelt should also include those external conditions which are significant *for* though not necessarily *to* the living being "such as the chemical composition of the soil, temperature, climate, light, irrigation, and hydromechanical factors."[61] In other words, Uexküll's attack on milieu had gone too far; in order for Umwelt to function as a viable concept it needed to reintegrate some—from the point of view of the subject, nonsignificant—determining factors.[62] In retrospect, the elision of the latter was instrumental in facilitating the semiotic appropriation of Uexküll: If the abstraction from materiality and physicality were one of the enabling conditions for the creation of Uexküll's Umwelt, the subsequent abstraction from mediality was one of the prerequisites for the enthronement of Uexküll as a pioneer of semiotics.[63]

Uexküll appears to have performed yet another anticipatory feat: His work foreshadows one of the cardinal insights of the later twentieth century—that, in Paul Watzlawick's words, one cannot not communicate. But if read in a more Kittlerian vein Uexküll also provides a sober media-technological rephrasing: One cannot not process incoming data. Uexküll is one of the early prophets of the modern hegemony of communication; yet his work may also serve to remind us of the flip side that Baggesen had already hinted at (and that reaches its apex in Niklas Luhmann's systems theory): that the increase of communication is tied to a corresponding increase of isolation. Once again, it is a literary text that exposes this dilemma.

Lonely Danish Worlds (Part II):
Time Runs in Our Veins Like Blood

Roughly a hundred years after Baggesen coined the term Umwelt Uexküll redefined it; another hundred years later another Danish author, Peter Høeg, completed the circle by teasing out the subtext already present in Baggesen's ode. Published in the wake of his bestseller *Smilla's Sense of Snow*—a novel that much like Süskind's *Perfume* centers on Umwelt-specific detection skills—Høeg's *Borderliners* relates the experiences of an orphan called Peter in Biel's Academy, a private school named after its founder-director. Biel is an idealist autocrat bent on turning "borderliners" like Peter—that is, mildly defective students other institutions have given up on—into respectable citizens by imposing an inhuman(e) time regime. Not since Thomas Mann locked up a motley crew of pre-war Europeans in a mountain sanatorium to learn about time, sex, and death has an isolated institution been so saturated with time. *Borderliners* reads as if Michel Foucault had rewritten *The Magic Mountain* and put Frederick Winslow Taylor in charge. Looking back, Biel's Academy appears to Peter as nothing less than the gruesome zenith of modern time management:

> I believe that Biel's Academy was the last possible point in three hundred years of scientific development. At that place only linear time was permitted, all life and teaching at the school was arranged in accordance with this—the school buildings, environment, teachers, pupils, kitchens, plants, equipment, and everyday life were a mobile machine, a symbol of linear time.
>
> We stood on the edge, we had reached the limit. For how far you could, with the instrument of time, push human nature.[64]

This apotheosis of linear time comes with its own twisted metaphysics according to which "God created heaven and earth as raw material, like a group of pupils entering Primary One, designated and earmarked for processing and ennoblement. As the straight path along which the process of evolution should progress, he created linear time. And as an instrument for measuring how far the process of evolution had advanced he created mathematics and physics."[65] To Peter, the academy becomes a place in which time runs "in our veins like blood."[66] Years after being expelled Peter encounters Uexküll's writings, which come to serve as a kind of retroactive antidote. This is not surprising given that Biel's Academy is a concentrate of the cultural decline Uexküll associated with the rise of a mechanical worldview based on the reduction of evolution to external shaping forces in combination with the apotheosis of impersonal linear time. By contrast, Uexküll argued that time fundamentally depends on what the subject is able to perceive, and hence project, as time. "Just as certainly as that there is no such thing as absolute space, so also it is certain that there is no such thing as absolute time; for both space and time are merely forms of our human intuition."[67] Biel's project, then, was doomed to fail from the start. But the more Peter delves into Uexküll, the more he comes to realize that autochronicity, like so any forms of autonomy, comes at the price of profound isolation. As terrible as it may have been to be "saturated by tight, tight time," it did enable a fundamental commonality.[68] Linear time—however Newtonian, anemic, and mechanical—binds us; to produce our own time results in loosening those ties.

Once you have realized that there is no objective external world to be found, that what you know is only a filtered and processed version, then it is a short step to the thought that, in that case, other people, too, are nothing but a processed shadow, and but a short step to the belief that every person must somehow be shut away, isolated behind their own unreliable sensory apparatus. And then the thought springs to mind that man is fundamentally alone. That the world is made up of disconnected consciousnesses, each isolated within the illusion of its own senses, floating in a featureless vacuum.

He [Uexküll] does not put it so bluntly, but the idea is not far away. That, fundamentally, man is alone.[69]

Such existentialist angst is alien to Uexküll, if only because his theory (like the monadology of Leibniz) constantly beckons toward the prearranged coordination of the isolated constituent elements and their equally harmonious environmental *Einpassung* ("fitting-into"). To lament the lonely bubbles is to miss out on their webs. But though Peter may be more aware of the hidden dimension of Uexküll's theories than Uexküll himself, he acknowledges his debt. "Jacob von Uexküll. A difficult name. Although it feels good to write it."[70]

Postscript: What's in a Name?

Maybe it all begins with that name: *Uexküll*. According to Gudrun von Uexküll it translates as "one village": "In Livonian and Estonian *uex* [*sic*] means 'one' and *külla* means 'village.'"[71] Barring a minor correction ("village" is *küla* whereas *külla* translates as "into the village"), this is probably the historically correct origin of the name. But for native speakers the flip side of Uexküll's theories, so prominently on display in the literary approximations, is just as present. In Estonian *küll* means "enough," hence Uexküll's name conjures up the saying "*üx [on] küll*—one [is] enough."[72]

A village of one. Community and self-sufficiency, coordination and isolation, planned integration and near-autistic solitude: the name contains the theory's essential polarity. Uexküll's work is both a singular appearance, an edifice removed from others, and a village where many paths intersect—from Helmholtz to Maturana and Luhmann, from Peirce to Sebeok, from Herder to Sloterdijk, from Leibniz and Spinoza to Deleuze and Guattari, from Driesch to Bertalanffy and on to second-order cybernetics. But the attractiveness of his work rests as much on what he said as on what he did *not* say. Uexküll tore into Darwin as only a German biologist could, yet unlike many of his peers he did not introduce a developmental or orthogenetic driving force to act as the internal alternative to the external forces of selection—and this enables his recruitment as a precursor of post-Darwinian evolutionary theory. He depicted a honeycombed multitude of species-specific Umwelten, but he did not offset the demotion of the human bubble by arguing for its innate superiority—and this moves him into the orbit of posthumanist theory. He was one of the first to provide a biological foundation for the study of signs, but he did not dwell on material enabling conditions located in the grey zone between significant Umwelt and indifferent Umgebung—and this secures his position as a pioneer of semiotics. Uexküll, in short, is a highly detachable theorist. It is easy to dip into his writings and extract certain portions. This, however, may result in an intellectual form of *Umweltvergessenheit*. To glimpse the hidden dimensions of the concept, you need to explore the Umwelt of Umwelt.

Introduction

1. This energetic gradient, the metabolic source of energy for most animals (rare exceptions include "planimals" such as the sea slug *Plakobranchus ocellatus* with its internal chloroplasts and *Convoluta roscoffensis*, a sunbathing worm, mouthless as an adult, whose energy is provided internally by chloroplasts), also drives our technological fossil fuel economy. But the geological record shows the gradient only arose some two billion years ago, as a result of accumulation of oxygen (O_2) as waste by the cyanobacteria that evolved to use hydrogen (H_2O) in water. The energy for this came not from the redox gradient but from the solar gradient, sunlight. Our aerobic and occasional anaerobic metabolism, which evolved in bacteria, represent only two of their many metabolic modes. Each mode suggests perception of the environment at a chemical level.

2. Friedrich Nietzsche, "Truth and Lie in the Extra-Moral Sense," in *The Portable Nietzsche*, trans. and ed. Walter Kaufmann (New York: Penguin Books, 1997 [1983]), 42–46.

3. Maurice Blanchot, "Literature and the Right to Death," in *The Gaze of Orpheus and Other Literary Essays*, ed. P. Adams Sitney, trans. Lydia Davis (Barrytown, NY: Station Hill Press, 1981), 46. Important for language is the persistence of the sign, which is part of its thingly nature and in principle expands the realm of potential signification—think of animal footprints being tracked that, while not written, can be read—sometimes, as in the case of dinosaur prints, by paleobiologists whose interests have moved beyond finding a food source.

4. Thomas D. Seeley, *The Wisdom of the Hive: The Social Physiology of Honey Bee Colonies* (Cambridge, MA: Harvard University Press, 1995).

5. Gilles Deleuze, *Spinoza: Practical Philosophy*, trans. Robert Hurley (San Francisco: City Lights Books, 1988). Here Deleuze's gloss is worth noting: Deleuze argues, if not for a master plan, for a "conceptual-affective continuum" (in Robert Hurley's translation), a nontranscendental plane which Deleuze tags the *"plan d'immanence"* (122). Deleuze argues that Uexküll, "one of the main founders of ethology"—which is "first of all the study . . . of the capacities for affecting and being affected . . . For example,

given an animal, what is this animal unaffected by . . . What are its nutriments and poisons? What does it 'take' in its world? . . . How do individuals enter into composition with one another in order to form a higher individual, . . . How can a being take another being into its world, but while preserving or respecting the other's own relations and world?"—is a "Spinozist when [Uexküll] describes a symphony as an immanent higher unity," a "plane [plan] of musical composition, a plane of Nature, insofar as the latter is the fullest and most intense Individual, with parts that vary in an infinity of ways" (125–27). The question of Umwelt blending applies to beings and, in philosophy, kaleidoscopically even to the appropriation and interpenetration of the worldviews that posit and question the nature of the Umwelt.

6. Kalevi Kull, "Jakob Von Uexküll: An Introduction," *Semiotica* 134 (1/4) (2001): 8.

7. Ibid., 12.

8. John Deely, "Umwelt," *Semiotica* 134 (1/4) (2001): 134.

9. Jakob von Uexküll, "The Theory of Meaning," *Semiotica* 42 (1) (1982): 68.

10. Ibid., 59.

11. Ibid., 57–58.

12. Paul de Man, *Aesthetic Ideology*, ed. Andrzej Warminski (Minneapolis: University of Minnesota Press, 1996). Hegel distinguishes between symbol, which is the natural, necessary relation of one object to another, and sign, which links sign to its referent through an arbitrary act of signification, the power of the mind or will. For example, de Man, discussing Hegel, writes, "The thinking subject is to be kept sharply distinguished from the perceiving subject, in a manner that is reminiscent of (or that anticipates) the distinction we have just encountered in the differentiation between sign and symbol. Just as the sign refuses to be in the service of sensory perceptions but uses them instead for its own purposes, thought, unlike perception, appropriates the world and literally 'subjects' it to its own powers" (97). (Charles Sanders Peirce, however, uses almost reverse terminology: calling symbol that which has an abstract relation to its referent, while reserving the term *icon* for something, like a picture of an arrow or a pointing hand on a computer, that physically resembles what it stands for—in this case something that points. An index for Peirce is something that clues us in as to the presence of an associated factor, such as dark shadows signaling fish in the Umwelt of a sea urchin.)

13. Uexküll, "Theory of Meaning," 73. Uexküll's relationship to Nazism was ambiguous. Although he did not embrace it, he seemed to accept it with ambivalent expedience. On the one hand, he had approved of limitations in universities for Jews, was friends with the Wagners and other families supportive of the Nazi regime, and had his work appropriated by student propaganda outlets as part of Nazi race biology. On the other hand, he described as "crass barbarism" the purge of researchers who were more than

25 percent Jewish, worried of his work "fall[ing] victim to the new race research," and argued that the universities, as Germany's "sense organs," were effectively being punched in the eye by the state. These comments, delivered in 1933 at the Nietzsche house at a state-sponsored meeting hosted by Nietzsche's aging sister, were interrupted and Uexküll's intellectual resistance to the regime was effectively silenced. (Anne Harrington, *Reenchanted Science: Holism in German Culture from Wilhelm II to Hitler* [Princeton, NJ: Princeton University Press, 1999], 71.)

14. Jakob von Uexküll, "The New Concept of Umwelt: A Link Between Science and the Humanities," *Semiotica* 134 (1/4) (2001): 118.

15. Uexküll, "Theory of Meaning," 59, 69.

16. Freeman Dyson, *Origins of Life* (Cambridge: Cambridge University Press, 1999).

17. Hans Jonas, *The Phenomenon of Life: Toward a Philosophical Biology* (Westport, CT: Greenwood Press, 1979).

18. Uexküll, "Theory of Meaning," 51.

19. Andrew J. Watson and James E. Lovelock, "Biological homeostasis of the global environment: the parable of Daisyworld," *Tellus B* (International Meteorological Society) 35, no. 4 (1983): 286–89.

20. Uexküll, "Theory of Meaning," 62.

21. Uexküll, "New Concept of Umwelt," 118.

22. Kull, "Jakob von Uexküll," 4.

23. Let us not forget the interconnected, intersubjective Umwelten of interacting minds. Language, a kind of group trace of interacting human intersubjectivities, reflects an Umwelt larger and more sophisticated than that of any individual human. What other semioses exist among different species, populations of cells, beings communicating across phyla and kingdoms? An index of the potential cognitive diversity of radically different Umwelten is suggested by the culturally important interactions between humans and certain fungi (e.g., *Psilocybes, Amanita muscaria*), as well as the plants we use for medicines, shelter, pigments, aesthetics, and inspiration. The interaction of humans and bacteria also alters human Umwelten. Historically, the black plague has left a cultural scar on the collective Western consciousness. (Antonin Artaud, *The Theater and Its Double* [New York: Grove Press, 1994].) Again, individual strains of parasitic and symbiotic bacteria alter human consciousness. Tertiary syphilis, for example, an effect of the activities of *Treponema* spirochetes, is speculatively associated with genius, for example in Baudelaire, Joyce, Poe, Gauguin, Napoleon, Paganini, Rabelais, and Tolstoy. (Deb Hayden, *Pox: Genius, Madness, and the Mysteries of Syphilis* [New York: Basic Books, 2003].) Other bacterial interactions may, after billions of years of evolution, have laid the groundwork for the neurosemiosis internal to human brains. (Lynn Margulis and Dorion Sagan, *Microcosmos: Four Billion Years of Microbial Evolution* [Berkeley: University of California Press, 1997].) This speculative notion attracted

the attention of Sebeok, who writes that the "key to semiosis in the micro-cosmos is symbiosis." (Thomas A. Sebeok, *Global Semiotics* [Bloomington: Indiana University Press, 2001], 24.)

24. Thure von Uexküll, "Introduction: Meaning and Science in Jakob von Uexküll's Concept of Biology," *Semiotica* 42 (1) (1982): 1–24.

25. Jakob von Uexküll, *Theoretische Biologie*, 2te Aufl. (Berlin: 1928), cited in Kalevi Kull, "Organism as a Self-reading Text: Anticipation and Se-miosis," *International Journal of Computing Anticipatory Systems*, vol. 1 (1998): 93–104. (See also www.zbi.ee/~kalevi/textorg.htm.)

26. Julius Fraser, "The Extended Umwelt Principle: von Uexküll and the Na-ture of Time," *Semiotica* 134 (1/4) (2001): 263–74.

27. Donald Favareau, "The Evolutionary History of Biosemiotics," in *Intro-duction to Biosemiotics: The New Biological Synthesis*, ed. Marcello Bar-bieri (n.p.: Springer, 2008).

28. Jacques Derrida, *Of Grammatology* (Baltimore, MD: Johns Hopkins Uni-versity Press, 1998).

29. Martin Heidegger, "Letter in Humanism," in *Basic Writings: From Being and Time (1927) to the Task of Thinking (1964)* (New York: Harper Col-lins, 1977), 213–66.

30. Avital Ronell, Derrida memorial (Columbia University, Manhattan, Octo-ber 2004).

31. In running with a dog I noticed I had a canine search image of my own, as I mistook the jingle from the keys in my own pocket for the clink of her collar. Uexküll's dog world breaks down largely into things that can be eaten, sat upon, and pose physical obstacles to movement. Today, there may be some additions to the canine Umwelt's functional tones. For ex-ample, cars may represent a threat to some dogs but are probably more associated with traveling with their human masters; they thus may be said to have a double valence. As evolution continues the realm of se-miosis expands. A woodpecker in upstate New York was killed because, mistaking itself for a rival, it repeatedly broke the rearview mirrors of cars. Contrariwise, English tits learned how to peck open the foil tops of delivered milk bottles, to their temporary survival advantage. The smell and texture of the soft underside of the paw of a dog may be a sign of loving affection for its owner, while sugar molecules may signal more to come to bacteria and yeasts. As evolution progresses, and more chemi-cal elements become involved in life's metabolism, the realm of semiosis grows. Symbols grow, as Sebeok says.

32. Uexküll, "Theory of Meaning," 20.

33. Stanley N. Salthe and Gary Fuhrman, "The Cosmic Bellows: The Big Bang and the Second Law," *Cosmos and History: The Journal of Natural and Social Philosophy* 1, no. 2: 309.

34. Alexander Zotin, *Thermodynamic Aspects of Developmental Biology*, Monographs in Developmental Biology vol. 5 (Basel: S. Karger, 1972).

35. Charles R. Darwin, *The Expression of the Emotions in Man and Animals* (London: John Murray, 1872).

36. Uexküll, "An Introduction to Umwelt," *Semiotica* 134 (1/4): 107–10.

37. J. C. Luvall and H. R. Holbo, "Measurements of Short Term Thermal Responses of Coniferous Forest Canopies Using Thermal Scanner Data," *Remote Sensing of the Environment* 27 (1989): 1–10.

38. The growth within a certain temperature range of Bénard cells and life, the growth and maintenance of autocatalytic reactions within certain electron potential gradients, and the appearance and "reproduction" (e.g., of typhoons) of cyclical dynamic systems within certain pressure gradients all tend to suggest that life's essence is shared with that of other natural complex systems—systems which don't have genes or brains. Because all these systems will appear, and grow, and even reproduce (e.g., Taylor vortices) when the gradient is within a certain range, and vanish when it isn't, they effectively have sensation (whether or not they have consciousness). The ability to maintain complexity within a certain temperature range or gradient suggests a cybernetic connection between metabolic activities and information manipulation. The connectedness and historicity of complex systems suggests that they are all in principle semiotic, insofar as aspects of their cyclical organization follow one another and thus for a perceiver reliably signal (in the sense of a Peircian index) what is to come.

39. Eric D. Schneider and Dorion Sagan, *Into the Cool: Energy Flow, Thermodynamics, and Life* (Chicago: University of Chicago Press, 2006).

40. Dorion Sagan, "The Science of Illusions by Jacques Ninio," *Science, Technology, and Human Values* 27 (Autumn): 546–49.

41. An interesting compound: dogs can detect it at ten parts per billion, whereas only at ten times that concentration do we notice it—which is just as well, as isobutyric acid is the smell of vomit as well as some of the finest French cheeses.

42. Sorin Sonea and Maurice Panisset, *Toward a New Bacteriology* (n.p.: Jones and Bartlett Publishers, 1983).

43. Tor Nørretranders, *The User Illusion: Cutting Consciousness Down to Size*, trans. Jonathan Sydenham (New York: Viking, 1991), 20–21.

44. Deely, "Umwelt," 125–35.

45. Paul Bains, "Umwelten," *Semiotica* 134-1/4 (2001): 137–67.

46. Ibid., 147.

47. Tyler Volk, *Death* (n.p.: Chelsea Green Publishing, 2009).

48. Kvond, "Human Centric Semiosis in the Name of Umwelten," May 26, 2009: kvond.wordpress.com/2009/05/26/human-centric-semiosis-in-the-name-of-umwelten/.

49. Uexküll, *A Foray into the Worlds of Animals and Humans*, Introduction.

50. Martin Heidegger, *The Fundamental Concepts of Metaphysics: World, Finitude, Solitude* (Bloomington: Indiana University Press, 1995); Theodor Adorno, *The Jargon of Authenticity*, trans. Knut Tarnowski (Evanston: Northwestern University, 1973), cited in Thomas Pepper, *Singularities:*

Extremes of Theory in the Twentieth Century (Cambridge: Cambridge University Press, 1997), 59.

51. Jacques Derrida, "'Eating Well,' or the Calculation of the Subject: An Interview with Jacques Derrida," in *Who Comes after the Subject?*, ed. E. Cadava, P. Connor, and J.L. Nancy (New York: Routledge), 111.

52. James Lovelock, *The Revenge of Gaia: Earth's Climate Crisis and The Fate of Humanity* (New York: Basic Books, 2007).

53. Francois Jacob, *The Possible and the Actual* (New York: Pantheon, 1982).

54. Jacques Derrida, "White Mythology," in *Margins of Philosophy* (Chicago: Chicago University Press, 1982), 207–71.

55. The potential for modeling cognitive processes based on the effortless proto-cogitation of nonequilibrium thermodynamic processes has not been lost on the US Department of Defense's research body DARPA, which has instituted a "PI"—Physical Intelligence—program that "aspires to understand intelligence as a physical phenomenon . . . [which] spontaneously evolves as a consequence of thermodynamics in open systems . . . If successful, the program would launch a revolution of understanding across many fields of human endeavor, demonstrate the first intelligence engineered from first principles, create new classes of electronic, computational, and chemical systems, and create tools to engineer intelligent systems that match the problem/environment in which they will exist." Special Notice DARPA-SN-09-35. (See also Katie Drummond, "Darpa: Heat + Energy = Brains. Now Make Us Some." *Wired*, May 8: www.wired .com/dangerroom/2009/05/darpa-heat-energy-brains-now-make-us-some/.)

56. Fraser, "Extended Umwelt Principle."

Translator's Introduction

1. Jakob von Uexküll, "Strolls through the Worlds of Animals and Men," ed. Thure von Uexküll, trans. Claire Schiller, *Semiotica* 89.4 (1992): 287–394.

2. Johann Wolfgang von Goethe, *Werke*, Hamburger Ausgabe, vol. 3 (Munich: Deutscher Taschenbuch Verlag, 1998), 409.

3. Torsten Rüting, "History and Significance of Jakob von Uexküll and of His Institute in Hamburg," *Sign Systems Studies* 32, 1–2 (2004): 54.

4. Ibid., 53.

A Foray into the Worlds of Animals and Humans

There are three different sorts of notes: those of Jakob von Uexküll, which receive no special marking; those of the editor of the *Rowohlt-Enzyklopädie* edition, bracketed and followed by "—Ed."; and those of Joseph D. O'Neil, bracketed and followed by "—Trans."

1. [Cf. Friedrich Brock, "Verzeichnis der Schriften Johann Jakob von

Uexkülls und der aus dem Institut für Umweltforschung zu Hamburg hervorgegangenen Arbeiten." *Archiv für die Geschichte der Medizin und der Naturwissenschaften*, Vol. 27.3–4 (1934). Leipzig: J. A. Barth. —Ed.]

2. "Reflex" originally meant the capturing and casting back of a ray of light by a mirror. Transferred to living beings, it means the capturing of an external stimulus by a receptor and the response effected by the stimulus through the living being's effectors. The stimulus is thereby transformed into a nerve excitation which must pass multiple points in order to get from the receptor to the effector. The path it takes in doing so is designated a reflex arc.

3. [Founder of modern physiology (1801–1858) here. —Ed.]

4. [See the Translator's Introduction. —Trans.]

5. The tick is constructed in every aspect for a long period of hunger. The semen cells which the female shelters during this waiting period remain lying bundled in semen capsules until the mammal's blood enters the tick's stomach; then, they emerge and fertilize the eggs resting in the ovaries. In contrast to the tick's complete adaptation to its prey object, of which it finally takes hold, it is extremely improbable that this ever occurs, in spite of the long waiting period. Bodenheimer is entirely right when he speaks of a "pessimal" world, i.e., one as unfavorable as possible, in which most animals live. But this world is not their environment, only their surroundings. An *optimal environment*, i.e., one as favorable as possible, and *pessimal surroundings* will obtain as a general rule. For the point is that the species be preserved, no matter how many individuals perish. If the surroundings of a certain species were not pessimal, it would quickly predominate over all other species thanks to its optimal environment.

6. The cinema provides proof of this. In the projection of a film, the images must jump out with a jerk one after the other and then stand still. In order to show them sharply focused, the jerky movement must be made invisible by passing a shutter in front of the film. The darkening that occurs thereby is not perceived by our eye if stopping and darkening the image both take place within an eighteenth of a second. If the time is prolonged, an insufferable flickering occurs.

7. [Elie von Cyon (1842–1912), a Russian physiologist, the discoverer of important nerves and nerve functions. —Ed.]

8. [Ernst Heinrich Weber (1795–1878), cofounder of modern physiology, research on the skin's sense of touch. —Ed.]

9. [This presentation only shows the way to a first understanding of the distinctions of seeing. Whoever wants to get an idea of the dynamic properties of sight, for example in insects, can find an introduction in K. von Frisch's work *From the Life of Bees* (5th printing: Springer Press, 1953). —Ed.]

10. [Hermann von Helmholtz (1821–1894), physiologist and physicist, discoverer of the ophthalmoscope, early advocate of Maxwell's wave theory, made important observations on the nature of energy, etc. —Ed.]

11. [Siegmund Exner (1846–1926), professor in the Department of Physiology, Vienna, starting in 1875. Wrote works in the field of optical physiology and on the function of the cerebral cortex. —Ed.]

12. [Karl Ernst von Baer (1792–1876), zoologist, founder of a modern theory of development which deviated from Darwinism. —Ed.]

13. [The term used here is *Vexierbilder*, images which can be seen either of two ways. In each case, something completely different is depicted, for instance, two human silhouettes facing each other or, in the middle, in the white space between the silhouettes, the image of a goblet. —Trans.]

14. [J. Henri Fabre (1823–1915), French insect researcher. —Ed.]

15. [Uexküll calls these *Nachtpfauenaugen*, which is a moth of the genus *Saturnia*. The two main species are *Saturnia pavonia* and *Saturnia pyri*, both of which are called emperor moths (small and large, or Viennese, respectively) in English. C. Schiller translates *Nachtpfauenauge* as "eyed hawk moth." —Trans.]

16. [Uexküll's language dates his text, as does my translation. He uses the German word *Neger*, which is apt in a text of this period, and in most cases in older texts sounds condescending and certainly culturally biased without indicating outright racial or ethnic animosity. —Trans.]

17. [Konrad Lorenz (1903–1989), zoologist and animal psychologist (i.e., animal behavior). —Ed.]

18. [Leo Frobenius (1873–1938), ethnologist and Africa specialist. —Ed.]

A Theory of Meaning

1. [E.G. Sarris, a collaborator of von Uexküll's, who occupied himself, starting in 1931, particularly with the behavior and training of dogs (also with the training of seeing-eye dogs). —Ed.]

2. [Werner Sombart, German sociologist (1863–1941). —Ed.]

3. [Walter Arndt (1891–1944), zoologist and physician. Curator of the Zoological Museum in Berlin, made a widely respected film in the 1930s on the development of slime mold. —Ed.]

4. [Hans Driesch (1867–1941), German philosopher and biologist, student and later opponent of Ernst Haeckel; joined biological experimentation with theoretical biology and *Naturphilosophie*. —Ed.]

5. [Hans Spemann (1869–1941), zoologist, Nobel laureate for medicine, eminent representative of experimental developmental research. —Ed.]

6. [This is from Act IV, Scene II of Schiller's *Wilhelm Tell*. I use the translation by Theodore Martin, available in the public domain at http://www.gutenberg.org. —Trans.]

7. [Arthur Stanley Eddington, English astronomer and physicist, leading representative of relativity theory (1882–1944). —Ed.]

8. [German-American biologist (1859–1924). —Ed.]

9. [Tropism = lawlike, directed movement in plants and lower animals in reaction to certain stimuli. —Ed.]

10. [Ewald Hering (1834–1918), German physiologist, worked particularly on the spatial sense of the eye and the perception of color. —Ed.]

11. [W. Wunder (1898–[?]), zoologist, specialist in fish breeding and pond management. —Ed.]

12. [Otto August Mangold (1891–[1962]), zoologist, student of Spemann, head of department in Heiligenberg (Max Planck Institute) in 1946. Work[ed] *inter alia* on embryo cells. —Ed.]

13. [1820–1903, English philosopher, subscribed to the idea of biological development. —Ed.]

14. [Karl von Frisch (1886–[1982]), zoologist, important sense physiologist, experiments on bees and fish. —Ed.]

15. ["Voice-leading" is the American English term for *Stimmführung*; the British equivalent is "part-writing," which William Drabkin defines as follows: "That aspect of counterpoint and polyphony which recognizes each part as an individual line (or 'voice'), not merely as an element of the resultant harmony; each line must therefore have a melodic shape as well as a rhythmic life of its own." William Drabkin, "Part-writing," *Grove Music Online. Oxford Music Online*, 31 Aug. 2009. http://www.oxfordmusic online.com/ . —Trans.]

16. [Goethe's verse is based upon Plotinus' *Enneads* and reflects his theory of vision in the *Farbenlehre* (Theory of Color), where it appears among animadversions against Isaac Newton's supposed errors and omissions (Goethe, *Werke*, Hamburger Ausgabe 13: 324–25). Goethe writes, "The eye owes its existence to the light. The light calls forth an organ for itself from among undifferentiated animal ancillary organs that will become like it [the light], and so the eye is formed in the light for the light, so that the inner light encounters the outer light."—Trans.]

17. [Uexküll uses the German word *Motiv* here where I translate "motif" or "motive." By using the same word in different contexts, which make it impossible to translate as the same English term, he is playing on the musical conceit in order to underscore the element of motivation that takes animal form and functioning beyond what he criticizes as merely mechanical and into the realm of subjectivity, ultimately of Nature as a subject. —Trans.]

18. [Jean Baptiste Antoine Pierre de Monet de Lamarck (1744–1829), French zoologist, introduced a new system for the animal kingdom, developed the first theory of heredity, represented the conviction that acquired characteristics could be inherited. —Ed.]

19. [Ernst Haeckel (1834–1919), German zoologist, reformer of biology, follower of Darwin. —Ed.]

20. [A "rocher de bronze" is an immoveable, unshakable element. Although in French, it is a German expression used in widely varied contexts. It is

attributed by Otto von Bismarck, among others, to Friedrich Wilhelm I, King of Prussia (d. 1740), who seems to have used the expression to refer to the sovereignty of the monarchy over the Junkers (Prussian landed nobility). (See Bismarck's speech in the Prussian *Landtag*, 22 January, 1864.) —Trans.]

21. [See the Foreword to *Foray*, which connects *Wirken* with *Werkzeug* and *Merken* with Uexküll's invented term *Merkzeug*. —Trans.]

22. [Hermann Braus (1868–1924), natural scientist and physician, professor in Heidelberg. Cofounder of developmental mechanics, author of a widely respected anatomy. —Ed.]

23. [Franz Nissl (1860–1919), psychiatrist, researched pathological changes, particularly in ganglion cells. —Ed.]

Afterword

1. Jakob von Uexküll, "Darwins Verschulden," *Deutsche Allgemeine Zeitung* 82/14.1 (1943): 1.

2. Ibid., 2.

3. Florian Mildenberger, *Umwelt als Vision. Leben und Werk Jakob von Uexkülls (1864–1944)* (Stuttgart: Franz Steiner, 2007), 33.

4. Jakob von Uexküll, *Theoretical Biology*, trans. D. L. Mackinnon (London: Kegan Paul, 1926), 322.

5. For example, Jakob von Uexküll, "Darwin und die englische Moral," *Deutsche Rundschau* 173 (1917): 215–43.

6. Jakob von Uexküll, *Die Lebenslehre* (Potsdam: Müller and Kiepenheuer, 1930), 157.

7. Gottfried Benn, *Das Hauptwerk. Vol. 4: Vermischte Schriften* (Wiesbaden: Limes, 1980), 192–93.

8. Helmut Lethen, *Der Sound der Väter: Gottfried Benn und seine Zeit* (Berlin: Rowohlt, 2006), 213–27.

9. This was not a gratuitous association on Benn's part. Among the objections leveled at the Umwelt concept during the Third Reich was the claim that it was too static and thus not in line with the envisioned dynamic expansion of the German race. Umwelt clashes with *Lebensraum* in much the same way as *Heimat* does. Those rooted in their Umwelt will not be able to strike out east to conquer new living space (cf. Mildenberger 202).

10. Throughout this essay I will stick to the German spelling (capitalized, and with the correct plural Umwelten). As Thomas Sebeok notes, the term is "notoriously hard to translate," though he is quick to add that "its sense is quite clear: It is captured, in varying degree, by such overlapping English terms as *ecological niche*, *experienced world*, *psychological* or *subjective* or *significant environment*, *behavioral life space*, *ambient extension*, *ipse-fact*, or, expressions that I prefer, *cognitive map* or *scheme* or even *mind*

set" (Thomas Sebeok, *The Sign and Its Masters,* preface by John Deely [Lanham: University Press of America, 1989], 194). Does such a cascade of synonyms clarify anything? All the more reason to stick to the original term.

11. For a survey of postwar "rediscoveries" of Uexküll see Mildenberger, *Umwelt als Vision,* 231–38. Malte Herwig has provided the most comprehensive summary of his influence on writers and artists, "The unwitting muse: Jakob von Uexküll's theory of Umwelt in twentieth-century literature," *Semiotica* 132 (2001): 553–92. The highly idiosyncratic appropriation by Deleuze has recently been discussed by Greaves and Buchanan. (Tom Greaves, "A Silent Dance: Eco-Political Compositions after Uexküll's Umwelt Biology," in *An [Un]Likely Alliance: Thinking Environment[s] with Deleuze/Guattari,* ed. Bernd Herzogenrath [Cambridge: Cambridge Scholars Publishing, 2008], 98–115; Brett Buchanan, *Onto-Ethnologies: The Animal Environments of Uexküll. Heidegger, Merleau-Ponty, and Deleuze* [Albany: State University Press of New York, 2008], 151–86.) Dorion Sagan has already presented Uexküll's role for post-Darwinian and biosemiotic research agendas; there is no need to repeat what he succinctly summarized.

12. Jens Immanuel Baggesen, *Poetische Werke in deutscher Sprache. Vol. II: Oden und Elegian,* ed. Carl and August Baggesen (Leipzig: Brockhaus, 1836), 102.

13. Leo Spitzer, *Essays in Historical Semantics* (London: Russell & Russell, 1948).

14. Jakob von Uexküll, "Weltanschauung und Gewissen," *Deutsche Rundschau* 197 (1923): 266.

15. Gudrun von Uexküll, *Jakob von Uexküll: Seine Welt und seine Umwelt* (Hamburg: Wegner, 1964), 134.

16. John Alexander Williams, *Turning to Nature in Germany: Hiking, Nudism, and Conservation, 1900–1940* (Stanford: Stanford University Press, 2007).

17. Niklas Luhmann, *Ecological Communication,* trans. John Bednorz (Chicago: University of Chicago Press, 1989).

18. Urmas Sutrop's paraphrase "[h]ere the Umwelt appears from a distance as an etheric castle, as the fate-hell of a poet," is incorrect. (Urmas Sutrop, "Umwelt—Word and Concept: Two Hundred Years of Semantic Change," *Semiotica* 134 [2001]: 452.) *Umwelt* is a dative object as required by the verb *erscheinen.* The Umwelt does not appear as anything to anybody, instead it is the "fate-hell" of the poet that appears as an "etheric castle" *to* the Umwelt.

19. Leif Ludwig Albertsen, "Umwelt," *Zeitschrift für deutsche Sprache* 21 (1965): 117.

20. See Joachim Fischer, *Philosophische Anthropologie: Eine Denkrichtung des 20. Jahrhunderts* (Freiburg: Karl Alber, 2008), 520–26.

21. Gerhard Arlt, *Philosophische Anthropologie* (Stuttgart: Metzler, 2001).

22. Theodor Litt, quoted in Rudolf Langenthaler, *Organismus und Umwelt: Die biologische Umweltlehre im Spiegel traditioneller Naturphilosophie* (Hildesheim: Georg Olms, 1992), 235.

23. Benn, *Das Hauptwerk,* 192.

24. Jakob von Uexküll, "Die neue Umweltlehre: Ein Bindeglied zwischen Natur- und Kulturwissenschaften," *Die Erziehung* 13 (1938): 64.

25. Jakob von Uexküll, *Niegeschaute Welten: Die Umwelten meiner Freunde* (Berlin: S. Fischer, 1936), 294.

26. Ibid., 201.

27. Roberto Esposito, *Bíos: Biopolitics and Philosophy*, trans. Timothy Campbell (Minneapolis: University of Minnesota Press, 2008), 17.

28. Jakob von Uexküll, *Staatsbiologie* (Berlin: Paetel, 1920), 28.

29. Compare, for instance, Uexküll's analysis of a bell ("Die neue Umweltlehre," 185–88) with Heidegger's more famous musings on a jug in "The Thing."

30. Jakob von Uexküll, *Staatsbiologie*, 2nd ed. (Hamburg: Hanseatische Verlagsanstalt, 1933), 71.

31. Esposito, *Bíos*, 18.

32. Ibid., 113.

33. The unnamed Hitler appears at the very end as a "famous surgeon" into whose hands Germany, a "critically ill patient," has laid her fate (Uexküll, *Staatsbiologie*, 2nd ed., 79). Uexküll's flattery was in vain. Similar to Heidegger's initial delusions regarding the position of postsecondary education in the Third Reich, Uexküll believed that Nazis would come to share his high opinions of the university as a sensory organ of the state. But despite his obsequious promotion to surgeon of the state, Hitler was neither particularly interested in the state nor in those institutions that trained the expertise necessary to cure it.

34. Uexküll, *Niegeschaute Welten*, 159–60.

35. Ibid., 165.

36. Ibid., 167.

37. Anne Harrington, *Reenchanted Science: Holism in German Culture from Wilhelm II to Hitler* (Princeton: Princeton University Press, 1996), 62.

38. Uexküll, *Theoretical Biology*, 336.

39. Rainer Maria Rilke, "Eighth Duino Elegy," *The Selected Poetry of Rainer Maria Rilke*, ed. and trans. Stephen Mitchell (New York: Random House, 1982), 193.

40. Giorgio Agamben, *The Open: Man and Animal*, trans. Kevin Attell (Stanford: Stanford University Press, 2004), 57–59.

41. See Langthaler, *Organismus und Umwelt*, 232–34.

42. Ibid., 166–225.

43. Rilke, *Selected Poetry*, 201.

44. Rainer Maria Rilke, *The Best of Rilke*, trans. Walter Arndt (Lebanon, NH: Dartmouth College Press, 1989), 69.

45. Further see Erich Unglaub, *Panther und Aschanti: Rilke-Gedichte in kulturwissenschaftlicher Sicht* (Frankfurt am Main: Peter Lang, 2005).

46. Quoted in Gudrun von Uexküll, *Jakob von Uexküll*, 132.

47. Rainer Maria Rilke, *New Poems*, trans. J. B. Leishman (New York: New Directions, 1964), 109.

48. Uexküll, *Niegeschaute Welten*, 267.

49. Werner Heisenberg, *The Physicist's Conception of Nature*, trans. Arnold J. Pomerans (Westport, CT: Greenwood Press, 1958), 24. On a more fundamental (and yet to be fully discussed) level, Uexküll's approach shares early quantum theory's discontent over causality that Paul Forman famously attributed to the intellectual environment in late Wilhelmine and Weimar culture (further see Forman, "Culture, Causality, and Quantum Theory, 1918 1927: Adaptation by German Physicists and Mathematicians to a Hostile Intellectual Environment," *Historical Studies in the Physical Sciences* 3 [1971]: 1–115).

50. Uexküll, *Niegeschaute Welten*, 300–301.

51. Uexküll's biology partakes in a "gradual delegation of the authority to decide how life is to be tackled from the genetic material to the organism itself." (Jesper Hoffmeyer, *Signs of Meaning in the Universe*, trans. Barbara Haveland [Bloomington: Indiana University Press, 1996], 59.) It is precisely this promotion of the world-shaping abilities of the subject that struck a chord with many modern artistic movements from expressionism to cubism. No wonder Uexküll became an "unwitting muse" to many new-fangled isms he, the arch-conservative, heartily disapproved of. (Herwig, "The Unwitting Muse," 554.)

52. Agamben, *The Open*, 45.

53. Patrick Süskind, *Perfume: The Story of a Murder* (New York: Washington Square Press, 1991), 22.

54. Sebeok, *The Sign*, 187–207; Hoffmeyer, *Signs of Meaning*, 54–58.

55. Sebeok, *The Sign*, 201; emphasis in the original.

56. Carlo Ginzburg, "Morelli, Freud, and Sherlock Holmes: Clues and Scientific Method," in *The Sign of Three: Dupin, Holmes, Peirce*, ed. Umberto Eco and Thomas Sebeok (Bloomington: Indiana University Press, 1983), 81–118.

57. Friedrich Kittler, *Gramophone, Film, Typewriter*, trans. Geoffrey Winthrop-Young and Michael Wutz (Stanford: Stanford University Press, 1999), 83.

58. Herwig, "The Unwitting Muse," 573.

59. Quoted in Arnold Gehlen, *Man: His Nature and Place in the World*, trans. Clare McKillan and Karl Pillemer (New York: Columbia University Press, 1988), 71.

60. Sebeok, *The Sign*, 194.

61. Langthaler, *Organismus und Umwelt*, 103.

62. At a certain point in twentieth-century German biology one of these determining factors was race and the notion of a specific racial environment sometimes captured in the term *Lebensraum*. This, incidentally, is where Weber—a biologist with a much greater affinity to Nazi ideology and one of Uexküll's chief antagonists during the Third Reich—was coming from (further see Mildenberger, *Umwelt als Vision*, 176–83). Not that Gehlen, who himself had fared well under the regime, saw the need to mention this.

63. It may also explain why some of those engaged in this semiotic endeavor are also quick to recruit Uexküll as a precursor of a "post-modern evolutionism" that either retires the allegedly excessive Darwinian dependencies on random external conditions or reinterprets them as a communicative and hence semiotic phenomenon (e.g., Kalevi Kull, "Uexküll and the post-modern evolutionism," *Sign System Studies* 32 (1/2) [2004]: 99–114).

64. Peter Høeg, *Borderliners*, trans. Barbara Haveland (New York: Farrar, Straus and Giroux, 1994), 260–61.

65. Ibid., 255–56.

66. Ibid., 227.

67. Uexküll, *Theoretical Biology*, 52.

68. Høeg, *Borderliners*, 35.

69. Ibid., 237–38.

70. Ibid., 235.

71. Gudrun von Uexküll, *Jakob von Uexküll*, 16.

72. I am grateful to Thomas Salumets for bringing this to my attention.

INDEX

Adorno, Theodor, 29
Agamben, Giorgio, 213, 235
amoebas: contrapuntal relation with
food, 192; meaning factors for,
170; reproduction of, 149, 156;
self-tones of, 192
anglerfish: contrapuntal relationship
with prey, 188; design rule of, 181
animals: actions available for, 96;
acts of observation, 232; carriers of
meaning in, 171, 201; in Cartesian
philosophy, 12; centrifugal
construction of, 156; construction
of environments, 222; contrapuntal relations of, 173, 177–79;
coordinate systems of, 99; directed
goals of, 19; dwelling worlds of,
139; effect worlds of, 162; factors
affecting, 245n5; familiar paths
of, 99; farthest planes of, 67–68;
functional cycles of, 36; goal-
oriented actions of, 86; house-door
compasses of, 57; marking of territory, 106–7; mastering of images,
99; mechanistic view of, 41–42,
163; moods of, 95; and musical
instruments, 187; nocturnal, 61;
perception of, 26, 42, 43; perception marks of, 165, 202; perception
organs of, 147; perception signs of,
53, 165; perception time of, 71–72;
perception worlds of, 2, 3, 20, 162;
production of effects in, 42, 47;
purposefulness of, 5; reflex, 75–76;

relation with mazes, 139; relation
with objects, 139–40, 173; search
tones of, 113; self-reflexive agency
of, 222; semioticity of, 28; structural plans of, 147; subjectivity
of, 231; Umwelten of, 7, 219–20,
221, 222
animal subjects, 42; as carriers of
meaning, 201; effect tones of, 188;
environments of, 50; perception
marks of, 49; perception tones of,
188; physiochemical effects on, 166
anthroposemiosis, 28, 32
apple trees: magical properties of,
128–29
Arndt, Walter, 251n3; slime-mold
film of, 149, 152, 156, 170, 192
Arosenius, Ivar: "Jul," 203–4
art: complementing of biology, 234;
meaning-germs in, 204
astronomers: environment of, 133,
134
autochronicity, 241
autodermin, 77

Bach, Johann Sebastian: St.
Matthew Passion, 195
bacteria: as carriers of meaning, 149;
consciousness among, 246n23;
metabolic modes of, 244n1
Baer, Karl Ernst von, 70, 185, 193,
251n12
Baggesen, Immanuel: use of *Umwelt*,
215–16, 217, 239–40

Jakob von Uexküll (1864–1944) was a Baltic German biologist whose work helped to establish the field of biosemiotics. He published widely in the fields of muscular physiology, animal behavior studies, and the cybernetics of life.

Joseph D. O'Neil is assistant professor of German studies in the Department of Modern and Classical Languages, Literatures, and Cultures at the University of Kentucky.

A writer and sleight-of-hand magician, **Dorion Sagan** has written extensively on evolution, cybersex, and the biology of gender.

Geoffrey Winthrop-Young is associate professor of Central, Eastern, and Northern European studies at the University of British Columbia.